Developing Multicultural Awareness
Through Children's Literature

Developing Multicultural Awareness Through Children's Literature

A Guide for Teachers and Librarians, Grades K–8

by
Patricia L. Roberts
and
Nancy Lee Cecil

McFarland & Company, Inc., Publishers
Jefferson, North Carolina, and London

British Library Cataloguing-in-Publication data are available

Library of Congress Cataloguing-in-Publication Data

Roberts, Patricia L.
    Developing multicultural awareness through children's literature :
a guide for teachers and librarians, grades K–8 / by Patricia L.
Roberts and Nancy Lee Cecil.
        p.   cm.
    Includes index.
    ISBN 0-89950-879-0 (sewn softcover : 50# alk. paper)   ∞
    1. Minorities—United States—Juvenile literature—Bibliography.
2. United States—Ethnic relations—Juvenile literature—
Bibliography.   3. Minorities—Study and teaching (Elementary)—
United States.   4. United States—Ethnic relations—Study and
teaching (Elementary)   5. Intercultural education—United States.
I. Cecil, Nancy Lee.   II. Title.
Z1361.E4R63   1993
[E184.A1]
305.8′00973—dc20   93-15144
                                                             CIP

Manufactured in the United States of America

McFarland & Company, Inc., Publishers
  Box 611, Jefferson, North Carolina 28640

Dedicated to our husbands,
James and Gary

CONTENTS

Extended Activity Unit: Grades 4–8

INTRODUCTION

Almost all of the people in the United States are the children, grand-children or great-grandchildren of immigrants from some other land. It is becoming increasingly clear, then, that young people, who will soon become the country's adult citizens and leaders, will need to be presented with broad concepts about cultural similarities and differences, and respect for the increasing diversity of the population.

The need for understanding of the radically changing demographics has perhaps never been greater than it is today. The riots in Los Angeles in response to the verdict in the Rodney King beating may have been only the beginning of a new round of problems having to do with recognition and understanding. The continued existence of the Ku Klux Klan, the pervasive anti–Semitism, and the daily "hate crimes" are not occurrences of an unfortunate past history, but part of the fabric of everyday life in America. Frustrated folks from every racial, ethnic and cultural group shake their heads and ask, "When will it all end?" The answer is that so long as fear and ignorance are allowed to fester in the hearts of people, individuals will most likely continue to perform atrocities against other human beings—who threaten them merely by being different from them-selves.

On a hopeful note, the authors of this text believe that the way chil-dren think and feel about diverse members of the United States can be positively affected by education—in the home, in the school, and in the larger societal context. Through education we can replace fear with curi-osity and broaden children's awareness of other people, their needs, their hopes, and their dreams. Educators are in an ideal position to lead the way toward breaking down the prejudiced and stereotyped thinking that leads to hate crimes, riots, dissension, and even war.

A humane, enlightened approach to education offering multicultural concepts threaded throughout the entire curriculum may eventually lead to a truly democratic society whose citizens not only tolerate, but actively value diversity. Specifically, we believe that a wide array of multicultural children's literature, with debriefing discussions and internalizing activities,

1

is the optimal curricular vehicle through which to present these broad concepts.

Students need to read and listen to literature that presents accurate and respectful images of individuals in all cultures. In addition to helping students gain an accurate and respectful image of others, the teacher may read or suggest stories to students that develop an understanding of what it is like to be "new" to an area and reflect the experiences of "newcomers."

A few researchers have recently started to look at multicultural literature and have asked, "What images are seen by children?" and, by implication for this book's focus, "In what books are there fair portrayals of people from different cultures?" Current research and findings are available and contribute some answers to the questions.

A major goal of education is to dispel ignorance. One does not fear that which one understands, whether it be nuclear physics, the Hmong people, or the history of the Jews. As more and more attention is focused on understanding different cultures as the demographics rapidly change in the United States, it is essential that children first learn to understand their own individual cultures. Based upon a strong sense of cultural identity and self-esteem, they can then begin to reach out and accept the cultures of others. When this occurs we will have come a long way toward eradicating cultural stereotyping and prejudice, which have profound negative effects on the whole society.

Building upon a foundation of empathy for diverse peoples in the United States, we should then be able to extend children's understanding readily to persons living in other countries. When this understanding is absent, those who speak a different language and display differing values often appear threatening to children. When that knowledge base of understanding has been provided through vehicles such as children's literature, however, people from other countries suddenly are seen as fascinating, interesting, and friendly.

While lack of understanding may lead to violence and conflict, multicultural understanding can only lead to harmony, unity and, played out to the fullest extent, world peace. According to Garcia (1981), multicultural education is a broad generic term for any program that not only confronts ethnocentric behavior, but fosters understanding and respect for ethnic and minority groups. Such inquiry leads children to begin to grasp the rich diversity of the population and to begin to appreciate, and actively value, the role of each group in enriching the societal milieu which we all share.

Wide exposure to people from different cultures not only leads to harmony, but to an understanding of a major multicultural axiom: There are greater differences *within* cultural groups than there are *between* cultural groups. When this simple yet profound concept is realized, children (and adults, as well) begin to look at people from different cultures in broader, less pigeon-holed ways. A case in point is taken from a recent article in *National Geographic* on the people from the Trobriand Islands of Papua, New Guinea (Theroux, 1992). The author's attempts at describing not only the personality traits but the physical traits of the Trobriand Islanders were in vain. He finally admits: "There is no 'typical' Trobriander. . . . The People are all sorts, some Negroid, some Papuan or Polynesian, some with straight hair and some with tightly curled hair; some are very dark and some are light brown; most tend to be small in stature, but some are tall. . . ." Such observations might well be generalized to *all* traits in *all* cultures; when children begin to appreciate the diversity within a culture, they are only then able to accept each representative from a discrete cultural group as a unique individual.

For teachers, the research findings on modifying cultural stereotypes have profound practical classroom implications. While once a teacher might have been able to expect a relatively homogenous classroom filled with average middle-class children, the teacher can now look forward to the challenge of a heterogeneous group of children with a diverse set of cultural backgrounds. Each child will be an individualist and have a unique history and many will have stories to tell about being stereotyped. If, indeed, children's literature may affect the understanding of cultural stereotypes for youngsters, an interested teacher or librarian might ask, What are the models that modify cultural stereotypes that youngsters could be seeing and reading about? If quality literature, such as books that have won the Caldecott and the Newbery awards, and others, are instructive vehicles, which characters can be used to help develop further understanding about modifying cultural stereotypes? To assist in this, teachers and librarians have turned to such resources as the *Classroom Teachers' Manual for Bibliotherapy* (Schultheis and Pavlik, 1977).

The positive aspects of developing multicultural concepts and modifying cultural stereotypes can be actively developed. Such modifications need to be reinforced by a strong teacher-model who demonstrates a personal conviction that each individual is good and worthwhile. A teacher can also foster multicultural concepts and the modification of cultural stereotypes by introducing children to works of literature that have at their core characters who are themselves models in the process of overcoming cultural stereotypes and presenting multicultural concepts. Follow-up discussion of the literature can show children that there are similarities among people of different cultures, and that they, like the literary characters, can modify cultural stereotypes.

Moreover, retelling the same stories through dramatic play suddenly can put children of different cultures into the roles of modifiers and allow them, for a while, to roleplay certain fictional characters that embody nonstereotypical behavior that they, too, will want to see in their community, city, state and world.

An example from literature that could be selected is *Somewhere in Africa* (Dutton, 1992, for grades 4–5) by Ingrid Mennen and Niki Daly. This book features Ashraf, a strong African American boy who, living in a big city, knows nothing about the world of African nature except what he learns from books he has borrowed from the public library. A follow-up discussion to this book would underscore the range of positive traits exhibited by Ashraf. Through Ashraf's adventures in the city streets, a reader is able to share the city's special beauty—the music, flowers, and fruit sellers. A child without Ashraf's background would likely perceive Ashraf's situation as terribly boring, uneventful, and perhaps strange and somewhat frightening, whereas the same circumstance would probably be viewed more optimistically by a child who could more easily relate to Ashraf's heritage and environment. Ashraf "stalks the shelves" in the library and looks at new titles from the "jungle of books" there but always chooses his favorite book, one that describes Africa as "wild and untamed." The teacher's role, then, would be to guide the girls and boys into seeing Ashraf as a type of child found in all cultures. The teacher would help the children brainstorm some possible comparative characters who found themselves in similar situations—trying to discover their heritage and the world outside their immediate environments. The teacher could then ask the students to speculate about the similarities of the characters. Finally, having those same students roleplay a positive "predictable" character like Ashraf would allow them to "try on" different cultural backgrounds, and perhaps over time, grow in their own understanding and appreciation of the heritage of others.

Using children's literature to teach is not new. Bibliotherapy, the use of books to help children understand and cope with the problems of everyday life, is a practice dating back to the time of Aristotle, when the libraries of ancient Greece carried inscriptions such as "the Medicine Chest for the Soul." There is little doubt that by empathizing with believable book characters, children may be able to understand themselves and others better. When children read about a character whose behavior causes him or her to succeed and "modifies" a cultural stereotype, as Ashraf's does, the children can reach into themselves to make adjustments in their own personalities. Obviously, the vicarious experiences of reading and dramatic play are less threatening to one's ego than the reality of everyday life. Moreover, the experiences are reversible. The readers can reflect for weeks upon the action taken by main characters and continue to come up with a myriad of actions that might also have been taken. And in fiction, as opposed to real life, no one sits in judgment of the readers' decisions.

The use of books to help prevent the development of a problem (Thomas, 1967) or to help children solve or at least better understand their problems by interacting with literature, has been documented by studies related to the use of books and their effect on children (Zaccaria and Moses, 1968). In working with challenging populations in the schools, children's literature has affected coping behavior (Cianciolo, 1965) and has been useful with retarded readers (Kantrowitz, 1967), with the emotionally disturbed (Koon, 1970), and as an aid in preventing dropouts (Faust, 1969). Literature for children also has been a positive influence on the academic achievement of the educable mentally retarded (Limper, 1970), junior high underachievers (Waite, 1965), readers with emotional blocks (Bruell, 1966), atypical readers (Nigen, 1979), and inner-city children (Brocki, 1969). Outside the schools, it has affected inmate students (Whipple, 1968) and adolescent girls in a correctional agency (Limper, 1970). Indeed, adolescents themselves have reported that they do respond positively to identification through literature (Koon, 1970).

Further, books have been aids in the general development of children's values, attitudes, and codes of conduct (Cooper, 1969; Bissett, 1969; Taba, 1950, 1955; Strickland, 1961; and Squire, 1968) as well as assisting in identification (Russell, 1949). In these reports, some books have been an influence on the child's mind and course of action and a help for a child needing to overcome conflicts. Fiction has been a treatment to alter attitudes (Beardsley, 1980; Bodart, 1980; Cornett and Cornett, 1980), to deal with school anxieties (Marrelli, 1965), and to solve personal problems (Appleberry, 1969). Other books have been a factor in changing attitudes toward minority groups, in diminishing fears, in helping students deal with deaths and in developing moral maturity (Berstein, 1978).

Recent studies of ways books affect children and ways cultural images are shown in children's books support a conclusion that some children can and do develop healthy perceptions about the heritage of others and can modify certain beliefs about the cultures of others. A teacher who believes and models the notion that we are the masters of our own fate can encourage children to develop such understandings of multicultural concepts. Additionally, carefully chosen children's literature, which has as its core those characters from different cultures, can provide fictional interactions that allow children to develop the understanding and appreciation necessary for meeting and accepting others from different cultural backgrounds in real life. With a guided discussion of a range of alternative situations, children can begin to see that they have the capacity to modify cultural stereotypes in their own lives. Also, by donning the role of fictitious friends in children's literature through dramatic play, children further increase their repertoire of modification skills.

In the following sections, teachers and librarians will find some helpful tools that will allow them to use children's literature as a vehicle for modifying cultural stereotypes. The sections contain short summaries of carefully selected children's books, each of which features main characters who contribute to an understanding of one's cultural heritage and ways to modify a cultural stereotype. The characters in the books present a point of view to combat stereotyping. The book summaries identify characters from different cultural backgrounds, their problems, and the resolutions. The summaries also indicate the grade level(s) for which each book would be most appropriate. The book summaries are divided into the following subsections: 1) African American Heritage; 2) Asian American Heritage; 3) European American Heritage; 4) Latino American Heritage; and 5) Native American Heritage.

The sections of the bibliography contain entries with examples of realistic/contemporary fiction, folk literature, historical fiction, and biography. Each book is followed by a target activity that can be used to help children internalize ways to modify cultural stereotypes.

A final section in the book provides extended activities — mini-units — for a selected few of the children's literature titles summarized in the previous sections. Skilled teachers and librarians may use these examples of mini-units as models for adapting the book summaries to their classrooms as they see fit. Each mini-unit example contains:

1) Bibliographical information
2) Brief summary
3) Vocabulary to be introduced
4) Materials needed
5) Motivational activities ("into" text to tap prior knowledge)
6) Purposes for reading or listening
7) Retelling activities ("through" the text to engage the reader actively)
8) Discussion questions ("through" the text to help the readers reflect on the text and compare it to their own lives)
9) Extended activities (using language arts to enrich the text "beyond" its original boundaries)
10) Interdisciplinary ideas (going "beyond" the text's boundaries to span other areas of the curriculum)

This guide is intended to be only a starting point for caring teachers and librarians who find themselves challenged by a growing number of children living with cultural stereotypes that cause them to be, to a larger and larger degree, desperately in need of understanding and appreciation for others. While even the most committed teachers cannot change the cultural stereotypes faced by all the children in their charge, they can, themselves, provide positive role models of adults who maintain fair views of people from different cultures. Furthermore, they can enhance their language curricula by molding quality children's literature into carefully crafted lessons that guide all children toward developing the skills necessary for developing multicultural concepts and modifying cultural stereotypes in today's changing world. This book is a plea and a call for action toward that goal.

Readings

Appleberry, M. H. (1969). "A study of the effect of bibliotherapy on third grade children using a master list of titles from children's literature." University of Houston. University microfilm 69-21, 746.

Beardsley, D. A. (1979). "The effects of using fiction in bibliotherapy to alter attitudes of regular third grade students toward their handicapped peers." Unpublished Ph.D. dissertation, the University of Missouri-Columbia. University microfilm 80-07, 128.

Bissett, D. J. (1969). "The usefulness of children's books in the reading program." Paper presented at the International Reading Association, April 30–May 3, Kansas City, Missouri.

Bodart, J. (1980). "Bibliotherapy: The right book for the right person at the right time — and more." *Top of the News* (36), 183–88.

Brocki, A. C. (1969). "New literature for inner-city students." *English Journal* (58), 1151–61.

Bruell, E. (1966). "How to block the reading blocks? Read." *Peabody Journal of Education* (44), 114–17.

Cianciolo, P. J. (1965). "Children's literature can affect coping behavior." *Personnel and Guidance Journal* (43), 897–903.

Cooper, B. (1969). "Using children's literature in the elementary school." *Georgia English Counselor* (17), 1–3.

Cornett, C. E. and C. R. Cornett (1980). *Bibliotherapy: The Right Book at the Right Time.* Fastback 151. Bloomington, IN: Phi Delta Kappa Educational Foundation. ED 192 380.

Faust, H. F. (1969). "Books as an aid in preventing dropouts." *Elementary English* (46), 191–98.

Garcia, R. (1981). "Education for pluralism: Global roots stew." *Phi Delta Kappan* (37), 14–23.

Kantrowitz, V. (1967). "Bibliotherapy with retarded readers." *Journal of Reading* (11), 205–12.

Koon, J. F. (1970). "Cues for teaching the emotionally disturbed: Turn on, tune in, drop out." *The Clearing House* (44), 497–500.

Nigen, G. A. (1979). "Bibliotherapy for the atypical reader." *Wisconsin State Reading Journal* (24), 12–16.

Russell, D. H. (1949). "Identification through literature." *Childhood Education* (25), 397–401.

Schultheis, M. and R. Pavlik (1977). *Classroom Teachers' Manual for Bibliotherapy*. Fort Wayne, IN: Benet Learning Center. ED 163 493.

Squire, J. R. (1968). *Response to Literature*. Champaign: National Council of Teachers of English.

Strickland, R. (1961). "What thou lovest well remains." *Elementary English* (38), 63–73.

Taba, H. (1950). *With Focus on Human Relations*. Washington, D.C.: American Council on Education, 1950.

———— (1955). *With Perspective on Human Relations: A Study of Peer Group Dynamics in an Eighth Grade*. Washington, D.C.: American Council of Education.

Theroux, P. (1992). "Under the spell of the Trobriand Islands." *National Geographic* (182), 117–36.

Thomas, V. (1967). "The power of the book." *The English Teacher* (12), 21–24.

Waite, D. D. (1965). "Therapy for reading ills." *Pennsylvania School Journal* (114), 64–65.

Whipple, C. M. (1968). "The effect of short-term classroom bibliotherapy on the personality and academic achievement of reformatory inmate students." Unpublished Ed.D. dissertation, University of Oklahoma.

Zaccaria, J. S. and H. A. Moses (1968). *Facilitating Human Development Through Reading: The Use of Bibliotherapy in Teaching and Counseling*. Champaign: Stipes.

Books for
Young Children:
Grades K–3

AFRICAN AMERICAN HERITAGE

1 Aardema, Verna. *Bringing the Rain to Kapiti Plain: A Nandi Tale.* Ill. by Beatriz Vidal. New York: Dial, 1981.

This is an accumulating tale from Kenya that tells of Ki-Pat, a herdsman and Kenyan hero, who pierces a cloud with his eagle-feathered arrow to bring rain. On a barren, parched, dry African plain, hungry cattle wait for a huge dark cloud mass and rain to make the plain green with grass. An appended note mentions the origin in terms of the country, a sign of sensitivity on the author's part. Search for this rhythmic tale in UNICEF Curriculum Guide: *African Folktales.* Folk literature. 3–5.

Target Activity: "Herdsman and Hero"

Explore what this hero from the African culture has in common with some of our own heroes in the culture of the United States. What traits of heroism will the students discuss? To show similarities and differences between the two heroes, draw two overlapping circles (Venn diagrams) and in one circle write the words Hero from Africa, and in the other, Heroes from other cultures. In the appropriate circles, write down the traits the African hero has (perseverance, ability to overcome obstacles, solving problems) and the traits the other heroes have. If there are traits that the heroes have in common, write those traits in the overlapping area of the circles. Discuss the traits as they are written in the circles.

2 Aaseng, Nathan. *Florence Griffith Joyner: Dazzling Olympian.* Minneapolis: Lerner, 1989.

Florence Griffith Joyner was the seventh of eleven children. Her mother wanted her children to do well so she was very strict. She did not allow the children to watch television on a week day and required them, even when they were teenagers, to be in bed by 10 o'clock. But her mother encouraged her children to develop their special talents, whatever they might be.

Dee Dee, as Florence was called, showed a talent for stubborn independence early since she could go without speaking for days when she felt like it. She loved reading, kept a diary, and knew how to be noticed because of her special style. She had a pet snake that she used to wear around her neck and hair styles that made her famous in her Los Angeles neighborhood. But her most famous talent she discovered when she was quite young — she was a very fast runner and won her very first track competition when she was only seven.

"Flo Jo," as she is sometimes called today, is known around the world for her athletic running ability. She has won many medals at the Olympics for excelling at track competitions. Her stubborn independence helps her work harder and harder as she prepares for races. She is still known, too, for her flamboyant style as an athlete. She has worn long painted fingernails and beautiful running suits in her races. When she is not running and preparing for races, Florence Griffith Joyner writes children's books. She always loved reading and writing in her diary and the person she was as a child is reflected in the successful adult she has become. Biography. 2–3.

Target Activity: "You Are Special"
After reading this story with the class, discuss how Florence Griffith Joyner wasn't afraid to be someone special even when she was a small girl. Have a discussion with the group about how each of them is special. Help them see that "special" can mean being helpful, kind, a hard worker, knowing when to say "no," as well as doing your best when drawing, playing sports, reading, or engaging in other activities. Have children develop a list on the board of the many ways they can be special. Then have them draw a picture or write a story about how Florence Griffith Joyner was special when she was a child.

Optional Activity: Ask young children to draw pictures of when they are special and have each complete a sentence for a picture that starts: I am special when I _____. Have children share their pictures/stories and sentences with the class.

3 Bang, Betsy. *The Old Woman and the Red Pumpkin.* Ill. New York: Macmillan, 1975.

This is a Bengali folktale about a wise old woman who outsmarts a jackal, a tiger, and a bear whom she meets on her way to her granddaughter's house. The old woman is helped by her granddaughter to outsmart the animals for the trip back home, but in the end, her own wits save her. Folk literature. K–3.

Target Activity: "Outsmarting Danger"
Before acting out the story, discuss with children the choices this old woman had to save her life: Did she have a weapon? Was there someone around to help her? Could she outrun the danger? What could she do? Discuss how the old woman understood the motives of the animals by appealing to their hope for a *good* meal and their greed for the *best* part.

4 Bang, Betsy. *The Old Woman and the Rice Thief.* Ill. by Molly Garrett Bang. New York: Greenwillow, 1978.

This is a Bengali folktale of an old woman who has a complaint for the local ruler. Every night, someone steals her rice and she wants to put a stop to it. On her way to the Raja, she finds scary friends who ask her to take them home with her. She does not find the Raja but returns home with her friends who find a place to be in and around her house. After that, she has no need of help from the Raja because she has these helpers who protect her rice. Folk literature. K–3.

Target Activity: "The Bigger Idea"

Before hearing (reading) the story, discuss with children how they feel about the "bigger idea" behind the following:

    a. Why would a thief break the law or "human courtesy rule" of not stealing from another?

    b. Why should a thief be punished for breaking the law and stealing? Would there be a time when a thief should not be punished?

    c. Why would a person want to "get even" when a thief does something that affects the person?

    d. Do you agree/disagree that it is wrong for a thief to steal? What are your feelings about stealing? About getting friends to help stop a thief?

    e. Think about a time when a thief might have a "bad" excuse and a "good" excuse for taking something from someone.

5   Bunting, Eve. *The Wednesday Surprise.* Ill. by Donald Carrick. New York: Clarion, 1989.

Grandmother and Anna work together secretly on a present for Dad's birthday. It is a present that only the two of them can give to Dad. Anna teaches Grandmother to read. Anna and Grandmother are persistent and persevere as each day they work together and Grandmother develops a new skills. She learns to read from Anna's instruction. Concept of the importance of adult literacy supports a positive vision of life. Contemporary realism. Pre–3.

Target Activity: "Oral History of Learning to Read"

With children, discuss the idea of oral history: They may interview an older person who is from a background or cultural group different from their own and report back to the class. In the interview, they may use such questions as:

    a. How long have you lived here?

    b. What was the town like when you first came?

    c. Where did you live when you were a child?

    d. What was school like?

    e. How did you learn to read?

6   Climo, Shirley. *The Egyptian Cinderella.* Ill. by Ruth Heller. New York: Thomas Y. Crowell, 1989.

Recorded by the Roman historian Strabo (first century, B.C.) this is an old story based on fact about a Greek slave girl, Rhodopis, who married the Pharaoh Amasis and became his queen. Some of it is partly fable, for it is believed that one of her fellow slaves was a man named Aesop who told her fables about animals. Because she is a Greek slave in Egypt, Rhodopis (meaning Rosy Cheeks) washes clothes in the Nile, tends the geese, mends clothing, bakes bread, and gathers reeds along the bank. Scorned by the Egyptian girls, she befriends the animals and dances for them. Her master, seeing her dance, gives her a pair of dainty leather slippers with the toes gilded with rose-red gold. When the Pharaoh and his entourage are nearby, the Egyptian girls row away to Memphis to visit the Pharaoh's court. Rhodopis polishes her shoes and puts them on the bank just as a great falcon soars away with one of her slippers in his talons. Unknown to her, the falcon flies to Memphis where Amasis, the Pharaoh, is holding court and drops the slipper into his lap.

Amasis, thinking it is a sign to find the maiden whose foot fits the shoe, announces it is the will of the gods that the maiden should be the queen. During his long search, Amasis visits every place along the Nile and the Egyptian girls try to cramp and curl their feet into the slipper. When he discovers Rhodopis and commands her to try on the slipper, Rhodopis puts her foot into the slipper with ease and shows him the other shoe. Saying that she is not fit to be queen, the girls protest and say she is a slave and not even Egyptian. "She is the most Egyptian of all," says the Pharaoh, "for her eyes are as green as the Nile, her hair is as feathery as papyrus, and her skin the pink of a lotus flower." Folk literature. 3 up.

Target Activity: "Something Positive"

The teacher encourages all in the group to be friends to one another. In the group each student prints his or her name on a paper. Each paper is passed to the right until it has completed the circle. Each student in turn writes something positive about the person whose name is on the sheet. Finally each student has his or her own "good word" sheet to keep. This is a list of written compliments for the student to take home, show to others, and keep as a souvenir of the lesson.

7 Gray, Nigel. *A Country Far Away*. Ill. by Philippe Dupasquier. New York: Watts/Orchard Books, 1989.

The book shows an African boy in the illustration, and below, a Western boy with the words, "Today was an ordinary day. I stayed home." A reader sees the African boy's village home with him tending goats. The Western boy is washing the car with his father. There are differences and similarities in two cultures for discussion and review cultures different from the reader's. Contemporary realism. 1–3.

Target Activity: "Find Similarities in Two Cultures"

Ask children to compare books with illustrations showing life in two cultures and to begin creative writing with the words, "The two countries I read about are alike because. . ." When finished, each child reads it to a reading partner. Discuss and make any revisions the writer wants to make.

8 Greene, Carol. *Desmond Tutu: Bishop of Peace.* Chicago: Children's Press, 1986.

Desmond Tutu was born in South Africa and quickly learned some sad things about his country: although 70 percent of the people in South Africa were black, they could not vote in national elections; they could not live wherever they wanted to or own land; the government could make them move at any time.

When Desmond was twelve years old, his mother worked as a cook in a missionary school for the blind. Seeing people caring about helping other people made Desmond decide to help other people, too. Tutu became a teacher, and then, inspired by a white Anglican priest, he was ordained as a priest. Tutu became the first black dean in the Anglican church. When the government was moving blacks from cities back to tribal lands, Tutu, who was not a bishop, asked the United States and countries in Europe to stop trading with South Africa. Though this made the South African government angry, the peaceful method worked. In 1984, Bishop Tutu was chosen to receive the Nobel Peace Prize. The citation with the award praised all South African blacks who had worked for peaceful change. Biography. 2–3.

Target Activity: "Speaking Out Against Injustice"

Bishop Tutu believes that all people should be free—no matter what color they are. "I cannot help it," he says. "When I see injustice, I cannot keep quiet. . ." (see p. 31). Discuss this quote from Bishop Tutu and the idea that sometimes, to create a peaceful world, one must speak out against injustice. With children, brainstorm some situations they have witnessed that were unjust, such as children taunting a disabled child, a bully knocking down a little child, calling someone of a different race names, etc. Invite groups of children to select an unjust situation from those that have been brainstormed. Ask them to select a "peacemaker" who witnesses the injustice and speaks out against it in a firm but gentle way.

9 Greenfield, Eloise. *Rosa Parks.* Ill. by Eric Marlow. New York: Thomas Y. Crowell, 1973.

Even when she was a little girl growing up in Montgomery, Alabama, Rosa hated the special rules by which black people were forced to live. With her mother's help, she was able to grow up proud of herself and other black people. Rosa Parks became known as the "Mother of the Civil

Rights Movement" because of a very brave act. One day in 1955, while riding home on the bus after a long day's work, Rosa refused to give up her seat to a white man. She was arrested and put in jail. Black people in Montgomery then decided that they would not ride the buses until the unfair rules were changed. Led by Dr. Martin Luther King, the Montgomery protests against the bus policies went on for months, despite arrests and threats, while the world watched. Rosa herself was arrested again and often threatened. Finally, the Supreme Court ruled that the bus company had to change its policy. It was a great victory for black people, started by one peaceful yet determined black woman. Biography. 2–3.

Target Activity: "Fighting Back Peacefully"

Discuss with children the fact that Rosa Parks accomplished positive changes for black people with her dignified refusal to be treated with disrespect. Ask children why they think this tactic was successful. Have children think of a problem that they may have had with siblings or with other children on the playground—or one that they witnessed—that was settled with hitting, kicking, or name-calling. For each situation, have volunteers offer how they think Rosa Parks might have dealt with the situation more peacefully, while successfully changing the negative behavior.

10 Guirma, Frederic. *Princess of the Full Moon.* Ill. London: Macmillan, 1970.

This is a favorite folktale told by the people of Upper Volta in Africa. People sit around the fire at night—the girls with the women and the boys with the men as is their tradition. As the tale of the beautiful princess is told, the children call out the names of each character to speak, because they have heard the story many times and enjoy anticipating what comes next. The story is a traditional tale of good disguised as ugly and bad disguised as handsome, with a foolish princess mistaking appearance for true worth. She learns her lesson, and in the end, she gets both goodness and beauty and is saved from evil. Folk literature. 2–3.

Target Activity: "The Beautiful Princess in Every Culture"

After discussing the story with the children, ask them to dictate (write) a description of the princess without using the word beautiful. What words best describe a princess from another culture? Consider the ones that are listed:

Africa: _____

Asia (China, Japan): _____

Latino/Hispanic: _____

Native Americans: _____

After the story, ask children to think back to some of the things in it that impressed them the most.

11 Hazen, Barbara Shook. *Why Are People Different?* Ill. by Kathy Wilburn. Racine, WI: Western, 1985.

In this story, little Terry is feeling bad about being different. He is African American and is sure that is the reason he is being ignored by his friends. His grandmother tells him that she always felt different because she was tall and a tomboy. She encourages Terry to notice that people all have their differences and that differences are often an advantage. When Terry begins to worry more about liking people and less about being liked, he makes friends with the children in his school. K–3.

Target Activity: "Accepting Differences"

Differences in people's skin color, hair color, language, dress, or religion, need not be frightening to children if they learn to be comfortable and value diverse people as human beings. Ask children to think of one way they, like Terry, have felt different from others. Invite them to brainstorm some ways that that difference might be considered an advantage, as Terry's grandmother suggested.

12 Heide, Florence Parry and Judith Heide Gilliland. *The Day of Ahmed's Secret.* Ill. by Ted Lewin. New York: Lothrop, 1990.

Ahmed, a butagaz boy who delivers cooking gas to customers in Cairo, has news for his family. After his rounds with his donkey cart, he goes home where he shows his family that he can write his name in Arabic.

Ahmed has been persistent and has persevered as he learns to write his name in Arabic. He waits for the right moment to tell his secret to his family. Contemporary realism. K–3.

Target Activity: "Children Achieve in Every Culture"

With the children, discuss some of the accomplishments they have made and the feelings they had when they did those things. Invite each to write her or his name on the writing board.

In teams of two, the children can create a scene in which Ahmed and his donkey deliver cooking gas to a customer in Cairo. Ask the students to change roles and play the scene again. Then joining with other groups, they will dramatize the loving family gathered around and watching Ahmed as he shows them he can proudly write his name. Invite each student to write the name, Ahmed, on the writing board and to pantomime or show the excitement to dramatize the boy's feelings about this accomplishment.

13 Isadora, Rachel. *Ben's Trumpet.* Ill. by the author. New York: Greenwillow, 1979.

Ben, a young black child in the inner city, sits on the fire escape and plays his invisible trumpet to the beat of the music from the nearby Zig Zag

Jazz Club. This is his favorite activity. Ben suffers the the ridicule of his peers and the lack of interest of his family. When the trumpeter of the club recognizes his potential, he has the chance to try out a real trumpet. In spite of his uninterested family and the teasing of his friends, Ben is persistent as he "practices" playing an invisible trumpet each night. Contemporary realism. K–2.

Target Activity: "People in Every Culture Enjoy Music"

With children, discuss some of their musical ambitions and interests. With a record player, tape recorder, or a radio, play some music from different cultures for the members of the class and ask them to observe and watch one another as they all listen. What do the students do when they want to keep time to the music? For each behavior that a student observes, the students will make a list of what the listeners do to keep the beat.

Listeners' Check List

by _____

date _____

What the Listener Did

_____

a.

b.

c.

Discuss: Which ways seemed to work best? Why do you think so? Did anyone persevere and keep the beat all the way through the song? Who? Invite that student to tell that class what made her or him persistent in this activity.

14 Keats, Ezra Jack. *Goggles!* Ill. by the author. New York: Macmillan, 1969.

Two young black boys, Peter and Archie, live in the inner city and find a pair of motorcycle goggles near their hideout in a deserted lot. They have to stand up to three older bullies who want the goggles. Willie, a dog, grabs the goggles and runs off with them as the boys head for their hideout. The boys trick the bullies into heading off in another direction and the two young boys and Willie run back to Archie's house to savor their escape and their find. Contemporary realism. Pre–1.

Target Activity: "Children in Every Culture Feel Afraid Sometimes"

The actions and feelings of the boys will seem close to home for young readers. Archie peers through the hole in a board in the fence to secretly observe the big boys chasing him. There is some security in being hidden behind the board of the fence. Ask the children to name some things that frighten them and then draw the frightening things to show what they would look like when seen through a peephole of a fence. Encourage the girls and boys to make their own drawings to gain insight into Archie's feelings as he hides from the chasing boys.

15 Keats, Ezra Jack. *A Letter to Amy.* Ill. by the author. New York: Harper & Row, 1968.

Peter wants to invite Amy to his birthday party, even though he knows his friends will make fun of her because she is a girl. But Amy is clearly very special to him, as evidenced by the fact that he sends her a special invitation, when he has just asked everyone else. Peter is a sensitive little boy who values his friendship with Amy. K–3.

Target Activity: "Helping Children from Other Cultures Feel Welcome"

Lead a general discussion with children about a time they went someplace and felt alone because they were the only girl, boy, child, American, black, Asian, etc. Brainstorm some words that could be used to describe how they felt. Pair children and have them roleplay this situation, or the one with Amy and Peter. Have one child play the "different" child and the other child portray a child trying to do and say things to make the first child feel welcome. Lead into a follow-up discussion about how children just arriving from other cultures could be made to feel welcome.

16 Lottridge, Celia Barker, reteller. *The Name of the Tree.* Ill. by Ian Wallace. New York: McElderry Books/Macmillan, 1990.

When a drought settles on an African plain, animals search for food and find a tree with every fruit imaginable. This Bantu folktale tells that the animals must learn the name of the tree before it will surrender its bounty. Muted grays and greens in illustrations show the dry land and hot African sun. Faced with the problem of learning a tree's name before it will surrender its wonderful edible fruit during the time of drought, the animals persevere after their long search. Recommended storytelling. Folk literature. K–3.

Target Activity: "Water Is Valued in All Cultures"

Explore what the Nandi culture and Bantu culture in Africa have in common with our own, the reliance on water, the resourcefulness of people (or animals posing as people in stories) when they are faced with this problem. Compare the solution in this story to the one in *Bringing the Rain to Kapiti Plain: A Nandi Tale* and identify the importance of water to all people.

17 McDermott, Gerald. *Anansi the Spider: A Tale from the Ashanti.* Adapted and Ill. by Gerald McDermott. New York: Holt, Rinehart & Winston, 1972.

Six wondrous deeds are performed by the sons of Anansi. Their names are See Trouble, Road Builder, River Drinker, Game Skinner, Stone Thrower, and Cushion. They save their father from a terrible danger. Each of the sons of the spider-hero is an expert in some way. Their names tell the children their expertise that is useful in solving problems. Folk literature. 3–4.

Target Activity: "Pattern of Six Is Found in Folktales from Different Cultures"

Before the story is reread, the children decide on motions and movements for the characters for an audience participation story. The names of the sons will lead the young children quickly into ideas for movements. When a character's name is mentioned in the rereading, the teacher pauses and gives the audience time to respond with the movements that identify the character. To further expand the pattern of six into folktales from other cultures, a teacher or librarian may invite children to find other folktales and record the information they find in the tales:

Pattern of Six (or Five)   *Title of Tale*   *Country-Culture*

18 McKissack, Patricia C. *Mirandy and Brother Wind.* Ill. by Jerry Pinkney. New York: Knopf, 1988.

Mirandy was hoping to win her first cakewalk, a dance rooted in African American culture in which the pair of dancers with the most flamboyant dances take home a cake. The trouble is, Mirandy's most logical partner, Ezel, is much too clumsy to be a partner who could help her win. Mirandy decides to try to catch Brother Wind and have *him* be her partner. Everyone she speaks to tells her, "Can't nobody put shackles on Brother Wind . . . he be free." She tries to put black pepper on his footprints to make him sneeze so she can slip up behind him and throw a quilt over him. She tries to catch him in a crock bottle, but he escapes. Finally, Mirandy traps Brother Wind in the barn. At the cakewalk, when another girl makes fun of Ezel's clumsiness, Mirandy defends him and claims him as her partner. She immediately regrets having said such a "tomfool" thing; she has caught Brother Wind. She goes to Brother Wind and makes a wish. She and Ezel dance with grace and style and win the cakewalk. A beautifully illustrated book that portrays a young black girl as highly resourceful and clever, yet compassionate. 3–4.

Target Activity: "Pursuing a Goal"

Have children retell the story, paying special attention to the attempts Mirandy made to catch Brother Wind. Ask them why they feel she did not give up. Ask them to take a couple of minutes to remember a time they really wanted to do something that seemed impossible. What was their goal? What did other people tell them about the possibility of pursuing their goal? Have each child share their goal with a partner. Let the partner be the "other person" who gives them reasons why their goal is impossible. Tell them to try their best to offer arguments as to why they should continue pursuing their goal. Compare the goals of the boys and girls in the classroom.

19 Mendez, Phil. *The Black Snowman.* Ill. by Carole Byard. New York: Scholastic, 1989.

Young Jacob Miller wakes up on a snowy Saturday, angry at being poor and black. "I hate being black," he tells his mother. Try as she may to humor him, he sulks. Then his brother cajoles him into making a snowman, which is black from dirty snow. Among the scraps they use to dress the snowman is a brightly colored kente cloth (material believed to have brought magic to the Ashanti people before they were sold into slavery). With this material as a symbol that life has meaning, Jacob can reassess his anger at being black and can look toward a more positive vision of life. Full page watercolors by Carole Byard add depth to this story. Contemporary realism. 1–3.

Target Activity: "Every Culture Has Magical Objects in Its Folktales"

With the children, discuss the kente cloth, the colored material that brought magic to the Ashanti people, and its power in the story. Discuss other tales from different cultures you and others can find with magical objects in them.

Tales	*Magical Object*	*Culture*

20 Monjo, Ferdinand. *The Drinking Gourd.* Ill. by Fred Brenner. New York: Harper, 1970.

Tommy is a little boy growing up in New England in the decade before the Civil War. In his barn, he is surprised to find a family of escaping slaves that have been hidden there by his father. His father explains that he is a "conductor" on the Underground Railroad and that, although he doesn't like to break the law, he feels he must, because he feels it is wrong to own people. Together Tommy and his father take the family to the next station. While the family and Tommy's father lie hidden in the hay truck, Tommy drives. Tommy is stopped by a U.S. Marshal and his men. They ask him if he has slaves hidden in the back of the truck. Thinking quickly, Tommy says that he is running away. The men laugh and tell him to go home. The family of slaves makes a safe escape. Historical fiction. 2–3.

Target Activity: "Judge Others Fairly"

Discuss the concept of slavery with children and make the point that it is wrong to judge people on the basis of the color of their skin. To play "Good and Bad," ask one child to briefly leave the room. Pick an arbitrary physical feature, such as eye color or hair color. Tell the students in one group, such as those with brown hair, that they are "good," while all others are bad. Allow the child who has left the room to return and try to figure out the basis on which the other children have been labeled as "good" or "bad." Let each group share their feelings about the arbitrary labeling.

Optional Activity: "The Code in *The Drinking Gourd* Song"

With the children, discuss the illustration that shows the light sketches of seven runaways who carry their bundles over their shoulders super-imposed over the drawing of the house and barn that gives a sense of the magnitude of the cause, the task, the danger, the importance, the symbol. Discuss the danger and the excitement on the journey as Tommy goes with his father and an escaping black family to take them on the next part of the journey. Discuss the ethical considerations of knowing one must break a law.

The Drinking Gourd was the code song that the slaves sang. The song was used to point the direction for escape by following the North Star, using the Big Dipper as a guide. The words to the song are in the book.

21 Pomerantz, Charlotte. *The Chalk Doll.* Ill. by Fran Lessac. New York: Lippincott, 1989.

Mother tells Rose stories of her childhood and her wish for a store-bought chalk doll. Rose compares her own life with the fun of her mother's — having a rag doll, drinking milk from a can, and special parties. She gathers scraps of materials and together Mother and Rose make a rag doll for her. The illustrations, which should be discussed, show the colorful Jamaican countryside with bright foliage and painted buildings — and the daily life — chickens at the front door, lizards on the walk, cows grazing, and donkeys used for transportation. Contemporary realism. 2–3.

Target Activity: "There Are Family Memories in Every Culture"

As a companion book to this one, read excerpts from your favorite book of poems or from *Childtimes* (Crowell, 1979), a book of memories of three generations written by Eloise Greenfield and her mother, Lessie Jones Little. A theme of the text is the social concerns of the family. After listening to some selected verses, encourage children to tell a memory they have had with a family member.

22 Roberts, Naurice. *Barbara Jordan: The Great Lady from Texas.* Chicago: Children's Press, 1984.

Barbara Jordan always wanted to be someone special, even as a little girl. She was the third and youngest daughter of parents who helped her and her sisters behave in a way so that they always would have self-respect and dignity. Barbara's father always said that if they worked hard they could be anything that they wanted to be in life. Barbara worked hard at school and when she didn't get the A she wanted, she learned to work even harder.

Barbara's family was black and poor, living in the South at a time when life was not fun for her people. Blacks were not allowed to go to the same schools as whites or eat in the same restaurants. Barbara knew that to get ahead in such a place, she would have to be well educated. When she was in high school, she decided to become a lawyer, like a black woman judge she had heard speak. She, too, wanted to help change laws that hurt her and other black people.

Barbara Jordan did become a lawyer. She was also elected as a Texas senator. She could now work to end segregation laws in the very place where they were made. Biography. 3 up.

Target Activity: "Models to Follow"

After reading the book, discuss with children the person who inspired Barbara Jordan's decision to become a lawyer and why being a lawyer was especially important to her. Ask children to think about a person they know, have seen on television, or have read about (like Barbara Jordan) who would be a good model (and discuss this concept) for them for their adult life. Ask children to share their ideas and then each write an essay about a good model. For example, an essay may begin with, "I think of _____ as a good model for me. She/he is _____ (a lawyer, etc.). I think being a _____ (lawyer, etc.) is an important job because _____.

Optional Activity: Have each child describe why he or she thinks a particular person is a good model. Encourage other children to ask questions about this person to see if they can then guess who the model is.

23 Seed, Jenny. *Ntombi's Song.* Ill. by Anno Berry. Boston: Beacon Press, 1989.

In South Africa in a rural Zulu life setting, six-year-old Ntombi takes a first journey to the village store to buy sugar for her mother. Told by other women that a monster lives in the forest, she is frightened by a passing bus, and spills the sugar into the sand. Deciding to earn the money to replace the sugar, she dances for tourists and sings a song her mother created for her when she was a baby and receives a coin. Watercolor illustrations. Contemporary realism. K–2.

Target Activity: "Mishaps Can Be Solved the Peaceful Way"

Look at the illustrations again so the students get a close-up view of the mishap that happened to Ntombi. Encourage them to relate the mishap in the story to one that has happened to them in their lives and to talk about one of the traits of resiliency—solving problems. Discuss the way each solved or could have solved the problem. Invite them to draw a picture of what each would have done to help Ntombi if he had been there when she spilled the sugar on the ground.

24 Smith, Kathie Billingslea. *Harriet Tubman*. Ill. by James Seward. New York: Messner, 1989.

Born in Dorchester County, Maryland, Harriet Tubman (1821–1913) did much to help her people. As a young girl she was a field worker and then escaped to the North. There, she decided to help others to escape from slavery. During the War Between the States, Tubman was a cook, servant, spy, and scout for the Union Army. After the war, she supported schools for freed slaves in North Carolina. She took trips into slave territory and led more than 300 slaves to freedom, thus earning her the name of "Moses." Illustrations are both in full color and black and white. A read-aloud biography. 2–3.

Target Activity: "In Every Culture, People Help Others Escape from Tyranny"

Pair this story of Tubman's life as a read-aloud biography with *Runaway Slave* (Four Winds, 1968) by Ann McGovern and discuss the ways the two authors create the excitement of Tubman's life drama.

For independent reading and study:
a. Read selections from books about the life of Harriet Tubman.
b. React to the selection in writing in a letter beginning "Dear Harriet." Place it in your student journal.

25 Stock, Catherine. *Armien's Fishing Trip*. Ill. by the author. New York: Morrow, 1990.

While visiting his aunt and uncle one weekend, Armien stows away on Uncle Faried's boat, the *Rosie*, because he has "salt water in his veins." He is determined to prove himself old enough to go to sea like the other fishermen out of Kalk Bay off the African coast. When one of the crew is swept overboard by rough seas, Armien solves the problem about how to call for help and sounds the alarm which alerts Faried who rescues the crew member. Contemporary realism. K–3.

Target Activity: "Heroes Rescue Others in All Cultures"

Invite children to look in the newspapers for articles about current rescues. Discuss the articles and talk about some of the traits the rescuers had to have to accomplish what they did. Relate the traits to some of the traits of resiliency: perseverance, overcoming obstacles, and problem solving.

Ask children to dictate a story that would fit the headline: "Rescue at Sea."
Read the dictated story together and discuss. Talk about ways the children's story relates to the incident in *Armien's Fishing Trip*.

26　Williams, Karen Lynn. *Galimoto*. Ill. by Catherine Stock. New York: Lothrop, Lee & Shepard, 1990.

In a small African village, seven-year-old Kondi decides to make a push toy—a galimoto. When his older brother tells him that he does not have enough wire to make a toy, Kondi goes on a search to get wire from other children and adults using his persuasion and know-how. He shows he is resourceful and gets the wire he needs. He coaxes a girl to trade her wire. He swaps his knife with a friend for more. He rummages for wire at a junk yard. When the moon and his friends ask him out to play, out comes the galimoto. His persistence is rewarded and his goal is reached. Kondi overcomes all the obstacles to reach his goal. Contemporary realism. K–3.

Target Activity: "Resourceful Children Are Found in All Cultures"

Before the book: Talk about building toys of all kinds. Ask students to describe the different shapes, sizes, and types of toys they have used. Have students draw some of the shapes of toys on the writing board and suggest some geometrical descriptions. Ask what sorts of things the students like to build (or toys they repair). Next, tell students that they will hear a story that involves making a push toy. Ask students to listen for ways the boy solves his problem to find wire to make the toy.

After the book: Invite students to retell the action in the story with questions that focus on the details in the story:

a. What were some of the problems that Kondi had in his search for wire to make the toy?

b. How did Kondi deal with each situation to find wire?

c. Have students suggest other items that could have been built with the wire.

d. Can students suggest words to make a list of other things made from wire?

Extending the story:

To encourage diverse thinking, tell students that a pipecleaner is like the wire that Kondi had, the more you change it (twist it, bend it, reshape it), the more things the pipecleaner can become for you. Ask students to sit together in a circle on the floor. Pass a pipecleaner from student to student. Ask each one to use the pipecleaner to tell something about himself or herself. For an example, hold the pipecleaner up like a baseball bat, and say, "I like to play baseball. This is what I use to hit the ball and make a home run."

Continue passing the pipecleaner around until all have had one turn.

Then, give each student a pipecleaner and ask each one to think of a problem and then solve the problem by bending the pipecleaner into an object that represents the solution to the problem. Those who "can't think of anything" could decide to take on Kondi's problem and make a small push toy—a galimoto. Ask each student to talk about the problem that he or she selected and show the pipecleaner object that "solves" the problem. Example, "I like to play baseball but I do not have a bat so I made a pipecleaner bat."

Optional Activity: "Inventory of a Problem"

Ask children to give as many examples as they can from another setting (perhaps from settings related to the cultural backgrounds of some of the students in the class) to show another way a similar problem could have been solved:

In a United States Setting (then consider other settings)

   a. What would be some of the problems that a small boy would have in this setting in his search for wire to make a toy?
   b. How would a small boy in this setting deal with the situation to find wire?
   c. What other items could be built with the wire?

27 Yarbrough, Camille (1979). *Cornrows.* Ill. by Carole Byard. New York: Coward, McCann & Geoghegan, Inc.

The author's poignant, almost poetic tale provides a reader with insights into how the hairstyle of cornrows, a symbol of Africa since ancient times, can today symbolize the courage of outstanding African Americans living in this country. In the distinctive hairstyle, every design has a name and means something in the powerful past and present richness of the African American tradition. Sister and little brother, Me Two, listen as their mama and "great-grammaw" share the story of the cornrows and in doing so, tell the children much about African American history. K–3.

Target Activity: "Hairstyles"

After hearing Yarbrough's richly woven tale of the history and significance of cornrows, children will have a better appreciation and respect for the hairstyle and the people who wear it. Through pictures in trade books and National Geographic magazine, explore hairstyles worn by other groups of people. Help children to find out the origins of these hairstyles by providing research materials or inviting resource people from various cultural groups to talk to the class about the significance of certain hairstyles in their cultures.

Optional Activity: "African American Illustrations"

Carole Byard's illustrations have perfectly brought the words to life in this story. She expertly uses charcoal drawings to capture the nuance and this story. She expertly uses charcoal drawings to capture the nuance and moods of her characters. Discuss with children the illustrations of the symbols in the story. Point out the royal stool, sculptured wave, ritual masquerade, and of course, the braided hair. Introduce children to other books for children that also have been illustrated by Carole Byard, such as *African Dream* by Eloise Greenfield, and *Three African Tales* by Adjai Robinson.

ASIAN AMERICAN HERITAGE

28 Chan, Chin-Yi. *Good Luck Horse*. Ill. by Plato Chan. London: Whittlesey, 1943.

Out of print but still available in some library collections, this pre–Hsia dynasty Chinese legend is told by Chin-Yi Chan because it is a favorite one of her son, Plato. The tale is of Wah-Toong, the lonely son of a rich merchant, who cuts himself a horse from paper which becomes a live horse when wind snatches it and drops it in a magician's garden. The Good Luck horse damages a garden, scares other horses and is known as a bad-luck horse. Running away, he meets a beautiful mare and returns with Good-Luck Wife to Wah Toong. When war breaks out, the horse talks with the enemies' horses who all plan to mingle with the opposition so that no battle can take place and peace is achieved without fighting. When peace is achieved without fighting, all realize that there is no difference between good and bad luck and that "There is only luck! And that means that every day must be lived so that a man always does his best." A story of resilience of Eastern culture. Folk literature. 1–2.

Target Activity: "What Meaning Do Certain Things Have for You?"

Ask the students questions designed to get to the meaning that certain things have for them, what the girls and boys are familiar with, or to get descriptions of experiences they have had which can be used by the teacher to interpret their background and their feelings or their understanding of concepts of "luck." For this story, ask the students to describe what a good-luck horse might do. Accept the collection of notions from the children, even the ones the teacher suspects come from watching television. Share the fact that every culture has rituals and superstitions around the concept of "luck."

29 Coerr, Eleanor. *Chang's Paper Pony*. Ill. by Deborah Kogan Ray. New York: Harper & Row, 1988.

Chang and his grandfather have just come to California from China during the time of the gold rush. They work in the kitchen of a mining camp where Chang is often teased by the miners. He is very lonely and asks his grandfather if he could have a pony, but there is no way they can afford one. A kind miner, Big Pete, offers to take Chang panning for gold if Chang will clean Pete's cabin. Maybe he can find enough gold to enable him to buy a pony. He finds no gold while panning, but while cleaning Big Pete's cabin he finds some gold nuggets in the cracks in the floorboards. He reluctantly turns these over to Big Pete. Big Pete surprises him with a pony. Educators who are interested in this historically accurate story may want to avoid the use of the illustrations of Chinese men shown with their hair in pigtails and performing menial tasks at the mining camp. K–3.

Target Activity: "The Immigrants in the Mining Camps"

Have children do research to discover the importance of the immigrant laborers, like the Chinese, to the mining camps. Ask them to explore what life was like for these immigrants who were often exploited. Help them to graph the different cultures that came to California during the gold rush to work in the camps.

Optional Activity: "Teasing Hurts"

Chang was often teased by the miners simply because he was Chinese. Discuss this inequity with children. Ask them to think about what they would do if they heard someone teasing another child about their culture, language, or race. Ask them to choose a friend and roleplay such an encounter for the rest of the class.

30 Demi. *Chen Ping and His Magic Axe.* Ill. by the author. New York: Dodd, Mead, 1987.

This is the story of Chen Ping, an honest, peace-loviong boy who is sent out to collect firewood by his greedy master, Wing Fat. On his way, Chen Ping loses his axe. Suddenly, an old man appears and offers to help. First, he brings up a silver axe and then a gold one, but Chen Ping is not tempted. When the old man brings up Chen Ping's axe, the boy admits that it is his.

Such honesty pleases the elderly man, who says, "Do not be surprised if you find your axe to be much more of a treasure than the others." When Chen Ping tells his story to Wing Fat, greed enters. What then happens to the greedy Wing Fat and the magical forces that prevail to help the honest Chen Ping makes a wonderfully rewarding story about the importance of always telling the truth when solving problems. K–3.

Target Activity: "I Can Find Magical Objects in Tales from Other Cultures"

With the girls and boys, the teacher discusses the folktale and the concept of honesty gaining the positive attention of others and being rewarded in time. The teacher invites the students to draw an outline of a large axe (shape should fill the page) and inside the outline, write the titles of folk-tales they have found that include magical objects in tales from other cultures.

31   Hillman, Elizabeth. *Min-Yo and the Moon Dragon.* New York: Harcourt Brace Jovanovich, 1992.

This is a "why" tale set in ancient China. The Emperor's wise men want someone to climb the fragile staircase to the moon and ask the moon dragon why the moon is falling. The lightest person in China is Min-Yo and she is selected to take gifts of food and a diamond to the dragon. The dragon likes the food but is unimpressed with the diamond because he has a cave full of them. Presently, he realizes that the weight of the diamonds might be making the moon fall and he and Min Yo throw them into the sky where they turn into stars. Pre–2.

Target Activity: "Why Tales in Different Cultures"

With enough copies of different "why" tales from different cultures, invite the children to join up with partners and read their tales. In the whole group, ask the children to retell the tale they read and record the title under a related heading about its culture of origin:

Why Tales in Different Cultures

African   Asian   European   Latino   Native American

Ask the children to explain why they think ancient people told these "why" tales in different cultures.

32   Hodges, Margaret, reteller. *The Golden Deer.* Ill. by Daniel San Souci. New York: Scribner's, 1992.

This is a story that reflects Buddhist origins and is from the *Jataka Tales.* Weary of going daily with their King of Benares to hunt, the people drive two herds of deer into a park and let the king hunt by himself. Each of the two herds is led by a magnificent golden stag, one of which is the Buddha. The king orders that the beautiful creatures be spared and the deer decide that one of them will be chosen each day and given to the king. When a young doe about to give birth is chosen, Buddha takes her place. At this, the king realizes he should protect all living creatures of the land, air, and sea. 2–3.

Target Activity: "All Cultures Appreciate Creatures of the Land, Air, and Sea"

With children, discuss ways people of different cultures show their appreciation for the living creatures of the land, air, and sea.

African heritage: Students offer favorites.

Asian heritage: In the Eyes of the Cat: Japanese Poetry for All Seasons (Holt, 1992) has poems about living creatures.

European heritage: The Folks in the Valley: A Pennsylvania Dutch ABC (Harpercollins, 1992) by Jim Aylesworth shows life in a pleasant valley that has been home to Dutch families for generations.

Latino heritage: Students offer favorites.

Native American heritage: The illustrations in *My Name Is Pocahontas*, by William Accorsi, show a unity with nature.

33 Ikeda, Daisaku. *The Cherry Tree.* Ill. by Brian Wildsmith. New York: Knopf, 1992.

In a Japanese village destroyed by war actions, the lives of the villagers are difficult. In the cold, Taichi and Yumiko, brother and sister, see their mother leave for work each day. Since the bombings, a tree has not bloomed and the children notice an elderly man wrapping straw around its trunk to protect it from the cold. The elderly villager believes that his kindness and patience will make the tree flower again and the children help him. In the spring, the tree blooms and the villagers come to see it and, like the tree, the villagers come back to life. K–3.

Target Activity: "A Need to Keep Hope Alive"

Discuss the main idea of the importance of keeping hope alive and elicit times from the children's experience when they thought life was difficult (and dreary) but things changed because someone had kindness and patience.

34 Leaf, Margaret. *Eyes of the Dragon.* Ill. by Ed Young. New York: Lothrop, Lee & Shepard, 1987.

A magistrate of a Chinese village summoned the greatest dragon painter to decorate the mighty wall around the village with a portrait of the Dragon King. The portrait was so skillfully painted it seemed almost alive and when the eyes of the dragon were painted in (due to the magistrate's demand and over the painter's objections), the portrait came alive and the dragon crumbled the wall into pieces. 1–3.

Target Activity: "A Prose-Poetry Cultural Connection"

One of the poems compiled by Laura Whipple in *Eric Carle's Dragons Dragons and Other Creatures That Never Were* (Philomel, 1991) can be read aloud. Ask the children to talk about what they heard in the story and in the poem. Point out that authors created stories and poems about their people's beliefs in dragons — good and destructive. Suitable for storytelling by the teacher are two stories from *Dragons and Other Fabulous Beasts*

(Grosset & Dunlap, 1980) by R. Blythe, "The Fire Dragon of the Burning Mountain" and "The Cock and the Dragon." In the first tale, a dragon was the keeper of the volcano fire and made the fire flame and the rocks fall. Trapped by fallen rock himself, he was freed by a brave girl, and in return, he promised to keep the volcano silent and not destroy the village and fields. In the second tale, "The Cock and the Dragon," a dragon flew into a Chinese farmyard, borrowed the horns of a rooster, and promised to return them but never did. Now, every morning, the rooster's descendents call out to the sky, "Bring back my horns!" and they have not given up for they still make a noisy demand each morning. Help the children see that the story is a "why" story and is an explanation of why a rooster crows and point out that storytellers (and poets) in every culture have tried to explain ways that things in nature happen with this kind of "why" tale.

35   Lee, Jeanne M. (1987). *Ba-Nam.* Ill. by the author. New York: Henry Holt & Co..

In Vietnam, there is a special day called "Thanh-Minh," which means "pure and bright." On this day, families visit the graves of their ancestors and present them with offerings. It is also a day when relatives get together to pray and fellowship with one another. For little Nan, this Thanh-Minh Day is special because it is the first time she is old enough to go along with her family. When they arrive at the graveyard, they are greeted by the gatekeeper, Ba-Nam, who is old, ugly and very scary to Nan. The child clutches her father's hand tightly when Ba-Nam pats her on the head. When Nan and her brother Keung get lost among the tombstones, it is Ba-Nam who guides their way back. Ba-Nam has earned Nan's trust; Nan has also learned that one must not be judged by one's outward appearance. Realistic fiction. K–3.

Target Activity: "Inner Beauty"

Despite her wizened face and black teeth, Ba-Nam becomes a kind and beautiful woman in Nan's eyes and becomes her friend. Encourage children to share a time when they met someone and got an initial impression of them, based upon the person's appearance alone, that turned out later to be misleading. Compare Nan's experience with that of Nat in *Miss Maggie* by Cynthia Rylant.

Optional Activity: "A Vietnamese Folktale"

For children who enjoyed hearing about Ba-Nam, introduce them to another book written by Jeanne Lee, *Toad Is the Uncle of Heaven* (Holt). This is a Vietnamese folktale that children will enjoy listening to and then retelling. For children interested in learning more folktales as well as crafts, games, and recipes from Vietnam, present *Look What We've Brought You from Vietnam* (Julian Messner) by Phyllis Shalant.

36 Louie, Ai-Lang. *Yeh Shen: A Cinderella Story from China.*
Ill. by Ed Young. New York: Philomel, 1982.

Versions of Cinderella from other cultures have many similarities
to this ancient tale (A.D. 618–907). It appears in *The Miscellaneous Record
of Yu Yang*, authored by Tuan Ch'eng-Shih, and predates European versions: a beautiful girl is treated badly by her stepmother, and when a
festival approaches, Yeh-Shen is left weeping at home to do the heaviest
and dirtiest of chores while Stepmother and Stepsister go off dancing. Her
wish to go to the festival is granted by an old man through the power of
magic fish bones. Her slippers are woven of gold threads in a pattern
similar to the scales of a fish, her gown is azure, and she has a beautiful blue
feathered cloak. When her foot fits into the beautiful slipper she loses at
the festival, she marries the king, who refuses to let the stepmother and
stepsister come to the palace to live. Folk literature. 2–3.

Target Activity: "The Cinderella Story Is Found in Different Cultures"
Make a comparison chart to show the Cinderella stories from different
cultures.

Cinderellas from Different Cultures

Titles of Books	Character	Setting	Magic	Problem	Resolution
1.					
2.					
3.					

Some of the versions of Cinderella the students may want to consider are:

Martin, Rafe. *The Rough-Faced Girl.* Ill. by David Shannon. Putnam, 1992.
   (Algonquin)
Mbane, Phumla. *Nomi and the Magic Fish.* Ill. by Carole Byard. New York:
   Doubleday, 1972. (Africa)
Nygren, Tord. *Fiddler and His Brothers.* Ill. New York: Morrow, 1987.
   (male Cinderella)
Perrault, Charles. *Cinderella.* Ill. by Marcia Brown. New York: Scribner's,
   1954. (France)
Philip, Neil. *Fairy Tales of Eastern Europe.* Ill. New York: Clarion, 1992.
   (Eastern Slavic Europe)
Steel, Flora Annie. *Tattercoats.* Ill. by Diane Goode. New York: Bradbury,
   1978. (England)
Steptoe, John. *Mufaro's Beautiful Daughters: An African Tale.* Ill. by the
   reteller. New York: Lothrop, Lee & Shepard, 1987. (Africa)
Whitney, Thomas P., translator. *Vasilisa the Beautiful.* Ill. by Nonny
   Hogrogian. (Russia)

37 Mahy, Margaret, reteller. *The Seven Chinese Brothers*. Ill.
      by Jean and Mou-sien Tseng. New York: Scholastic, 1990.
      Seven brothers walk, talk, and look alike. Each has a special power.
When the third brother is sentenced to be beheaded by the emperor, the
fourth brother (who has bones of iron) takes his place. When sentenced to
drowning and burning, he is replaced by a different brother who survives.
Rich watercolors show the ceremonial robes of court. Recommended
storytelling. Folk literature. K–3.
      Target Activity: "Special Talents"
      Discuss the special talents of the brothers in the story and ask children
to contribute additional information about other talents of characters they
know about from folk literature. See Gerald McDermott's *Anansi the
Spider: A Tale from the Ashanti* (Holt, Rinehart & Winston, 1972). In
McDermott's retelling, the brothers' names are See Trouble, Road Builder,
River Drinker, Game Skinner, Stone Thrower, and Cushion. Begin a word
map about special talents of brothers in folk tales to record the information
the children contribute. Display the map so additional facts can be added
during the week.

38 Mosel, Arlene. *The Funny Little Woman*. Ill. by Blair Lent.
      New York: Dutton, 1972.
      In this Japanese tale, a little woman pursues a rice dumpling and
is captured by the wicked Oni, green underground creatures who live in
dark caverns. A captive, the woman must cook for them with a magic paddle that makes grains of rice. Trying to escape, she leaves in a boat floating
on an underground river. To recapture her, the Oni suck the river water
into their mouths and leave the woman's boat in the river's waterless bed.
The funny little woman has a contagious laugh and it makes the Oni laugh
too. Laughing, they spill all the water back into the river bed. She floats
back to her home and becomes the richest woman in Japan by making rice
cakes with her magic paddle. Folk literature. 1–3.
      Target Activity: "Humor Is Found in Folktales from Different Cul-
tures"
      Share folktales about being humorous and then read some of the
verses of J. Prelutsky's *Something Big Has Been Here*. For example, in "The
Turkey Shot Out of the Oven," the unknown narrator promises to plan
ahead the next time he or she stuffs a turkey and promises "never again to
stuff a turkey with popcorn that hadn't been popped."

	Country-culture	*Titles of folk tales with humor*
a.		
b.		

Optional Activity: "Adventurous"

Share stories about being unselfish, breaking enchantments, or ways to escape magical creatures. Invite the girls and boys to make a list of book characters they know of who were adventurous. Ask them to tell which characters they prefer and why. Further, ask the children to reflect upon which characters gave them the strongest feeling of adventure.

39 Stamm, Claus (1990). *Three Strong Women: A Tall Tale.* Ill. by Jean and Mou-sien Tseng. New York: Viking.

Forever-Mountain is a fine, strong man and the best wrestler in Japan — as he would be the first to tell you. But when he decides to play a joke on Maru-me, a round girl with laughing eyes, she decides to take him home and teach him what real strength is. After three months with Maru-me, her mother, and grandmother, Forever-Mountain sets out for the championships, a truly invincible man who has learned much about humility. There is an abundance of wisdom, wit and charm in this new edition. Folk literature. K–3.

Target Activity: "Telling a Tall Tale"

The illustrations in this tale are just right for having children retell the story, in their own language, with the help of the pictures. Then encourage children to create their own highly exaggerated tale about themselves, using Stamm's beginning phrase "Long ago, in Japan . . ." and ending with "And we lived happily ever after."

Students who need to read more tall tales as models for writing the stories may be interested in the different characters and their exaggerated behaviors and inventions in:

Bowleg Bill: Seagoing Cowpuncher (Prentice, 1957) by Harold W. Felton, a tall tale of nonsense about a cowboy who solves his problems in a unique manner.

John Tabor's Ride (Knopf, 1989) by Edward C. Day, an account of a young seaman's first whaling voyage, from an 1846 book of whaling adventures.

Mike Fink: A Tall Tale Retold (Morrow, 1992) by Steven Kellogg, a story of the King of the Keelboatmen who floated cargo downriver to New Orleans and his adventures of facing former king Jack Carpenter in a wrestling match and racing H. P. Blathersby and his powerful steamboat.

Mr. Yowder and the Train Robbers (Holiday, 1981) by Glen Rounds is about the self-proclaimed "World's Bestest and Fastest Sign Painter" and his run-in with robbers and rattlers.

Paul Bunyan (Morrow, 1984) by Steven Kellogg, a detailed story with doublepage illustrations.

Pecos Bill (Mulberry Books, 1992) by Steven Kellogg, a recount of how Bill invented cattle drives, lassos and rodeos.

40 Tompert, Ann. *Grandfather Tang's Story*. Ill. by Robert Andrew Parker. New York: Crown, 1990.

Chou and Wu Ling are fox fairies who can change their shapes into various animals. Boastfully, each one tries to outdo the other: Wu Ling changes into a rabbit, so Chou becomes a barking dog. To escape, Wu Ling turns into a squirrel and runs up a tree. As Wu Ling and Chou become caught up in this spiteful competition, they do not realize the danger that lurks nearby: just as they turn into geese, a pair of hunters shoot and wound Chou. The two realize that their friendship is much more important than the silly competition which has resulted in Chou's injury. Folk literature. K–3.

Target Activity: "Cooperation vs. Competition"

Through discussion after reading the story, guide children into understanding that the reason the two friends in this story got into trouble was that they were trying to outdo one another rather than attempting to get along peacefully. Have children make a list of games they know of that require competition and another list of those that require cooperation. Ask them to tell which games they prefer and why. Further, ask children to reflect upon which types of games promote a feeling of peace and harmony among friends.

41 Wallace, Ian. *Chin Chiang and the Dragon's Dance*. Ill. by the author. New York: Atheneum, 1984.

From the time Chin Chiang was very tiny, he had longed for the day he would be able to dance the dragon's dance. Now the first day of the Year of the Dragon had arrived and it seemed his dream was about to come true. But instead of being excited, Chin Chiang was so frightened he wanted to melt in his shoes. He was sure he could never dance well enough to make his grandfather proud of him. Though Chin Chiang had practiced at length with Grandfather, he was sure he would trip and disgrace his family. So, while everyone else was busy preparing for the evening's festivities, Chin Chiang ran away, down the street to the public library. Hiding on the roof of the library he ran into an elderly woman, Pu Yee, who gave him the quiet courage to face his fears. Chin Chiang is an appealing little boy whose problem, while set squarely in the Chinese culture, will be one with which all children can easily relate. Contemporary realism. Pre–3.

Target Activity: "Pictures Tell the Story"

The author-artist's brilliant watercolors illuminate this tale and present young children with a bit of the flavor and color of Chinese rituals and celebrations. Encourage attention to the illustrations by inviting the children to retell the story in their own words, using the illustrations. Invite children who speak languages other than English to use the pictures to tell the story in their own language.

Optional Activity: "Dragons in Different Cultures"

Discuss the idea with children that different cultures have recognized dragons as being good creatures, neutral creatures, or dangerous destructive ones. For those girls and boys who are interested further in these huge creatures, guide them to books about ways dragons are shown in stories of different cultures. Show that almost every country had dragons in its myths. For instance, in some countries in the East, it was believed that the wise dragons, rich and powerful, lived high up in the sky. They had the neck of a snake, the claws of an eagle and the horns of a stag. Often, these dragons were neutral and could take human form. In China, for example, the dragon was a kingly emblem and was once thought of as an important being. In the countries in the West, stories were told about dragons who were frightening creatures with scales and wings. In some of the countries, the dragon was a symbol of destruction. In other countries such as Wales, the symbol of the dragon was important enough to be placed on the national flag.

42 Xiong, Blia, reteller. *Nine-in-One Grr! Grr!*. Ill. by Nancy Horn. Adapted by Cathy Spagnoli. Chicago: Children's Book Press, 1989.

In this Hmong folktale, the world began when a lonely tiger journeyed to the great god Shao to discover if she will have cubs. Shao says that she will have nine cubs a year if she can remember his words. To remember, the tiger says a memory chant on the way home with the words — nine-in-one, Grr! Grr! The Eu bird (a black bird) asks Shao to change what he said because he fears if the tiger has nine cubs each year, the birds will all be eaten by them. Since Shao cannot change what he said, the black bird flies to the tiger and substitutes the words "one-in-nine" and alters natural history and the rest of creation. Illustrations have intricate borders and are reminiscent of story stitching or the stories told in needlework. Folk literature. 1–3.

Target Activity: "Black Bird's Problem"

Invite children to discuss the problem faced by the black bird and the way it was solved. Encourage boys and girls to think of other ways the story could have solved the problem for the bird. On the chalkboard, write down the ideas dictated by the children. Ask children to draw scenes of ways the problem could have been solved.

43 Yacowitz, Caryn, adapter. *The Jade Stone.* Ill. by Ju-Hong Chen. New York: Holiday House, 1992.

The humble stone carver, Chan Lo, is told by the Emperor to carve a dragon of wind and fire but the carver can carve only what he "hears" in the jade stone. He hears carp noises from the stone and carves three carp. The Emperor, before issuing punishment for the carver's disobedience, says, "I will let my dreams decide." In his dreams, the Emperor sees the sources of the carver's inspirations and rewards the carver with the title of Master Carver. Folk literature. K–3.

Target Activity: "Carving Only What Is Heard in Stone"

With a collection of medium sized rocks and pebbles from a gravel company or landscape business, the children can look at, touch, or sprinkle the rocks with water to change the colors seen. They can hold the rocks to their ears to simulate the carver who "listened" to the jade stone before carving it. Ask the children to announce what objects could be carved from their stones and then, on paper, design the carving with their crayons.

44 Yashima, Taro. *Crow Boy.* Ill. by the author. New York: Viking, 1955.

A small Asian boy, Chibi, is an isolate at school and spends the time looking at the ceiling, his desk, or out the window. Every day he walks miles to school and notices what is around him. He has six years of perfect attendance and receives attention from a new teacher, Mr. Isobe, who recognizes Chibi's knowledge of nature and discovers that Chibi can imitate the voices of crows. Chibi does so with the others in the school talent show. With this, he earns respect of others and himself and is nicknamed "Crow Boy." With the help of a kindly sixth grade teacher, a lonely boy wins the admiration of his classmates. Contemporary realism. K–2.

Target Activity: "Helping Others Who Are Shy"

With children, review the story again and look at the illustrations closely. Talk about any questions the students have and invite the students to draw a picture of what they could have done to help Crow Boy. After the drawings are completed, the students team up in pairs and talk about what they drew with each other. Display the illustrations in the classroom.

45 Yolen, Jane. *The Emperor and the Kite.* Ill. by Ed Young. Cleveland, Ohio: World, 1967.

This book features a very tiny but resourceful little girl named Djeow Seow, the youngest and frailest of the offspring of the emperor of China. Djeow Seow is so small that she is "not thought very much of— when she is thought of at all." When her father is captured and imprisoned by evil men, the child's older, bigger, and stronger siblings flee to a neighboring kingdom, sobbing and sighing. But little Djeow Seow, unnoticed by the men who imprisoned her father, cleverly thinks of a plan to rescue him. She patiently weaves a long, strong rope of her own hair, attaches it to the tail of her kite, and then flies it up to her father, who then slides down to freedom. Once insignificant to her father, Djeow Seow now always sits on a tiny throne by her grateful father's side. Her peaceful solution to her father's problem has saved his life. Folk literature. K–2.

Target Activity: "Resourceful Children Are Found in Every Culture"

With the children, discuss what was done by Djeow Seow. Draw a visual display of a large kite with a long kite-tail. Along the tail of the kite draw lines radiating outward, and on each line, invite the children to write some of the events in the story in their own words.

Optional Activity: "Think, Pair and Share"

Ask the children to contrast the responses of Djeow Seow and her siblings to the conflict. Which was the more positive solution? Give children ten minutes to brainstorm all the solutions they can think of in response to Djeow Seow's problem. Then have each child select a partner. With the partner, have each child share the solutions they have brainstormed. Next, ask children to work together to select the solution that would be the most peaceful and resourceful response to Djeow Seow's dilemma. Finally, ask one child from each pair to present the pair's optimal solution to the class. Invite discussion about the differing merits of each solution.

EUROPEAN AMERICAN HERITAGE

46 Bulla, Clyde Robert. *A Lion to Guard Us.* Ill. New York: Scholastic, 1983.

This book tells the story of a plucky young heroine named Amanda and her determination, against all odds, to stay together as a family with her beloved brother and sister despite the grim reality of her mother's death which leaves them in poverty. Amanda holds fast to her dream of tracking down her father, who had left the family behind. The author uses a simple prose style and develops her characters well against the backdrop of the story of the founding fathers and mothers of the Jamestown colony and the families that were left behind in England. Historical fiction. 2–3.

Target Activity: "Children with Courage Live in Every Culture"

Discuss with children the word "courage." Ask children to retell, in sequence, the things that Amanda did that took courage. Read children the picture storybook *Rose Blanche* (Creative Education, Inc., 1985), by Robert

Innocenti. Have children also retell the ways in which Rose showed courage. Ask children to pretend that they are on a committee to award a medal for courage to one of these two young girls. Which one would they choose? Why? Invite children to write a paragraph telling about who they would choose and why. Allow them to read their paragraphs to the rest of the class. Using a bar graph, chart the number of children who chose Rose and who chose Amanda. Discuss the difficulty children had in making their choices. Finally, invite children to find books featuring children from other cultures who have performed heroic deeds.

47 Estes, Eleanor. *The Hundred Dresses.* Ill. by Louis Slobodkin. Scarsdale, New York: Harcourt, Brace, 1944.

Wanda hates having to wear the same faded blue dress each day to school. Her mother learns that she has told a classmate that she has one hundred dresses all lined up in her closet. This starts a daily teasing by the other girls. When the Petronskis move to the city, Wanda's father writes a note to her new teacher saying, "No more holler Polack. No more asky why funny name. Plenty of funny names in big city." Wanda leaves her old school before the winner of the drawing and coloring contest is announced. Wanda is the winner with her one hundred "all different and beautiful" dress designs.

In this Newbery book, the reader feels compassion for Wanda as Peggy picks at Wanda each day and as Maddie just stands by. Finally, Maddie realizes her conduct is as shameful as Peggy's even though Peggy has tormented Wanda more. Maddie decides she will never again stand by and say nothing when she sees another person being mistreated. Contemporary realism. 2–4.

Target Activity: "Never Stand By and Say Nothing When Someone Is Mistreated"

Invite the students to respond in writing to such questions as:
   a. How would you have felt if you had been Wanda and been forced to wear the same dress/shirt day after day?
   b. What would your reaction have been if you had to move to the big city?
   c. Have you ever known anyone or read about anyone who was mistreated because he seemed to be different from others around him? Has mistreatment happened to you? When did this happen? Who helped you when you needed it? How will you help someone when you see this happening in the future?

48 Gag, Wanda. *Gone Is Gone.* Ill. by the author. New York: Coward-McCann, 1935.

Set in Bohemia, this is the story of Fritzel, a man who decides that housework is easier than his work in the fields. His wife, Liesi, agrees to change roles with him for a day. Fritzel has a series of misadventures during the day and when Liesi returns from the field, he begs, "Please let me go back to my work in the fields and never more will I say that my work is harder than yours." Leisi agrees that Fritzel should return to his work and she to hers and says, "If that's how it is, we surely can live in peace and happiness for ever and ever." Folk literature. 1–3.

Target Activity: "What's Gone Is Gone"

With children all chiming in and saying the words, "What's gone is gone," invite children to modify the culture of the characters, using simple props which indicate the culture, and act out some of the situations in the story. Replay each scene with settings in different cultures. Change the characters and objects to those appropriate to the culture.

For another version of this tale, read aloud Abe Gurvin's retelling with *The Husband Who Was to Mind the House* (Young Readers Press, 1968).

49 Goffstein, M. B.. *A Little Schubert.* Ill. New York: Harper and Row, 1972.

In Vienna many years ago, Schubert learned to play the piano and violin at home. Franz Peter Schubert lived in a room with few furnishings and without heat. He made his living by teaching. This is the life story of the famous composer (1797–1828) who heard music differently from other people. It tells the way he composed his ideas by writing down his music as quickly as he could.

When Schubert was fourteen years old, he began to compose music. At nineteen, he wrote some of his most well-known works. Biography. K–2.

Target Activity: "Every Culture Has Its Musical Composers"

With the children, listen to parts of the story of Schubert's life with a recording of the operetta *Blossom Time,* written by Sigmund Romberg. The theme song is a variation of Schubert's work called "Unfinished Symphony." It is referred to as "unfinished" because it has only two (not the usual three or four) movements of music expected in a classical symphony. Other versions of Schubert's melodies are heard in the operetta. After listening to parts of the operetta, discuss the melodies and the way the mood of the selections makes us think of actions. With the girls and boys, the teacher can create an informational chart for a resource in the classroom.

Optional Activity: "Great Musicians"

Cultural Heritage	Musician
1. African American	Marian Anderson, concert singer
	Aretha Franklin, singer of popular music

Cultural heritage	Musician
	Edward Kennedy "Duke" Ellington, conductor and composer
	Ulysses Kay, classical composer and conductor
	Bessie Smith, blues singer
	William Grant Smith, composer and first African American to conduct a major orchestra in a performance of his own composition
2. Asian American	Students offer suggestions.
3. European American	
4. Latino American	
5. Native American Indian	

50 Goldin, Barbara Diamond. *Cakes and Miracles: A Purim Tale*. Ill. by Erika Weihs. New York: Viking, 1991.

In this original story set in the late 1900s, Herschel, blinded by illness, is bored. Herschel likes to mold riverbank mud into shapes and landscapes. After dreaming that an angel tells him to make what he sees in his imagination, Herschel uses his mother's dough to sculpt unusual cookies in shapes of the images he sees in his mind and helps his mother sell them for Purim. (The festival of Purim is celebrated in March. Presents are given to friends, family, and the poor.) The text shows the love between mother and son as well as Herschel's strength of spirit in overcoming his disability. Recipe for *hamantashen*, the three cornered pastries, included. Historical fiction. Pre–3.

Target Activity: "People of Different Cultures Can Celebrate with a Spirit of Happiness and Merrymaking"

Students read the recipe for *hamantashen* three times, once silently as teacher reads it aloud, next in choral reading with the total group, and third, with each student reading one line. For those interested in this project as a homework activity, ingredients may be collected and cookies made at home. Invite students to bring one (or more) of their sculpted cookies to class to show and to discuss. Have children tell how their cookie shape shows something they saw in their imagination. Each cookie may be displayed along with the student's writing on an index card telling something about the shape chosen for the cookie.

51 Grimm, Jakob, and Wilhelm Grimm. "The Elves" in *The Complete Brothers Grimm Fairy Tales*. Edited by Lily Owens. New York: Avenel, 1981. 5–6.

This familiar story is also known as "The Elves and the Shoemaker." It is the tale of the little people who helped the shoemaker and his wife. Every night, the little people made shoes for the couple, until one night, the couple gave them a gift of beautiful clothes. The elves then disappeared and were never seen again. Folk literature. 1–3.

Target Activity: "Theme of 'Good Elves Helping Good Humans' in Folktales"

With the students, roleplay some of the characters in the story. Change the situation by changing the culture in which the story was set.

Read other versions of the story: *The Elves and the Shoemaker* (Clarion, 1984) by Paul Galdone; *The Elves and the Shoemaker* (Four Winds, 1975) by Freya Littledale with illustrations by Brinton Turkle; "The Elves" in *Household Tales,* by Jakob and Wilhelm Grimm, trans. Margaret Hunt (London: Bell & Son, 1884); and *Favorite Tales from Grimm* (Four Winds, 1982) retold and ill. by Mercer Mayer.

52 Grimm, Jakob, and Wilhelm Grimm. *Hansel and Gretel.* Retold by Rita Lesser. Ill. by Paul O. Zelinsky. New York: Dodd, 1984.

Near a large wood, a poor woodcutter listens to his wife who wants to take his two children to the thickest part of the woods and leave them. Despite repeated attempts to leave the children in the woods, the children manage to find their way home. Left once again, the children wander three days and arrive at a cottage made of bread and cakes, with windowpanes of clear sugar. An old woman, really a witch who waylays children, fattens them up with milk, pancakes, sugar, apples, and nuts. Her plan is to eat the children, but Gretel foils her plan.

This classic tale of an evil witch, a selfish mother, a weak father, and two resourceful children tells of the problem-solving done by the two children. Faced with the prospect of seeing if the oven is "hot enough," Gretel tricks the witch into showing it to her. Gretel gives her a push into the oven, shuts the iron door, and bolts it. She releases Hansel from his cage, and they collect the witch's pearls and precious stones. They return to their father who had missed them terribly. Folk literature. 1–3.

Target Activity: "Mock Court Case"

With students, a teacher or librarian may discuss the news event where a class of fifth graders in the Mount Diablo (California) school district responded to two complainants who lived in the school district. The two women said they were witches and asked the school board to ban the story of Hansel and Gretel because it degraded them. To consider this point of view, the students staged a mock trial in which Hansel and Gretel were charged with murdering the witch who had lured them to her sugar house. After deliberation, the student jury said the two children had acted in self-defense by pushing the mean old witch into the oven before she pushed them in. Engage the children in staging a mock trial of their own.

53 Grimm, Jakob, and Wilhelm Grimm. *Rapunzel: From the Brothers Grimm.* Retold by Barbara Rogasky. Ill. by Trina Schart Hyman. New York: Holiday House, 1982.

Twelve-year-old Rapunzel is shut up in a high tower by a witch, Mother Gothel, in punishment for her father's theft of her rampion plants. Hearing Rapunzel's singing and overhearing Mother Gothel's command to "let down your hair," a prince sees a pair of golden yellow braids tumble down from a tiny window in the tower. The prince calls out a command, climbs the tresses, and steps through the window. The prince asks for her hand in marriage and Rapunzel asks for a skein of silk each day to make a ladder for her to descend. Mother Gothel discovers the prince, cuts off Rapunzel's hair, and confronts the prince. When the prince falls from the tower he is blinded by his fall into a thorny thicket. After a year, the prince finds Rapunzel, banished, and living in wretchedness with her baby twins, a boy and a girl. Not able to see, he is drawn toward her by her singing. When she sees him she weeps with joy and embraces him. Her tears fall on his eyes and in a moment they are healed. The prince takes Rapunzel and the twins away to his kingdom where they all live happily. See also other versions such as Wanda Gag's early translation of "Rapunzel" in *Household Tales* (Coward-McCann, 1936). Folk literature. 2–4.

Target Activity: "Changing the Setting of the Story"

With a group, discuss different settings (geographic regions, countries) in which the story could take place and discuss the strength and resourcefulness of the character. As a choice, read *Petrosinella: A Neopolitan Rapunzel* (Warne, 1981, 3–5) by Gambattista Basile, a variant of the story from Italy. Discuss with children the effects that changes in the setting would make in the story:

If the story took place in:	*Then:*
African country	
Asian country	
European country	
Latino country	
Native American tribal/national region	

54 Grimm, Jakob, and Wilhelm Grimm. *Rumpelstiltskin.* Ill. by Paul O. Zelinsky. New York: Dutton, 1986.

Parents boast that their daughter has an ability to spin and is told

that she must spin straw into gold or lose her head. Crying, the girl notices
a creature who offers to do the spinning for her. In return, she will give
him her firstborn child when she marries the King. When he comes to
claim his child, he returns three times to give her three chances to guess
his name. If, at the end of the third time, she hasn't guessed his name, the
child will be his. Each time, she tries to solve her problem by bargaining
and by guessing the creature's name. Before the last day of the bargaining
time, a maid follows the creature and hears him singing his name. She
returns and tells the queen. The queen "guesses" the right name at the
third and last meeting. Folk literature. 1–3.

Target Activity: "Finding the Answer to a Riddle"

With the students, read Rumpelstiltskin's refrain from a favorite version or from Jakob and Wilhelm Grimm's "Rumpelstiltskin" in *Household
Tales* (Macmillan, 1926). In this refrain, the little man cried out:

> "Today do I bake, tomorrow I brew.
> The day after that the Queen's child comes in;
> And oh! I am glad that nobody knew
> That the name I am called is Rumpelstiltskin."

With children, discuss switching the cultural settings in the story.
Discuss the effect such changes have. Discuss the effect as it relates to
cultural stereotyping of characters in stories.

55 Grimm, Jakob, and Wilhelm Grimm. "The Wolf and the Seven Little Kids" in *Household Tales.* Trans. by Margaret Hunt. London: G. Bell & Son, 1884.

Tricked by the wolf into opening the cottage door, one kid hides
under the table, the second springs into the bed, the third into the stove,
the fourth into the kitchen, the fifth into the cupboard, the sixth under the
washing bowl, and the seventh into the clock case. The wolf satisfies his
appetite and swallows them all except for the kid hiding in the clock case.
When mother returns, she and the remaining kid follow the wolf and find
him snoring in the meadow. Mother sees something moving and struggling
inside his stomach. "Ah, heavens," she says, "is it possible that my poor children whom he has swallowed down for his supper can still be alive?"

After fetching scissors, needles, and thread, the goat cuts open the
wolf and all six kids spring out alive. What rejoicing there is! They then em-
brace their dear mother. Mother suggests that the kids find some stones
"to fill the wicked beast's stomach" while he is asleep. When the wolf
awakens, he begins to walk and finds that the stones inside him knock
against each other and rattle. When the wolf reaches the well and stoops
down to drink, the heavy stones make him fall into the water and there is

no one to rescue him. The seven kids call out, "The wolf is dead! The wolf is dead!" and dance for joy around the well with their mother.

Target Activity: "Different Animals Are Featured in Folktales of Different Cultures"

With children, engage in researching some of the animals that are prevalent in stories from different cultures.

Country	Animal
Italy	blackbirds
Japan	badgers
Other:	Other:

Ask children to offer suggestions as to *why* the animals used in the folktales might vary from culture to culture.

56 Gurvin, Abe, reteller. *The Husband Who Was to Mind the House.* Ill. by the reteller. New York: Young Readers Press, 1968.

This retold version of Wanda Gag's *Gone Is Gone* (Coward-McCann, 1935) challenges the normal stereotypes of "male" jobs versus "female" household work, which is thought to be easier and less stressful. The husband in the story makes a big fuss one evening, complaining that his wife never does anything. "Don't be angry," replies his wife, Goody. "Tomorrow we will change places. I'll go out and cut hay all day and you can stay home and mind the house." The husband assumes this will be easy and sleeps late the next morning. What ensues is a true comedy of errors, with the pig getting loose in the kitchen, the butter churn overturning, the baby screaming, the water spilling in the fireplace pot, and the husband forgetting to feed the cow. When Goody comes home, she finds the cow dangling from the roof from a rope, the result of another of her husband's mistakes. The book ends by asking the reader to "guess who stayed home to mind the house from now on," implying that the husband has a newfound respect for his wife's work *and* her ability to perform it. 2–3.

Target Activity: "Women in Other Cultures"

Have groups of children select a culture other than their own. Instruct them to find out as much as they can about the role of women in this culture through interviews with women of the culture, trade books on the culture, and other sources.

57 Huck, Charlotte. *Princess Furball.* Ill. by Anita Lobel. New York: Greenwillow, 1989.

When a beautiful princess grows up, her father, the king, promises to marry her to an ogre in return for a fortune. To avoid the detested idea of marrying the ogre, the princess asks for a dowry that no one can fulfill: three dresses and a coat made of the skins of a thousand different kinds of wild animals. One dress is to be as "golden as the sun," the second as "silvery as the moon," and the third as "glittering as the stars." The king brings her the dresses and coat and the princess runs away. Wrapped in her fur coat and carrying the three dresses, her mother's golden treasures (tiny spinning wheel, a ring), and seasoning for soup, she flees to another kingdom and falls asleep in a hollow tree where she is found by a young king's hunters and their white dogs. Taken back to the castle, she works as a servant to the servants. When the king gives three gala affairs, the princess wears her three dresses and the king says, "I cannot live without you." They are married and live happily ever after.

Princess Furball solves her problem of an unwanted marriage by escaping from it; at the castle, she uses her mother's golden talisman and the seasoning for the soup to reveal her cleverness, and finally, her identity to the king. The king kneels on her fur coat to propose to her. Folk literature. 2–3.

Target Activity: "Change the Golden Treasures to Valued Objects from Another Culture"

After reading the story, the teacher may discuss the descriptive language of the tale with the students and review the words telling about the golden treasures. The golden treasures are considered and the girls and boys are invited to think of their own words to describe the objects. With the whole group, the teacher may lead the discussion about the group's selection of objects that represent other cultures:

Culture	*Examples of Objects Valued*
African heritage	magic hat, drum
Asian heritage	magic fish bones
European heritage	magic slippers
Latino heritage	magic llama
Native American Indian heritage	magic bow and arrow

58 Jacobs, Joseph. "Teeny-Tiny." In *Anthology of Children's Literature* by Edna Johnson, et al. Boston: Houghton Mifflin, 1970.

Retells the story of the "teeny-tiny" woman who lived in her house in a village and found a bone to make soup for her supper. A voice from the cupboard calls out, "Give me my bone," and obligingly, the woman says in her loudest voice, "Take it!" This is a repetitive form of a cumulative tale enjoyed by many children. Pre–1.

Target Activity: "Nicknames Sometimes Hurt"

With students, discuss the times when "teeny-tiny" could be a nickname that some girls and boys would not like assigned to them. Further, discuss the idea that some students do not like the new nicknames given to them by others and read excerpts from a contemporary realistic story, *Lanky Longlegs* (Atheneum, 1983) by Karin Lorentzen. In the story, Di, a European nine-year-old, does not like a nickname she is called by Martin, a new boy at school. Soon, Di's dog has puppies and Martin buys one. Martin and Di's relationship improves. Di's two-year-old brother is quite ill with a fatal blood disease. After his death, Di comforts herself and dreams that he has disappeared into a sunbeam, but her real comfort comes from Martin, who brings a gift for the last puppy in the litter which Di wants to keep for herself.

Discuss the value of talking to the student to find a nickname the student likes. Talk about Di's objections to the nickname "lanky longlegs." Invite students to work with partners and refer to the list on the board to discuss and think of different ways to confront the objections that are listed. With the whole group, ask the students to report what was discussed in their partnership meetings. Let them think of a favorite nickname they themselves would like and distribute name tags so they can write their new names and display them to others.

59 Jacobs, Joseph. *Aesop's Fables.* "The Lark and Its Young." London: Batsford, 1954.

A mother lark had a nest of young birds in a field of ripe grain. One day, she found the little birds quite excited for they had heard the owner say it was time to gather in the grain. "Do not worry," said Mother Lark, "if he is depending on his neighbors, the work will not begin today. But listen carefully to what the owner says each time he comes and report to me." The next day, the little birds heard the owner say, "This field needs cutting badly; I'll call my relatives over to help me. We'll get them here tomorrow." The little birds told their mother and she said, "Never mind. I happen to know the relatives are busy with their own grain. They won't come. But keep your ears open and tell me what you hear." The third day, the owner came and said to his son, "We can't wait any longer. We will hire some men tonight and tomorrow we will begin cutting the grain." When Mother Lark heard these words, she said, "Now we'll have to move. When people decide to do things themselves instead of leaving work to others, you know they mean business." Folk literature. 1–3.

Target Activity: "Dictate a New Fable for Another Setting"

With students, discuss the idea that Mother Lark knew the nature of humans and kept informed about what was going on. Talk about times when people have decided to do things themselves instead of leaving work for others to do. Then focus more specifically on the setting and the most familiar animals associated with different cultures to create a new story:

Cultures   *Familiar Animals*

_____

_____

New Fables

_____

Ask the children to dictate a retelling of the story and switch the setting to another country. Record the children's dictation on a chart or on the board. Discuss the effect the change has on the story. The children may show their "change-of-setting expectations" through their discussion. As a culminating review, return to the list and invite the children to identify stories with settings in different cultures.

60 Jaffe, Nina. *In the Month of Kislev: A Story for Hanukkah.*
   Ill. by Louise August. Viking, 1992.
      In Europe, in the town of Kislev, the people are celebrating Hanukkah (also spelled Chanukah)—a Jewish holiday also called the Feast of Lights. It is celebrated in early December and includes the lighting of candles over eight nights and recognizes the winning of religious freedom in 165 B.C. Mendel, the peddler, and his family are not celebrating for there is no money and Mendel's children stand under the window of Feivel, a haughty wealthy merchant, to smell the wonderful smell of the golden latkes. On the last night, Feivel finds the children outside the window, and insists that Mendel's family receive a consequence from Rabbi Yonah. But the tables are turned and Feivel learns a lesson about Hanukkah. Historical fiction. Pre–3.
      Target Activity: "People of Different Cultures Recognize the Winning of Freedoms"
      With children, discuss their ideas of the meaning of the word *freedom.* Write their ideas about freedom and the related celebrations in different cultures on the board, chart, or overhead transparency.

Freedoms	*Celebrations*
Religious freedom	Jewish American: Hanukkah (Feast of Dedication)
Freedom from slavery	Jewish American: Passover (Festival of Unleavened Bread)
Harvest Thanksgiving	Shevuoth (Feast of Weeks)

Review the historical background of Maccabee's leadership: In 165
B.C., a small group of patriots and their leader, Judah the Maccabee,
defeated the army of Antiochus Epiphanes, a Syrian emperor, who had
substituted idol worship for the worship of one god and had desecrated the
temple in Jerusalem. In this remembrance celebration, the head of the
family lights a single candle each evening after nightfall and, each evening,
the number is increased by one until the last night when all eight are burning. After the review, invite the children to identify stories that exemplify
the "winning of freedoms" by characters from different cultures. List the
characters on the board. Ask children to tell *why* they think "freedom" is
important to people and *why* the characters devoted their actions to "winning freedoms."

61 Lasker, David. *The Boy Who Loved Music*. Ill. by Joe Lasker. New York: Viking, 1979.

In eighteenth-century Austria, in the summer palace of Prince
Esterhazy, Joseph Haydn, an Austrian composer, was the music director.
When the Prince stays at his summer palace far into the fall and does not
seem to be interested in returning to Vienna where the musicians want to
be, Haydn, a great master of the symphony, composes the *Farewell Symphony*. There is a surprise ending as Haydn hints that the musicians of the
orchestra would like a vacation, for in the final movement, the musicians
leave the stage, one by one, after blowing out the candles on their music
stands. Only two musicians are left, leaving Haydn with no orchestra to
conduct. The music persuades the Prince to return to Vienna with his
musicians and the court.

Haydn loved to get a little humor in his music. As examples, in the *Surprise Symphony*, Haydn puts in a loud chord in a slow quiet movement to
"make the ladies jump" and he solved the problem of the musicians' desired
return to Vienna with his ending of the *Farewell* symphony. Biography.
2–3.

Target Activity: "Comparing Music from Other Cultures"

Bring in music from the Hispanic, Asian, African American and Native
American cultures or, if you have children from these cultures represented
in your class, invite them to do so. Start by playing the *Surprise Symphony*
for children. Ask them to brainstorm in words and phrases how this music
makes them feel. Keep this word bank on a chart paper. In later sessions,
play the music from the four other cultures. Also invite children to
brainstorm words and phrases that come to their minds. Finally, when all
the music has been listened to, review the chart for a "word bank" from
which children can write a paragraph comparing or contrasting any two
selections of music.

62 Lawson, Robert. *They Were Strong and Good.* Ill. by the author. New York: Viking, 1940.

The author presents his relatives in this biography to show the ancestors who had to be strong and who helped build the beginnings of the United States. This is the story of a mother and a father and their mothers and fathers and the country that they helped build. A Scotch sea captain, a little Dutch girl, a Minnesota girl, and an Englishman who was a preacher in Alabama are all presented as ancestors of the author. Brief biography.T 1–2.

Target Activity: "Ancestors Are Respected in Every Culture"

With some of the interested girls and boys, discuss the backgrounds of adult relatives in their homes (i.e., aunts, uncles, grandmothers, mothers and father and their mothers and fathers). Invite interested children to make a display of intergenerational stories they find.

Intergenerational Stories

African American heritage   Asian American heritage

_____   _____

(story)   (story)

European American heritage   Latino heritage

_____   _____

(story)   (story)

Original Native American heritage

_____

(story)

63 Lee, Betsy. *Mother Teresa: Caring for God's Children.* Minneapolis: Dillon Press, 1983.

This is the story of a Yugoslavian girl named Agnes Gonxha Bojaxhiu whom we now know as Mother Teresa. Agnes grew up in a very loving and religious family. She was a happy child who enjoyed going to church and school because she liked the stories she heard about Jesus. The priests told her that Jesus loved little children, the sick, and the poor. She decided when she was twelve to leave her family to become a nun. She went to India, a country with many poor people. This was a place where she thought she could show God's love by loving others in need.

Once in India, she became a teacher but after many years she realized that to serve the poor she would have to live with them and live like them. She left the protection of the school and the church and has, since then, served the needy, the sick, and the dying in the streets of Calcutta, India. For many years, she has inspired people all over the world to serve, like her, poor and desperate people. Mother Teresa has been honored with the highest award the world can give its heroes for her selfless work with the most desperate of all people. Biography. 2–3.

Target Activity: "How Can I Help Others"

After reading aloud about Mother Teresa, discuss how she helped other people who were the most in need. Discuss how we can help others who are smaller than we are, or those who seem to need a friend. Have the children tell how they have tried to help someone in need. Have them tell how they have been helped by a friend, a teacher, or a family member. Have them write/draw a thank-you note for the help they have received and or draw a picture of the person whom they are thanking on the note. Ask them how thanking a person who has been kind helps that person feel special. Discuss how helping people and thanking people makes us all feel good because we know we are important. Ask children to mention stories they have read (heard) about people from different cultures who have helped others and been "special."

64 Leighton, Maxinne Rhea. *An Ellis Island Christmas.* Ill. by Dennis Nolan. Viking, 1992.

In Poland, Krysia wants to see her father again and Mother says, "First we must cross the ocean to get to Ellis Island in America." Papa is waiting for them in America and the rest of the family journeys on a long, stormy ocean voyage. On Christmas Eve, the passengers are on deck to see the Statue of Liberty as the ship approaches the dock where long lines of people are waiting to be accepted into America and a "new world." Krysia sees a woman crying, turns away, and worries if she will be allowed to stay in America and see her father. Historical fiction. 1–3.

Target Activity: "A Young Immigrant's Experience"

With students, a teacher may discuss the book's illustrations and ask students to search for evidence that points out:

  a. Krysia's look of uncertainty as a young immigrant traveling to a new place.
  b. the family members' look of wonder at the Statue of Liberty, America, and the idea of a "new world."
  c. the family members' look of hope about a "new" life in a new place.
  d. other feelings and messages.

65 Provensen, Alice, and Martin Provensen. *The Glorious Flight: Across the Channel with Louis Bleriot, July 25, 1909.* New York: Viking, 1983.

In 1901, in Cambrai, France, Louis Bleriot has one wish — to build a flying machine. He builds a machine with wings that flap like a chicken turned by a small motor; a gliding machine that is towed into the air by a motorboat; a machine that has two motors and two propellers but will only go in circles on the water; and finally, a machine with a powerful motor and propeller that takes him across the English Channel. Historical fiction. 2–4.

Target Activity: "Inventors Are Found in All Cultures"

The teacher asks the student to listen to the story again for information about who, what, and where. Then the information is reviewed again to be put together to make a sentence that "sums up" what was read. In other words, the students will connect the informational items in a way that summarizes information from the story. To extend the idea that inventors are found in all cultures, the students are invited to search for related historical fiction and biographies in the library.

66 Rehyer, Becky. *My Mother Is the Most Beautiful Woman in the World.* Ill. by Ruth Gannett. New York: Howell, Soskin, 1945.

All are preparing for a Ukrainian harvest feast and six-year-old Varya gets separated from her mother in the fields. When found by rescuers, Varya describes her mother as "the most beautiful woman in the world" and all search for the mother until the child sees her rounded "almost toothless" mother who is beautiful only in the eyes of her daughter. Folk literature. K–2.

Target Activity: "The One Who Is Most Beautiful to Me"

Ask children to talk about who is "most beautiful" to them and to describe the person. Talk about the descriptive words. Talk about why this person is "most beautiful." What does this person do for the child? Using pictographs from diverse peoples found in *National Geographic* magazine, discuss the idea that "beauty differs" from culture to culture and that there is no universally accepted way to be beautiful.

67 Shulevitz, Uri. *The Treasure.* Ill. by the author. New York: Farrar, Straus & Giroux, 1978.

In this folktale, Isaac is compelled by a dream to look for a treasure under the bridge near the Royal Palace and makes the long journey to the capital through forests and over mountains. There, he finds no treasure but hears the words of a palace guard who says, "The treasure is buried under a stove in the house of a man named Isaac." He returns home and finds the money which he uses to build a house of prayer with the inscription, "Sometimes one must travel far to discover what is near." Folk literature. 1–3.

Target Activity: "People in All Cultures Can Find Treasure in Their Houses"

With children discuss the meaning of treasure as more than money buried under a house. Invite the girls and boys to tell of something (other than money) that is a "treasure" at their house. A treasure can be a generous brother, a caring sister, an understanding mother, a hard-working father, a musically talented relative, etc. Ask the children to complete a sentence that starts with, "The treasure in my house is . . ." Then ask the children to draw illustrations to show the treasure. When finished, the children get together in pairs and trade their work for discussion and feedback. Invite the children to take their work with them to show the drawing to someone in the home.

68 Zemach, Margot. *It Could Always Be Worse.* Ill. by the author. New York: Farrar, Straus, Giroux, 1976.

In this hilarious folktale, a poor unfortunate man lives with his mother, his wife, and six children in a one-room hut. Because the hut is so crowded and noisy, the man, his wife, and his children argue frequently. The man finally goes to the rabbi for help; he can stand the situation no longer. The rabbi suggests he bring the barn animals—chickens, the rooster, and the goose—into the house. The man follows his advice and the intolerable situation is even worse, so he again appeals to the rabbi for help. In two follow-up sessions, the rabbi suggests that the man add a goat, and then a cow to the animals living in the house. Now with everyone quarreling even worse than before, the man is at his wit's end. He again runs to the rabbi for help. The rabbi tells him to now let all of the animals out of the hut. That night everyone sleeps peacefully. The man returns to the rabbi to thank him for making his life ". . . so quiet, so roomy, so peaceful . . . What a pleasure!" Folk literature. K–3.

Target Activity: "It Could Always Be Worse"

Part of the detriment to peace in people's lives is that they tend to focus on what they have to complain about rather than what they do not have to complain about. Discuss this concept with children and how it was true for the man in the folktale.

Using the writing board or overhead projector, brainstorm with the children some things that they always complain about that tend to cause arguments with their family or friends. After the brainstorming session, encourage the children to pick one of the brainstormed items and consider how the situation about which they complained could be even worse. Ask them to write (or dictate) a paragraph magnifying the problem, as the rabbi did for the poor unfortunate man. Encourage the children to end their paragraph with some new insights into the problem that may not seem so bad after all.

LATINO AMERICAN HERITAGE

69 Ada, Alma Flor. *Abecedario de los Animales.* Ill. by Vivi
Escriva. Madrid, Spain: Espasa Calpe, 1990.
This beautifully illustrated alphabet book is written in Spanish but
it is possible for non–Spanish-speaking children and teachers to understand the gist of the entries through the pictures. Because Spanish is a
phonetically regular language, it is also possible for a teacher who speaks
no Spanish to read the text adequately. Ideally, a child in the class who does
speak Spanish can assist with the pronunciations. K–3.
Target Activity: "Learning About Another Language"
This colorful book is perfect for introducing children to another
language and to demonstrate to them how it is possible, through contextual
clues, to figure out what unfamiliar words might mean. As the book is read
aloud, ask children to postulate what certain words might mean from how
the words are used and the pictures that accompany them. Have children
try to memorize one animal that corresponds to the letter in Spanish. Invite
any Spanish-speaking children to coach other children with correct enun-
ciation.

70 Adler, David A. *A Picture Book of Simon Bolivar.* Ill. by
Robert Casilla. New York: Holiday House, 1992.
In this biography, the boyhood of Bolivar is portrayed through
scenes with other children and with his tutor. The achievements of Bolivar
are portrayed and some of his quotes are included. The scenes of his later
years show Bolivar only in his military uniforms. 2–3.
Target Activity: "Leaders Are Leaders"
With the children, review the life of Bolivar that is recounted in the
print and pictures. Discuss a comparison of Bolivar's achievements with
the life of George Washington or Abraham Lincoln. Elicit events from the
children and write a list on the board under the three headings:

Simon Bolivar	George Washington	Abraham Lincoln
1.	1.	1.

Ask the children to team up as partners and discuss the lists with the
challenge of summarizing the achievements of these leaders. Ask all to re-
join as a whole group and invite the partners to tell their summaries.

71 Bloeckner, Carolyn. *Fernando Valenzuela.* Mankato, MN:
Crestwood House, 1985.

Fernando Valenzuela was the youngest of twelve children born in Sonora, Mexico. He and his brothers played on their town's baseball team from the time they were very young. As the youngest, Fernando was often overlooked as a pitcher, although he did well. When he was fifteen, Fernando went to play in a tournament in a neighboring town. Scouts there picked him to play on an all-star team representing the Mexican state of Sonora. He made his way up through the Mexican leagues and was finally discovered by a scout for the Dodgers. Fernando played well for the Dodgers and by his third year received a million-dollar contract, making him the highest-paid third-year player in history. Fernando married his hometown girlfriend and began to concentrate on learning to speak English. He also began to reach out to others. He spent much time talking to school children about the importance of education. He had quit school after fifth grade and felt he had missed out on a lot. He handed out buttons with his picture on them to school children. They contained this motto: "My best pitch is to stay in school." Fernando Valenzuela is a favorite with Mexicans and Mexican Americans; they are proud of all he has achieved. He continues to dazzle everyone with his pitching, leading to what the author describes as "Fernandomania." Biography. 2–3.

Target Activity: "Stay in School"

Many minority children admire sports stars of their own ethnic or racial background and hope that they can emulate their idol's success; however, only a minuscule number ever make it to the big leagues. Discuss this fact with children, and ask them why they think Valenzuela's motto is a good one. Even though Valenzuela became a great sports star, how might his life have been easier if he had been educated? Have children imagine that they have become famous in sports, music, or another field. What motto might *they* put on a button so that their fans would be influenced positively? Allow them to make these buttons. Laminate them and put safety pins on the back.

72 Carreno, Mada, reteller. *El Viaje del Joven Matsua (The Travels of the Youth Matsua).* Ill. by Gerado Suzan. Mexico City: Trillas, 1987.

When Matsua and his family leave their land because there is no longer water, they travel to another place and wonder if the Tarahumara will receive them well. As they grow closer, Matsua discovers a young Tarahumara trapped on a cliff, threatened by a large vulture. Matsua's family is welcomed by the family of the boy Matsua has rescued. Folk literature. 1–3.

Target Activity: "Similarities in Characters in Folktales"

With the children, compare the main character in this story to the herdsman in *Bringing the Rain to Kapiti Plain: A Nandi Tale.* What traits do they have in common? Ask children to outline the shapes of their right and left hands on paper. In the outline of one hand, write the word "herdsman," and in the outline of the other, write "Matsua." Under each name, place key words that identify the traits of each. Discuss as the traits are identified and written. Have children trade papers with study partners and discuss what was written.

73 Ets, Marie Hall. *Bad Boy, Good Boy.* Ill. New York: Thomas Y. Crowell, 1967.

This is an enriching story of a little boy, Roberto, who spoke only Spanish in an English-speaking school. His confusion and feelings of isolation constantly got him into trouble. Even when he was trying to be good, it seemed he got into trouble. His getting into trouble would cause disharmony at home and soon life in Roberto's home was not at all happy. Things changed when Roberto's father was persuaded to let him spend time at the Children's Center where the child began to learn to speak English. His father is proud of him and he is proud of himself. K–3.

Target Activity: "Not Understanding Is Frustrating"

To allow children to truly tune in to Roberto's feelings of anger and frustration at not being able to understand what was going on around him, the teacher can do a simulation for the children in the class. Selecting a passage to read from another language (the teacher needs only to be able to read the passage phonetically), the teacher reads without much inflection and without showing children the pictures or in any other way giving them ideas as to the context of the passage. After reading several pages, ask the children how they were feeling as they listened to the passage that they were unable to comprehend. Discuss with children that this is how Roberto felt and how any child feels when she or he suddenly must live in a culture with an unfamiliar language.

74 Ets, Marie Hall, and Aurora Labastida. *Nine Days to Christmas.* Ill. by Marie Hall Ets. New York: Viking, 1959.

To celebrate a posada, a traditional Mexican Christmas party, Ceci, a kindergartner, selects a piñata shaped like a large golden star at the market and fills it with fruit and candy. Not willing to see the piñata broken, Ceci hides behind a tree when it is time to break it open. Pre–2.

Target Activity: "A Story Shows Us Another Culture"

With the children, review the illustrations on an opaque projector and talk about ways this holiday is celebrated by Ceci's family. Look for indicators of the story's culture and discuss what is found—the markets, gardens, and parks.

75 Havill, Juanita. *Treasure Nap.* Ill. by Elivia Savadier. Boston: Houghton Mifflin, 1992.

Alicia and her baby brother listen to their mother tell a story of her childhood before a nap. When Mother was small, she went to the mountains to see her grandfather who made bird cages and *pitos,* the pipes used to call birds. Alicia knows an old pipe and bird cage are in an old trunk and she finds them. When she plays a tune on the pipe, a parrot flies to her. K–3.

Target Activity: "Family Heritage"

This Hispanic family is proud of its heritage. They make connections back to their grandparents and great-grandparents. Invite children to ask the adults in the home to tell them a story about an object they have kept from their childhood.

76 Maury, Inez. *My Mother the Mail Carrier—Mi Mama la Cartera.* New York: Feminist Press, 1976.

In this bilingual book, Lupita's mother is brave, strong, and a good cook. She loves outings and likes her work, carrying mail. Lupita wants to be a jockey when she grows up. Lupita sees a positive vision of life through her mother's abilities at home and at work. She wants a nonstereotypical occupation and, like her mother who likes her work, knows she will like her job of being a jockey too. Contemporary realism. Pre–3.

Target Activity: "Some People in All Cultures Want Nonstereotypical Jobs"

Look in the newspaper for articles about jobs people do. Discuss the character traits you think the person needs to do his or her job. Relate those character traits to traits of resiliency. What job/worker would need perseverance to overcome obstacles? to solve problems? to maintain a positive vision of life? Point out nonstereotypical jobs and discuss the extent to which culture affects a job sought by a person of a selected cultural background. Should there be any limits to the jobs that people with a selected cultural background can do? What does it take to do those jobs?

77 Politi, Leo. *The Butterflies Come.* Ill. New York: Charles Scribner's Sons, 1957.

Reading this charming story, children enter the world of two Hispanic children, Stephen and Lucia, who live on the Monterey Peninsula in California and make friends with the woodland creatures—particularly the orange-and-black Monarch butterflies. The children participate in the annual butterfly festival and create an original play of a butterfly. K–3.

Target Activity: "Coming Back Year After Year"

The nature facts about the Monarch butterflies in this story are true: every year the butterflies journey south to spend the winter; in the spring, they go north and lay their eggs on the milkweed plant. After reading this story to children, share these facts with them. Then introduce a comparison between the butterflies and some Hispanic migrant families who go back and forth, north to south, every year, too, to follow the crops. Why do these families migrate every year? Do the children think the families ever tire of all the moving around? Do the butterflies tire?

78 Politi, Leo. *Juanita.* Ill. by the author. New York: Charles Scribner's Sons, 1948.

This lighthearted story tells of a young Hispanic girl and her family in Los Angeles. Five-year-old Juanita's mother has made her a dress for her birthday and her father has given her a white dove. The story tells about the Blessing of the Animals, a ceremony that takes place every year on the day before Easter Sunday. Juanita will get to walk in the procession this year with her dove. The book contains much of the atmosphere of Hispanic Los Angeles, develops an appreciation for the ceremonies and lifestyle, and also includes many Spanish words. K–3.

Target Activity: "Juanita's Song"

Included with the text is a song, "Duermete, Nina" that Maria Gonzalez sings to Juanita to try to get her to go to sleep. Teach this song to the children. If any Spanish-speaking children are in the classroom, invite them to sing the song entirely in Spanish.

Optional Activity: "Juanita's Story Gives Us Another Languauge"

With children, review the story and the Spanish words and expressions. Point out that Politi followed the Spanish words with English translations. Introduce additional Spanish words with the songs that are included in the story. Perhaps the girls and boys will be interested in learning the birthday song, "Las Mananitas"; the dove song, "La Paloma"; or the Spanish lullaby, "Duermete, Nina," sung to Juanita by her mother.

79 Politi, Leo. *The Nicest Gift.* Ill. by the author. New York: Charles Scribner's Sons, 1973.

It is the Christmas season in the barrio of East Los Angeles. The mercado (market) is busy with festivities — people are dancing and singing, and the toy stores are overflowing with piñatas, puppets, and other toys. Carlitos, his mother, and his dog Blanco are there too, visiting with their friends and window-shopping. Suddenly, Blanco disappears. Carlitos and his family search everywhere for Blanco, but Christmas Day arrives and still the animal has not been found. Then, when they have almost given up hope, they find the dog in church, curled up in the warm straw near the nativity scene. Carlitos has his beloved dog back — the "nicest Christmas gift he could ever have wished for." K–3.

Target Activity: "Christmas in Other Cultures"

Help children to recount the festivities that take place in this book that make Christmas special for some Hispanic people. If there are Hispanic children in the class, ask them to compare and contrast their own Christmas traditions with that of Carlitos' family. Finally, bring in several people from the community who are from diverse cultures and who celebrate Christmas, or another religious remembrance, in other ways.

80 Politi, Leo. *Pedro: The Angel of Olvera Street.* Ill. New York: Charles Scribner's Sons, 1946.

This story, which is also available in Spanish, concerns a Chicano boy, Pedro, who lives in the heart of Los Angeles. Every Christmas there is a posada procession, a Mexican tradition. On this particular Christmas, Pedro is a little red-winged angel who leads the procession, for rumor has it that he "sings like an angel."

Target Activity: "Christmas Traditions"

This story tells much about Christmas tradition in old Mexico. Compare Christmas traditions as presented in this story with those that children enjoy in their own families. If Mexican American children are in the class, ask them to compare their traditions with those in the book. Are they familiar with these traditions? Have they heard relatives talk about them? Invite children from other cultures into the classroom to share any religious traditions they know of from their own cultures.

81 Politi, Leo. *Song of the Swallows.* Ill. by the author. New York: Charles Scribner's Sons, 1949.

This is the story of the friendship between Juan, a little boy in the California town of Capistrano, and Julian, the old gardener and bell-ringer at the mission of San Juan Capistrano. It is Julian who tells Juan of old days at the mission. Together they ring the bells to welcome the swallows as they come flying in from the sea on St. Joseph's Day.

The lovely pictures show the mission, the California coastline, and the swallows' return. The warm relationship between Juan and Julian is one with which most every child can relate. K–3.

Target Activity: "La Golondrina" (The Swallow)

Included in this text are the words and music to "La Golondrina," a song that Juan has learned in school. It is a song about the swallows returning again. Either the classroom teacher or the music teacher can teach this song to the children in the class. The children may want to act out the story, incorporating the song into their skit.

82 Prico, Mariana. *The Wise Rooster/El Gallo Sablo.* Ill. by Lee Smith. New York: The John Day Co., 1962.

In Latin America, every year at Christmas time (Navidades), the grandmothers gather their little children together and tell them lovely Christmas legends, stories of long ago, that were told to them by their own grandmothers in Spain. So in this tale, Grandmother Mena takes her granddaughter Alicia on her lap and tells her the story of the night the animals talked. This story is told in both Spanish and English. Folk literature. K–3.

Target Activity: "Stories from Our Relatives"

Encourage children to share stories that have been handed down from their relatives. Invite any children who wish to do so to tell their stories in their native language if it differs from English.

Optional Activity: "Guest from Another Culture"

Encourage the children to invite a grandmother, aunt, or other relative to come into the classroom and tell about a custom, legend, or ritual celebrated in their family which has been handed down for several generations.

83 Rohmer, Harriet, adapter. *The Legend of Food Mountain/ La Montana del Alimento.* Ill. by Graciela Carillo. San Francisco: Children's Book Press, 1982.

The lively tale tells the story (in both English and Spanish on alternating pages) of the creation of the earth by the great god, Quetzalcoatl. The people were at once hungry, but Quetzalcoatl didn't know what to feed them. When he saw a giant red ant carrying kernels of corn in her mouth, he asked her where she found the corn. The ant pointed to Food Mountain. The red ant showed the god how to get inside the mountain and together they drug out a pile of bright-colored corn. The people liked it. Quetzalcoatl was overjoyed and tried to bring back Food Mountain to the Western Heaven so that his people would always have food. The Lightning God broke Food Mountain open at last, but no one was there to guard it, so the rain dwarfs stole the food. From that time on, the people of the earth have had to call for rain in order to get food, or so the story goes. Folk literature. 2–3.

Target Activity: "Flannelboard Story"

Have the children make cardboard cutouts of the characters in the story:

> Quetzalcoatl
> giant red ant
> God and Goddess of the Calendar
> Lightning God
> (4) rain dwarfs

Glue velcro™ on the back of the cutouts and use them on a flannel-board to allow children to retell the story in Spanish, English or other primary languages used by children in the classroom.

84 Sargent, Jessie F. *Kids of Colombia.* Reading, MS: Addison-Wesley, 1974.

This engaging text with black-and-white photographs presents the customs, activities, and homes of Colombian children. Besides finding out that Colombian children play games, love their families and friends, and like animals just as they do, readers discover the differences in the cultures.

Colombian children wear *ruanas,* or colorful vests, and they often ride in a donkey cart called a *zorra.* The book is an excellent introduction to a different culture in a friendly, positive way. K–3.

Target Activity: "Likenesses and Differences"

While having children recount the factual information in the book, organize the information into "Likenesses" and "Differences" on the writing board or overhead. For example, the children in Colombia play a ball-and-stick game called *La Coca,* a difference; the children play games and go to school and these would be listed under likenesses.

85 Schoberle, Cecile. *Esmeralda and the Pet Parade.* Ill. New York: Simon and Schuster, 1990.

Esmeralda, Juan's high-spirited pet goat, is always getting into mischief. If the laundry is pulled down from the line or Papa's slippers have disappeared or the flowers have been eaten, everyone is pretty sure that Esmeralda did it. When it is time for the annual Santa Fe pet parade, Juan's friends try to convince him not to include Esmeralda, for they fear she will spoil their chances of winning the prize for best-dressed pet. Trying to escape from the unfamiliar leash, Esmeralda bolts through the city knocking over rummage sale tables and under clotheslines, picking up the clothes with her hooves and horns as she goes. Esmeralda wins the award for the "Most Unusual Costume," as Juan beams and even his grandfather, who is constantly berating the goat, is pleased. K–3.

Target Activity: "Children Everywhere Love Animal Companions"

Through this touching story of Juan and his beloved pet, children can begin to see that they share something in common with children of every culture: a love of pets. Ask children to interview an older friend or relative from another country who has recently come here. Have children ask the person if she or he ever owned a pet, what the pet was, and some of the experiences they had with their pet. Have children share the responses to their interviews in class.

86 Stanek, Muriel. *I Speak English for My Mom*. Ill. Chicago: Whitman, 1988.

Lupe Gomez helps her mother who speaks and reads only Spanish. Lupe helps her with trips to the dentist and with shopping, even though Lupe acknowledges she would rather play. Speaking and reading only Spanish, Mrs. Gomez needs her daughter's help as she completes the tasks and activities in her daily life. Even though she would rather play with her friends, Lupe is persistent and stays with the job of translating for her mother. Contemporary realism. Pre–3.

Target Activity: "Showing Sensitivity to the Language of Others with *A Show of Hands*"

Children can learn sensitivity to signers and speak sign language by using *A Show of Hands: Say It in Sign Language* (Harper & Row, 1980) by Mary Beth Sullivan and Linda Bourke. With the book, children will see that some people communicate by reading lips and speaking and others use sign language—a language made up of hand shapes and movements. This language is for everybody because it is expressive, beautiful when seen by others, and fun. Children may practice making the hand and finger signs for some of the letters (pp. 54–55) or practice spelling their names or sending a message to someone in the room. Reminiscent of Lupe who translated for her mother in a previous book, *I Speak English for My Mom,* the book can help children translate for another student who is using only sign language. Encourage interested students to learn to speak another language.

87 Vernon, Adele, reteller. *The Riddle*. Ill. by Robert Rayevsky and Vladimir Rayevsky. New York: Dodd, Mead, 1987.

In this tale from Catalan, a king asks a poor charcoal maker how he manages on so small a wage; the poor peasant answers with a conundrum. The riddle goes:

> How is it possible for a peasant who earns only ten cents a day to take care of his family, pay back a debt, save for the future, and still have something to throw out the window?

The king wants the courtiers in his court to solve the riddle and tells the peasant not to reveal the answer to the riddle until the peasant has seen the king's face one hundred times. Later at court, believing that the peasant has told the answer to one of the members of the court, the king brings the peasant to court to be punished for his disobedience. The peasant protests his innocence and maintains that he has seen the king's face one hundred times. The peasant explains: he saw the king's face printed on each of the one hundred gold coins that the courtier gave him for telling the answer to the riddle. Upon hearing this cleverness, the king rewards the peasant with three bags of gold. One bag is for his debts, one for his old age, and the last one for him to throw out of his window. 4–6

Target Activity: "Cleverness Is Appreciated in All Cultures"

With the children, read the story for the first time, and stop after the page where the peasant's riddle is presented to the king. Allow the children time to think of solutions to the riddle and list their ideas on a chart, transparency, or the board. Continuing the reading, stop again at the point in the story where the king discovers that the peasant has disobeyed him and wants the peasant brought to court. Encourage the girls and boys to talk together to try to explain what they *think* happened. Moving on, read the peasant's explanation to the king for his behavior and stop again to let the children talk among themselves about the explanation the peasant gives for his behavior in telling the secret of the riddle to the courtier. Encourage them to talk further about their reasons for justifying/not justifying the behavior of the peasant.

Invite the children to identify the books they have read (stories heard) about clever characters from different cultures and list their ideas for a class chart:

Books with Clever Characters   *Cultures*

a.

b.

c.

88 Winter, Joseph. *Diego.* Ill. by Jeannette Winter. New York: Knopf, 1992.

This portrays the life and work of Diego Rivera, a painter known for his colossal style, with a concentration on his early years. Later illustrations focus on his activities as a young man. They show Rivera painting on his scaffolding, and beckoning visitors. 1–3.

Target Activity: "English and Spanish Tell the Story"

Point out to children that the story is told in Spanish and has English captions beneath the paintings. Read some of the Spanish translation aloud and show children that it is easy to follow even if one lacks fluency in the language.

NATIVE AMERICAN HERITAGE

89 Accorsi, William. *My Name Is Pocahontas*. New York: Holiday House, 1992.

This is a fictionalized biography told by Princess Pocahontas and it begins with her childhood. The princess tells of her friendship with Captain John Smith and of her marriage to John Rolfe. The story ends with Pocahontas' trip to England as Rolfe's wife. Fictionalized biography. K–2.

Target Activity: "Princess Pocahontas"

With children, discuss the word princess and elicit what the word means to them.

Write their ideas on the writing board. Ask the children to fold a sheet of art paper into thirds to make three columns. In the left-hand column, ask the children to draw something that reminds them of the word princess. In the middle column, ask them to draw something they think they will hear about in the story that will be related to Princess Pocahontas. Ask the children to listen to the biography.

After the reading, ask the children to return to their papers and report to the whole group if what they drew was in the story. If so, ask children to put a check in the third column. If not, ask children to draw another sketch that does relate to the princess. Collect the drawings for a class book about Pocahontas.

90 Baylor, Byrd. *Hawk, I'm Your Brother*. Ill. by Peter Parnall. New York: Charles Scribner's Sons, 1976.

In the Santos Mountains, Rudy Soto wants to fly like a hawk and spends hours watching them. He steals a baby redtail hawk from its nest. Seeing the hawk caged and resentful, Rudy releases the bird and watches it fly away and feels he is flying together with the bird in spirit. They call to one another as one brother would call to another.

Rudy's observations of the wild hawks in flight makes Rudy yearn for the birds' sense of autonomy as exemplified through their ability to fly. To Rudy, flying is a symbol of a sense of control over life. Contemporary realism. 2–3.

Target Activity: "Modifying Cultural Stereotypes with Baylor's Books"

Surround the students with books by Baylor, read excerpts from them and discuss the feelings and the message developed by Baylor in her books. Determine any feelings elicited that are similar to those of the students' and record the students' interpretations on the board.

Baylor's Book	feelings like mine	message in book

The Desert Is Theirs
Hawk, I'm Your Brother
When Clay Sings
The Way to Start a Day

In a book, *The Desert Is Theirs* (Charles Scribner's Sons, 1975), there is a relationship of humans and earth shown through the Papago Indian culture with an emphasis of sharing with the earth and not taking from it. With the students, discuss what humans can learn from the animals and plants. How does this theme (learning from nature) relate to the earlier Baylor story? Other titles by Baylor to consider for an author's display are: *Desert Voices* (Scribner's, 1980); *If You Are a Hunter of Fossils* (Scribner's, 1980); *I'm in Charge of Celebrations* (Scribner's, 1986); *The Other Way to Listen* (Scribner's, 1978); *The Way to Start a Day* (Scribner's, 1978); and *When Clay Sings* (Scribner's, 1972).

91 Blood, Charles. *The Goat in the Rug.* Ill. New York: Macmillan, 1980.

Glenmae, with the assistance of her goat, Geraldine, creates a rug design that is unique. The story shows the tradition of Navajo weavers through hundreds of years. Being creative like other weavers of her tribe, Glenmae designs a rug that is uniquely hers. Using her talents, Glenmae finds she has a positive view of life. Contemporary realism. Pre–3.

Target Activity: "Traditions of the People"

Ask children to talk about the way Geraldine helped Glenmae create the rug design. Discuss what was learned about the tradition of the Navajo weavers from the story. Engage children in discussing any family traditions they know about from their own experiences.

92 Clark, Ann Nolan. *In My Mother's House.* Ill. by Velino Herrera. New York: Viking, 1941.

Though out of print, the book may be found in some branch libraries. It shows the thoughts of a young boy's life as a Pueblo Indian: "I string them together/ Like beads./ They make a chain,/ A strong chain,/ To hold me close/ To home,/ Where I live in my Mother's house." Illustrations and text have details from the world of Pueblos about the Council, Fire, Home, Mountains, Pasture, Pipeline, People, Wild Plants. Contemporary realism. 1–3.

Target Activity: "A Strong Chain to Home"

With children, discuss the things in their lives that link them to their families and their homes. Invite the children to draw their own large links. Ask them to write one fact inside each link. Each fact is to tell about something in their lives that ties them to their families and their homes (friendship, teasing, family jokes, pets, good cooking, atmosphere, care when they are hurt or injured, and so on). Display the "Strong Chains to Home" in the classroom.

93 Cohen, Caron Lee. *The Mud Pony.* Ill. by Shonto Begay. New York: Scholastic, 1988.

A poor boy in an Indian camp shapes a pony of mud and cares for it. When he is separated from his people, the white-faced mud pony comforts him in a dream, and then comes to life, a gift from Mother Earth. The pony guides him to his parents and directs him in becoming a great warrior, hunter and chief. When it is time for the pony to return to the earth, the chief removes the blanket with which he has always covered her, and she disappears in shrill winds and rushing rain leaving a patch of white clay on the wet ground. Folk literature. 1–3.

Target Activity: "Boy-Heroes from Different Cultures"

With the children, discuss:

a. Why do you think there was a need for warriors and chiefs in this story? What are the qualities of the boy-hero in this story?

b. Ask a student to retell the action in this story and, if needed, guide the teller through the events: 1) the white-faced mud pony comes to life, 2) it guides the boy to his parents; 3) it directs him in becoming a great warrior, hunter, and chief; and 4) it returns to the earth. Suggest to the girls and boys that they create the conversation that might have taken place at these times and engage in acting out and talking in brief "dialogue dramas."

94 Davis, Deborah. *The Secret of the Seal.* Ill. by Judy Labrasca. New York: Crown, 1989.

Using initiative and resourcefulness, Kyo, a young Eskimo boy, protects his playmate—a seal pup—from his uncle, the hunter. Young Kyo goes out to kill his first seal and finds a bond between himself and the female seal that he names Tooky. Kyo tries to prevent the capture of his new animal friend which brings a clash between traditional and modern values and a conflict in loyalties. Contemporary realism. 1–3.

Target Activity: "Traditional Values Versus Modern Values"

Encourage children to discuss the ways Kyo solved his problem about

his seal pup playmate. How will the children try to explain the clash between traditional and modern values that occurred in the story? What are
some of the main reasons that the children believe Kyo got into a conflict
of loyalties? Invite children to relate experiences from their lives to the
story.

95 de Paola, Tomie. *The Legend of the Bluebonnet*. Ill. by the author. New York: Scholastic, 1983.

In this retold Comanche legend, a drought and famine have killed
the mother, father and grandparents of She-Who-Is-Alone, a small girl. All
she has left is a warrior doll that her mother once made for her. One evening, the shaman of the camp tells his people that the famine is the result
of the people becoming selfish. They must make a sacrifice of the most
valued possession among them and life will be restored. No one volunteers
a valued possession except She-Who-Is-Alone, who offers her warrior doll.
Deep in the night she makes a burnt offering of the doll and then scatters
its ashes over the fields below. Where the ashes have fallen, the ground
becomes covered with bluebonnets. The Comanche people take the flowers
as a sign of forgiveness from the Great Spirits. From that day on, the little
girl is known as One-Who-Dearly-Loved-Her-People. The small girl gives
up the thing she loves best in all the world for her people. She spends a
frightening night alone on a hill offering her doll as a burnt offering to the
Great Spirits, clearly a courageous act of self-sacrifice and unselfishness.
Folk literature. K–3.

Target Activity: "Stories of Precious Possessions Are Found in All
Cultures"

Bring to students' minds other stories they have read or heard where
the main character has a most precious possession, e.g., Tera and her pig
Wilbur in *Charlotte's Web* by E. B. White; Sarah and her unicorn in *Sarah's
Unicorn* by Bruce and Katherine Coville; the child and his carrot plant in
The Carrot Seed by Ruth Kraus; Dick and his cat in *Dick Whittington and
His Cat* by Kathleen Lines. Have children rewrite *The Legend of the
Bluebonnet*, superimposing a new character and her or his prized possessions in a famine of modern times. Ask students to describe the famine. Tell
what the character says when he or she offers his or her prized possession
as a sacrifice to end the famine. How does your character feel? Describe
the night on the mountain. What happens as a result of the character's
sacrifice? How does your character feel about saving his or her people?
What has your character learned from the experience?"

96 de Paola, Tomie, reteller. *The Legend of the Indian Paint-brush*. Ill. by the reteller. New York: Putnam Group, 1988.

This is the story of Little Gopher, who cannot be like other children, but who, through his art, has a special gift for his people. Little Gopher finds his place among his people by painting their deeds. He is lonely, but faithful and true. He is rewarded with magical brushes left on a hillside. They hold colors and allow him to paint his vision of the evening sky. Discarded, they take root and multiply and bloom in colors of red, orange, and yellow. Simple poses of the characters show the dignity of the Indians' spirit. Folk literature. K–2.

Target Activity: "Understanding the Native American Spirit"

Invite children to see the ways primary colors turn into other colors with the overhead, a clear glass or plastic container, water, and drops of food coloring. Drops of red and yellow food coloring in the water in the container are swirled and the overhead projects the mingling as the colors turn into orange. Encourage children to use the colors of red, orange, and yellow, and other shades to create their own visions of the evening sky. Ask them to portray deeds of people in their lives. Remind them that no matter how small or young they are, their visions are important ones. After completing this activity, ask children to discuss how their colorful vision compares with Gopher's. How do they feel about the "Indian Paintbrush?"

97 Esbensen, Barbara Juster. *The Star Maiden.* Ill. by Helen K. Davie. Boston: Little, Brown, 1988.

This is an Ojibway Indian tale concerning the origin of a flower in the north lake country. A star maiden watches the earth and wants to make her home with the tribe who prepare to welcome her. The rose on the hillside where she first comes to rest is too far from the village and a flower on the prairie is too near the trampling feet of the buffalo. Finally, she finds the peaceful surface of a lake and calls her sisters down to live with her where they can be seen today as water lilies. Folk literature. K–3.

Target Activity: "Patterns in Ojibway (Chippewa) Tales Can Be Found in Other Tales"

To continue a study on Ojibway Indian legends, discuss the poetic use of words in this story. Discuss the illustrations which are framed on three sides with patterns authentic to the tribe. Read another legend about a positive vision of life, Esbensen's *The Ladder in the Sky* (Little, Brown, 1989).

98 Ginsburg, Mirra. *The Proud Maiden, Tungak, and the Sun.* Ill. by Igor Galin. New York: Macmillan, 1974.

This is a Russian Eskimo tale of why the tundra is no longer cold all year. It starts in typical fashion with a beautiful maiden who does not want to marry any of the men in her village. Her father becomes very angry with her and her mother who tries to protect her. He calls down the wrath of Tungak, an evil spirit. The maiden runs away from the demands of Tungak and marries into the family of the Sun. When they later visit her family the season changes because they bring the sun with them. 1–3.

Target Activity: "Exploring the Tundra"

Bring in pictures from an encyclopedia, the *National Geographic* magazine or other books showing the Russian tundra region. Discuss the lifestyle of the people who live there. Brainstorm with children why the people might create tales about the weather and the seasons in that region.

99 Goble, Paul, reteller. *Her Seven Brothers.* Ill. by the reteller. New York: Bradbury, 1988.

A lonely Cheyenne Indian girl makes clothing decorated with porcupine quills for seven brothers she has never seen. After many months, she travels north with her mother to find the seven brothers. When she finds the trail she wants, the girl says goodbye to her mother with the words, "Soon you will see me again with my brothers; everyone will know and love us!" In the land of pines, she finds the tipi of the brothers, gives them their clothing, and is well cared for by them. One day, the chief of the Buffalo nation wants to marry the sister. When the brothers refuse to let her go, the chief threatens to return with the whole Buffalo nation and kill them. Later, a shaking of the earth announces the rumbling of the Buffalo people stampeding toward the tipi. When the youngest brother shoots an arrow up in the air, a pine tree appears and grows upward as fast as the flight of the arrow. The girl and the brothers climb up just as the Chief of the Buffalo strikes the tree a mighty blow and the tree starts to topple over. The youngest brother shoots arrow after arrow into the sky and the tree continues to grow taller and taller until they are up among the stars. There, they jump down from the branches onto the prairies of the world above the Earth. The girl and her brothers are still there and can be seen as The Big Dipper. If one looks quite closely, one of the stars is near a tiny star that is the smallest brother walking with his sister who is never lonely now. Folk literature. 2–3.

Target Activity: "Meaning in Designs from Different Cultures"

Use the Cheyenne designs (circa 1900) as an example of cultural expression. Since other living creatures shared the Earth with humans, the creatures were included in the designs of Native Americans. Sometimes two of each are drawn, or to show abundance, many are drawn. With the whole group, a teacher may encourage artistic expression with: What design would you make for a tipi? Would your design include the members of the Buffalo Nation, the faithful dogs, the nearby deer, the porcupine "who climbs trees closest to Sun himself"?

Interested students may draw sketches of their designs and show them to others. Encourage the students to discuss their designs with someone and explain their reasons for drawing what they did.

100 Goble, Paul, reteller. *Iktomi and the Boulder: A Plains Indian Story*. Ill. by the reteller. New York: Orchard Books/Watts, 1988.

The vain Iktomi, a Plains Indian who gets into the worst kind of trouble, has overdressed for his journey. When he grows too warm, he offers his blanket as a gift to a boulder. When it begins to rain, Iktomi pretends the gift was only a loan. While congratulating himself on his foresight to bring the blanket, the boulder comes to reclaim the gift. Iktomi tries to elude the boulder, but it pins his legs. As the moon rises, bats appear and Iktomi tricks them into attacking the boulder. The bats break the boulder into small stones. This explains why bats have flat faces and there are rocks scattered over the Great Plains. Ink and watercolor illustrations show movement. Folk literature. K–3.

Target Activity: "Trickster Characters Are Found in All Cultures"

As an example of a trickster character, a teacher may discuss the background information in the foreword about Indian trickster characters and Iktomi. Point out that the book has large type and an informal narrative voice, with asides from the storyteller and the character Iktomi. The dark print tells children what happens; the light print gives the asides for the teller and invites comments from the audience. Invite children to tell about other trickster characters from other stories. Build a chart of information to show what they know about this type of character in literature.

Continue the focus on trickster tales of Native Indians with Goble's *Iktomi and the Berries: A Plains Indian Story* (Orchard Books, 1989). In *Berries*, the Lakota trickster is dressed inappropriately in full ceremonial clothing to hunt prairie dogs. He plans a feast to impress his relatives. After several failures, Iktomi sees buffalo berries in the water and dives for them. He is unaware that they are a reflection. Returning to land, he beats the berry bushes in anger with his bow. Berries are still harvested today in the Plains by beating the bushes. As mentioned earlier, the italic text invites listeners to make comments.

101 Green, Timothy. *Mystery of the Navajo Moon*. Ill. by the author. New York: Northland, 1991.

This story points out the universal dreams that children have of taking magical rides. Wilma Charley, a young Navajo girl, looks out the window of her hogan at a "Navajo Moon" and is given a diamond star one night. The next night, she is given a white pony and goes for a magical ride into the sky. As she reaches for a moonflake, she falls and wakes up to find herself in bed, with the moonflakes and the diamond star under her pillow as evidence that her dream really happened. K–3.

Target Activity: "Children of All Cultures Dream of Magical Rides"

With children, discuss the universal wishes of young children to take magical rides. Point out that children in different cultures might wish to ride in different ways. Talk about magical rides on the gander of Mother Goose, on a flying carpet, an oversize peach, and a silver pony. Invite children to use their crayons and draw sketches of a magical ride they wish for.

102 McDermott, Gerald. *Arrow to the Sun: A Pueblo Indian Tale.* Ill. by the adapter. New York: Viking, 1974.

This is the desert world where humans, nature, and spiritual forces are entwined. The yellow sun is the people's god. It is worshipped in a circular ceremonial chamber (the kiva). A spark of life from the sun becomes the sun god's son on earth. He decides to search for his father and, during his quest, he meets Corn Planter who silently tends his crops, Pot Maker who silently makes clay pots, and Arrow Maker who silently creates a special arrow into which the boy changes shape. He proves he is the son of the sun god by passing through four chambers of ceremony and takes on the sun's power. He returns to earth as an arrow returning with all the colors in the rainbow. The people celebrate with the dance of life. Folk literature. 2–3.

Target Activity: "Transformation Stories"

A common motif in many Native American tales, as in this one, is the transformation of human to animal or human to some inanimate object, such as the arrow. Help students to understand that this was once part of the beliefs of many Native Americans. Using *Arrow to the Sun* as a model, have children write a transformation tale where they change into an animal or object in order to "prove themselves," as the sun god's son did in this Native American tale.

103 Miles, Miska. *Annie and the Old One.* Ill. by Peter Parnall. Boston: Little, Brown, 1971.

Annie lives on the Navajo Indian reservation with her grandmother, called the "Old One," her father, her mother, and a herd of sheep. She helps tend the sheep and garden and goes to school. She lives a happy life until she learns from her grandmother that when the new rug being woven by her mother is completed, her grandmother will go back to Mother Earth. Since her grandmother means so much to her, Annie feels she must do something to prevent this from happening. She attempts to keep her mother from weaving the rug by misbehaving at school and letting the sheep out of the corral at night. Both these ploys fail. Annie then resorts to stealthily unweaving the rug at night. She is caught in the act by the Old One. The Old One then takes Annie out into the mesa and points out the natural evolution of seasons, time, and destiny. With this, Annie realizes that "she was a part of the earth and the things on it. She would always be a part of the earth, just as her grandmother had always been, just as her grandmother would always be, always and forever." Annie gains a deep, unspoken realization of the inevitability of earth's natural order, and accepts this way of life. The next morning, Annie starts weaving the rug. Contemporary realism. 2–3.

Target Activity: "Annie Grows Up"

Discuss what students have learned about Annie. Write descriptive traits on the board. Brainstorm some ideas about how Annie will be feeling when the rug is finished; several years later, when Annie is grown up and has children; or when Annie is an "Old One." Determine what values Annie has learned from the Old One and how she will carry them into later life. Ask children to choose one of Annie's later stages and write several sentences about what her life is like at that time.

104 Oliver, Rice D. *Lone Woman of Ghalas-hat.* Ill. Fullerton, Calif.: R. C. Law, 1987.

This is the true story of an Indian woman from a tribe that lived on the island of San Nicolas off the coast of California. In 1835, this young Indian woman, from the tribe called Ghalas-hat, was moved with her people off their home island. As the boat left the island, she found that her baby was missing. She dove into the water and swam back to the island but discovered that the baby was dead. The woman, later called Juana Maria, lived alone on the island for eighteen years until she was discovered by a white man who had heard about her. This Native American woman faced difficult times alone and the book tells us about her strength as a person, the values of her culture, and how she survived. 2–3.

Target Activity: "No Happy Ending"

Understanding the plight of Native Americans through the experience of this woman (and her story with no happy beginning or ending but with a view of our history) can help children understand that settling America was a costly affair—for the fighters and for the families who lived here originally. Some topics for discussion:

    a. Ask the children to explain why the tribe was moved. In what other cultures has this happened to the people?

    b. Ask what happened to the rest of the tribe as a result of this move. Has something similar happened to people in other cultures?

   c. Ask children to recount the ways this woman responded when her child was in danger and compare the ways to responses of other mothers from other cultures when their children are in danger.

   d. Ask children to discuss ways Juana Maria was able to fend for herself because of her ingenuity during the long years on the island. In what other cultures has something similar happened?

   e. Ask children in what ways people can be both strong and gentle. Give examples from Juana Maria's story and then from stories with settings in other cultures.

   f. Ask children in what ways they can compare the values Juana Maria's culture taught her with developing a respect for nature.

   g. Have children draw pictures of the various parts of the story by folding a paper in half and half again so that there are four places to draw on. Have them write a title under each drawing.

   h. Older students, grades 4 and up, may want to compare Juana Maria's story with the story of Karana, the girl in *Island of the Blue Dolphins,* and with survival stories set in other cultures.

105 Parish, Peggy. *Good Hunting Blue Sky.* Ill. by James Watts. New York: Harper & Row, 1989.

Blue Sky is going hunting for the first time in his young life. He tells his father, "Today I will bring home the meat." He shoots an arrow at a turkey and the turkey flees. He shoots at a deer and he, too, flees. Blue Sky decides to go after bigger quarry. When he sees a bear, he realizes it is too big, and Blue Sky climbs a tree. Feeling he has failed, Blue Sky starts toward home when suddenly he is charged by a ferocious wild boar. Thinking quickly, Blue Sky leaps onto the boar's back and rides it all the way home, where his father shoots the boar with his bow and arrow. All the people in the village are invited to the feast. Blue Sky tells them about the hunt. They change the young boy's name to Big Hunter. K–3.

Target Activity: "Growing Up"

Explain to children that in the original Native American culture, some young boys had to bring home an animal to prove they were growing up. Have children brainstorm some things that they can do now that they couldn't do, or weren't allowed to do, when they were younger. Have them draw a picture of themselves doing the activity and then share it with the rest of the class. This sharing underscores the idea that the students are growing up and capable.

106 Penney, Grace Jackson. "How the Seven Brothers Saved Their Sister." In *Tales of the Cheyenne.* Boston: Houghton Mifflin, 1954.

In this tale from the Cheyenne, the role of women is revealed as brothers are changed into the seven stars, the Pleiades. Double-Teethed Bull, strongest of all the buffalo, takes Red Leaf and runs away with her. The brothers build four strong corrals to provide a safe place for their sister when they rescue her. Moskois rescues Red Leaf and when the buffaloes charge the corral, they climb a tall tree reaching into the sky. There they became seven stars, with the girl as the head star. 2–3.

Target Activity: "Scenes from Traditional Tales Can Be Rewritten"

A teacher may assign parts in a reader's script developed with the help of the students. Students may rewrite some of the traditional scenes and change the setting to another culture. If desired, pairs may act out or read aloud both dialogues. With the whole group, the partners should discuss the effects of the change of setting with members of the audience.

107 Sleator, William. *The Angry Moon.* Ill. by Blair Lent. Boston: Little, Brown/Atlantic Monthly Press, 1970.

A rainbow appears and takes Lapowinsa to the sky when she angers the moon. To retrieve the girl, Lupan shoots his arrows toward the moon. He notices that a chain of his arrows forms a ladder on which he climbs into the sky. Reaching the top, he is taken by a small boy to his grandmother's house, where Lupan receives four objects to aid in the rescue of Lapowinsa. Lupan follows the sobs of Lapowinsa to the moon's home, substitutes a pine cone in her place in a smoke hole and they begin their escape. When the pine cone burns, the angry moon pursues them. A fish eye becomes a lake to block the moon's progress, a rose turns into a tangled thicket to slow the chasing moon. A stone grows deep into steep mountains and the children make their escape and return to earth to tell their story to succeeding generations. Lupan is an active character who has a positive characteristic of caring for another as he comes to the aid of Lapowinsa. Lupan is independent, brave, strong and competent. His grandmother portrays a positive adult female role and the story deals thoughtfully with the problem of caring for others. 2–3.

Target Activity: "Lupan Expresses a Range of Feelings"

The questions/activities that follow are examples of the types which teachers and librarians can prepare to encourage children to talk about how they feel about some of the ideas related to the book before it is read or heard:

    a. Why do some people come to the aid of or rescue others?

    b. Why is a person often punished when he or she angers others?

    c. Without using the word angry, write or talk about what the title, *The Angry Moon,* means to you.

    d. Create an "angry" research project and include these things: a list of words that best describe an angry person and a list of things that cause a person to become angry. Tell how you recognize anger. Tell what you would do to overcome anger in another person.

After reading or listening to the story, the students may be asked to think back to the rescue event and then write their impressions about a person who came to the aid of or rescued another person. Take time to discuss the children's work and point out examples that modify gender stereotypes.

A teacher or librarian may read these sentences about some of the things Lupan experienced in the story. After hearing each sentence, invite the students to "tell how you think Lupan felt and more about what he did." "As Lupan was feeling this way, tell how you think the young girl felt."

   a. Lupan discovers that a rainbow appears and takes the young girl to the sky when Lapowinsa angers the moon.

   b. To retrieve the girl, Lupan shoots his arrows toward the moon.

   c. Lupan notices a chain of his arrows makes a ladder upon which he climbs into the sky.

   d. Reaching the top, Lupan is taken by a small boy to his grandmother's house.

   e. At his grandmother's house, Lupan receives four objects to aid in the rescue of Lapowinsa.

   f. Lupan follows the sobs of Lapowinsa to the moon's home, substitutes a pine cone in her place in a smoke hole and they begin their escape.

   g. When the pine cone burns, the angry moon pursues them.

   h. Lupan sees that a fish eye becomes a lake to block the moon's progress, and a rose turns into a tangled thicket to slow the chasing moon. A stone grows into a steep mountain.

   i. Lupan and Lapowinsa make their escape and return to earth.

   j. They tell their story to the succeeding generation.

Books for
Older Children:
Grades 4–8

AFRICAN AMERICAN HERITAGE

108 Aardema, Verna. *Bringing the Rain to Kapiti Plain: A Nandi Tale.* Ill. by Beatriz Vidal. New York: Dial, 1981.

This is an accumulating tale from Kenya that tells of Ki-Pat, a herdsman and Kenyan hero, who pierces a cloud with his eagle-feathered arrow to bring rain. On a barren, parched, dry African plain, hungry cattle wait for a huge dark cloud mass and rain to make the plain green with grass. An appended note mentions the origin in terms of the country, a sign of sensitivity on the author's part. Search for this rhythmic tale in UNICEF Curriculum Guide: *African Folktales.* Folk literature. 3–5.

Target Activity: "Herdsman and Hero"

Explore what this hero from the African culture has in common with some of our own heroes in the culture of the United States. What traits of resiliency will the students discuss? To show similarities and differences between the two, draw two overlapping circles (Venn diagrams) and in one circle place the word "herdsman" and in the other, the name of a hero chosen by the students. In the appropriate circles, write down the traits the herdsman has (perseverance, ability to overcome obstacles, ability to solve problems) and the ones the hero has. If there are traits that the two have in common, write those traits in the overlapping area of the circles. Discuss the traits as they are written in the circles.

109 Anderson, Joy. *Juma and the Magic Jinn.* Ill. by Charles Mikolaycak. New York: Lothrop, Lee & Shepard, 1986.

In a setting in Muslim Africa, there is a motif (symbolism of three) for this tale of a boy whose three wishes show him that there is more magic at home than can be conjured from the family jinn jar. Full-color illustrations with map. Being able to ask for three wishes gives the boy a sense of control over his life and a sense of autonomy. He is persistent as he faces his problems and seeks a positive vision of life. Folk literature. 4 up.

Target Activity: "About Responsibility"

Discuss with the students: Suppose you had the responsibility of looking after a friend's valuable jinn jar. Tell how you think you would feel if something happened to it. What would you do to try to repair the damage done? What lengths would you go to if you didn't want anyone to know? Where would you draw the line?

Invite the students to discuss what they would wish for if each had three wishes. Invite them to draw pictures of their wishes, to discuss their drawings with an art partner, and to write sentences about their wishes. Invite them to read their sentences to their partners. Ask children to search the class and school libraries for other stories from other cultures that also have a motif of the "symbolic three."

110 Armstrong, William. *Sounder.* Ill. by James Barkley. New York: Harper & Row, 1969.

Caught stealing meat from a white man's smokehouse to feed his hungry family, a black sharecropper is arrested and taken away. His protective dog Sounder leaps at the sheriff's wagon where his master is chained. One of the men shoots the dog, leaving it disfigured and crippled, and without the spirit for barking. When the sharecropper receives a sentence of working on a gang, his wife endures, and each year his son searches for him after the crops are in. During a search, the boy meets an old black man who becomes his friend and teacher. Six years later, the father walks home, partially paralyzed and deformed from a dynamite blast in the prison quarry. When Sounder recognizes him the dog bays a welcome. The father and Sounder both die soon after. After seeing that his mother and the young children have wood and are prepared for the winter, the boy returns to his teacher.

Taking place in the South with unnamed characters, *Sounder* has courage, human dignity, as well as tragedy and some cruelty. Told to the author when he was a child by a gray-haired teacher, this oral history retells part of the teacher's childhood and the binding relationships with others. Contemporary realism. 5–8.

Target Activity: "Hungry Children"

The boy's father in this story stole some meat from a smokehouse to feed his hungry family. Discuss this incident with the students. Do you think the man wanted to steal? What else might he have done? Share with the students the fact that the poverty rate for black children was 39.8 percent in 1989 compared with 12.5 percent for white children (Source: the Children's Defense Fund). Do they think that is fair? What can be done about it? Do they ever think it would be all right to steal to feed hungry children? Ask them to support their answers with examples.

111 Brandenburg, Aliki. *A Weed Is a Flower.* Ill. New York: Simon and Schuster, 1965, 1968.

This biography of George Washington Carver gives information about his birth, early childhood and adult life. His story tells of slavery and freedom and poverty and success. Working as an agriculturalist chemist, Carver convinced farmers to grow peanuts as a crop, and in his laboratory, made approximately 300 products such as soap and ink from peanuts. Additionally, he gained recognition as a painter and was elected a Fellow in the Royal Society of Arts in London, an honor given to few Americans.

Born of slave parents on a farm near Diamond Grove, Missouri, Carver earned his way through school and was graduated from Iowa State College of Agriculture and Mechanical Arts. He joined the staff at Tuskegee Normal and Industrial Institute in Alabama and contributed his life savings to the George Washington Carver Foundation for Agricultural Research, a museum of his discoveries. Today, the George Washington Carver National Monument is on 210 acres of the farm where he was born. Biography 4–5.

Target Activity: "Find Your Cultural Heroes"

With the whole group, a teacher may discuss the idea that one way to become a cultural historian is to find heroes who can be models for you. The children can discuss people in their lives (a family member, a neighbor, a national personality, a teacher) who can be heroes and heroines for them. Point out that these special people also can be from the past and engage children in recording what they find about heroic people on a chart similar to the one that follows:

Heroic Trait	*Name*
determined educator; fighter for equal rights	Mary McLeod Bethune
powerful speaker against slavery	Frederick Douglass
scholar, writer, leader asking for equal rights	William E. B. DuBois
great explorer	Matthew Henson
campaigner against slavery	Sojourner Truth
conductor on Underground Railroad	Harriet Tubman
great African general	Shaka Zulu
other:	Others:

Optional Activity: "George Washington Carver's Activities"

On page 56 of Carver's biography is a selection of activities that are reminiscent of those that the scientist engaged in during his childhood. Have the students try their hand at making peanut butter or growing a sweet potato vine, as suggested in the text. Similarly, have students show their appreciation for Carver's artistic talent and love of plants by asking them to draw pictures of the plants that they like, paying close attention to the shapes and colors of the leaves, stems, and flowers.

Optional Activity: For the students who have shown much interest in George Washington Carver and his life as a scientist, direct them to the following trade books:

Adair, Gene (1989). *George Washington Carver, Botanist.* Chelsea House.

Graham, Shirley, and George D. Lipscomb (1971). *Dr. George Washington Carver, Scientist.* Julian Messner.

Kremer, Gary R. (1987). *George Washington Carver: In His Own Words.* University of Missouri Press.

Mitchell, Barbara (1986). *A Pocketful of Goobers: A Story About George Washington Carver.* Carolrhoda Books.

112 Clayton, Ed. *Martin Luther King: The Peaceful Warrior.* Ill. by David Hodges. New York: Archway, 1968.

When he was a young man, Martin Luther King, Jr., dreamed of a career of helping people. He hoped that by becoming a minister he would have an effective voice against racial prejudice. Following the example of the Indian leader Mahatma Gandhi, Dr. King chose nonviolence as the basis of his fight for civil rights. Dr. King soon became one of the most prominent leaders of the civil rights movement. In 1955, he helped to organize the famous Montgomery, Alabama, bus boycott. Freedom rides, sit-ins, and protest marches strengthened the battle against discrimination. As a result, the United States Congress passed the historic Civil Rights Bill in 1964. For his life's work, Dr. King received the prestigious Nobel Peace Prize. After King's death, to honor this great leader, Congress established a national holiday to commemorate the birthday of this man who courageously led a peaceful struggle for equal rights for all Americans. 5–8.

Target Activity: "We Shall Live in Peace"

After discussing the momentous events of the life of Martin Luther King, Jr., with children, share with them the freedom movement song "We Shall Overcome" that was always sung at the close of civil rights meetings. The last verse of the song suggests that peace will someday exist. Ask students if they think that if Martin Luther King, Jr., were to return today he would feel that day had arrived. Why or why not? Invite them to write a short essay to support their answer.

113 Climo, Shirley. *The Egyptian Cinderella.* Ill. by Ruth Heller. New York: Thomas Y. Crowell, 1989.

Recorded by the Roman historian Strabo (first century, B.C.) this is an old story based on fact about a Greek slave girl, Rhodopis, who married the Pharaoh Amasis (and became his queen). Some of it is partly fable, for it is believed that one of her fellow slaves was a man named Aesop who told her fables about animals. Because she is a Greek slave in Egypt, Rhodopis (meaning Rosy Cheeks) washes clothes in the Nile, tends the geese, mends clothing, bakes bread, and gathers reeds along the bank. Scorned by the Egyptian girls, she befriends the animals and dances for them. Her master, seeing her dance, gives her a pair of dainty leather slippers with the toes gilded with rose-red gold. When the Pharaoh and his entourage are nearby, the Egyptian girls row away to Memphis to visit the Pharaoh's court. Rhodopis polishes her shoes and puts them on the bank. A great falcon soars away with one of her slippers in his talons. Unknown to her, the falcon flies to Memphis where Amasis, the Pharaoh, is holding court and drops the slipper into his lap.

Amasis, thinking it is a sign to find the maiden whose foot fits the shoe, announces it is the will of the gods that the maiden should be the queen. During his long search, Amasis visits every place along the Nile and the Egyptian girls try to cramp and curl their feet into the slipper. When he discovers Rhodopis and commands her to try on the slipper, Rhodopis puts her foot into the slipper with ease and shows him the other shoe. Saying that she is not fit to be queen, the girls protest and say she is a slave and not even Egyptian. "She is the most Egyptian of all," says the Pharaoh, "for her eyes are as green as the Nile, her hair is as feathery as papyrus, and her skin the pink of a lotus flower." Folk literature. 3 up.

Target Activity: "Something Positive"

The teacher encourages all in the group to be friends to one another. In the group each students prints his or her name on a paper that is passed to the right (or left) of the person next to him or her. Each student in turn writes something positive about the person whose name is on the sheet. Finally each student has his or her own "good word" sheet to keep. This is a list of written compliments for the student to take home, show to others, and keep as a souvenir of the lesson.

114 Douty, Esther M. *Charlotte Forten: Free Black Teacher.* Champaign: Gerrard, 1971.

Charlotte Forten was from an African American family from Massachusetts. Having been born in the North in 1837 before the Civil War and the freeing of the slaves in the South, she was fortunate to be part of a free black family. This family consisted of her grandparents, her aunts and uncles, her cousins, and a brother. They were all highly educated professional or business people. They also had many well known whites and other free Northern blacks as friends. All of the people who gathered in her house at various times were very interested in helping the slaves of the South to be set free. Charlotte was most impressed with escaped slaves she met who were hidden by her family and their friends.

Since the schools where she grew up after her mother's death were segregated, Charlotte was, for the most part, educated at home by her aunt. Since she had no schoolmates, she read and wrote in a journal a great deal. She also attended meetings of the Female Antislavery Society with this aunt. By the time she was eighteen, Charlotte was a teacher but she continued to write in her journal. She wanted her people to know and remember stories of the heroic slaves who fought for their freedom and their friends who helped them in this fight. Historical fiction. 4 up.

Target Activity: "Keeping a Journal"

Discuss with the students how Charlotte Forten's journal writing helped her remember the important stories of the struggle of individual people to be free and to free the slaves at the time before the Civil War. Ask students to keep a journal of special things that they know about, read, or see that they might want to remember later. These events could be as usual as: a description of a good game with friends; a party at school; a good book they read; or an idea they would like to remember. Request ideas about sources from them.

Optional Activity: Have the students interview an adult family member or friend about a special African man or American woman they knew as a child. The students can write the story down or draw a picture about the person to show to the adult who shared the story. They can tell the story to the class.

115 Felton, Harold W. *Mumbet.* Ill. by Donn Albright. New York: Dodd, Mead, 1970.

This is the true story of a courageous black woman in the late 1700s. As a slave, she had a comfortable life with the Ashley family. But because she valued freedom she approached a young lawyer, Theodore Sedgwick, and asked him to help her become free. In 1781, Elizabeth Freeman won her freedom in the courts of the state of Massachusetts. It was the first time anyone of her race had dared to try to achieve freedom that way, but Elizabeth had been told that the Constitution said that all were "born free and equal" and she knew that included her. After the successful trial, she joined the Sedgwick household, where her talents with the children and in the kitchen earned her the affectionate nickname Mumbet.

Elizabeth Freeman never wavered in her belief that she should be free. Her courage in the face of fear continued when the house was raided and Elizabeth cleverly and courageously talked the ruffians out of taking anything. Historical fiction. 4–6.

Target Activity: "Why I Should Be Free"

After reading *Mumbet* with the class, use the chalkboard or overhead projector and cluster the ideas children have about the word "freedom." Ask them if they are free to do anything they wish. Ask them to select one thing that they would like to do that they are not allowed to do because they are too young or because their parents cannot afford it. Have them select a partner to be their "lawyer." With their lawyer, have them build a case for why they should be allowed to do their selected activity. Allow each pair to "present their case" to the rest of the class, who will offer arguments against the present case. Explain the terms associated with the legal profession. Emphasize the reasonableness of arguments. Focus on order. Use graphics on the board with headings of argument and counter argument, and write down the arguments with students also recording the information. A jury, consisting of nine class members, may decide whose arguments are stronger, while a judge, selected by the teacher, presides. End the activity with a discussion about how they would feel if the only reason they were not allowed to do their chosen activity was that they were black (or had green eyes, etc.).

116 Fox, Paula. *The Slave Dancer*. Ill. by Eros Keith. Scarsdale, New York: Bradbury, 1973.

Abducted in New Orleans in 1840, thirteen-year-old Jesse Bollier is taken to the *Moonlight,* a slave ship headed for West Africa. He is to play his fife for captured Africans so they will dance and exercise. Through the words and actions of Jesse and the others, the readers vicariously experience life on a slave ship. The slave trade in Africa and the United States was grim and becomes quite real to the reader. The sailing nightmare includes a tightly packed ship, shackled slaves with the "bloody flux," slaves thrown over the side of the ship, and the vessel, damaged in a terrible storm, sinking off the coast of Mississippi. One of the slave boys, Ras, and Jesse are the survivors. After being cared for by an old black man, Ras is sent North on the Underground Railroad and Jesse walks home to New Orleans. With a grim tone, the story narrated by Jesse is preceded by a history that lists the ship's name, its officers, crew, cargo, date of the wreck, and the survivors.

Target Activity: "How to be a Culture Historian"

With students, discuss being a cultural historian as one of the world's most important jobs and mention that "the job can be yours" if you want to start now. Invite interested students to find out how much they already know about a particular culture. For students interested further in an African American heritage, *The Slave Dancer* provides background information to talk about. Why is Jesse Bollier on board the *Moonlight,* a slave ship? Do you believe the reason was a good one? Why or why not? Why do you believe that Ras had to be sent North on the Underground Railroad? Why was Jesse sent to New Orleans? List the cargo, date of the wreck, and the survivors.

117 Greene, Bette. *Philip Hall Likes Me, I Reckon Maybe...* Ill. by Charles Lilly. New York: Dial, 1974.

Eleven-year-old Elizabeth "Beth" Lorraine Lambert is liked by Philip Hall, who is best in everything at school and who lives on the Hall dairy farm adjoining the Lambert poultry and pig farm in Arkansas. Because he likes her, he lets her do his chores every evening. Beth (with Philip's help) captures thieves, pickets the local stores that sell poor

merchandise, and wins the 4-H calf-raising contest. Recognizing Beth's accomplishments, Philip gets used to being second best and teams up with
Elizabeth for a square-dancing contest. Contemporary realism. 4–6.

Target Activity: "I Reckon Maybe..."

With the students, the teacher discusses the ways Philip Hall shows
Beth that he likes her. After discussion, the teacher invites the students to
start a list of names of friends and the ways they show their friendship. The
list is titled, "I Reckon Maybe..."

"I Reckon Maybe..."

Likes Me	Because
(name)	(ways to show friendship)

a.

b.

118   Greenfield, Eloise, and Lessie Jones Little. *Childtimes: A Three-Generation Memoir.* New York: Crowell, 1979.

From the late 1800s to the 1940s, three generations of black
Americans tell their early life experiences. Each of the book's three parts
"catches up to the past" and each is focused on the "threads of strength"
of one generation: a grandmother, mother, and daughter. Greenfield and
Little's conclusion tells us of the "great sadness" and "great joy" in the lives
of these women with these words: "It's been good, stopping for a while to
catch up to the past. It has filled me with both great sadness and great joy.
Sadness to look back on suffering, joy to feel the unbreakable threads of
strength. Now, it's time for us to look forward again, to see where it is that
we're going" (p. 175). Historical fiction. 4–8.

Target Activity: "Interview an Historical Resource Person to Learn
More About Culture"

Knowing the history of a culture is a resource that can be located and
discussed with people who have contributions to make. Share with children the hope of the authors, Greenfield and Little, and their words about
other children stopping and telling the story of their time and place with:
"Maybe years from now, our descendants will want to stop and tell the story
of their time and their place in this procession of children. A childtime is
a mighty thing" (p. 175).

To learn about the culture of a community personality whose
"childtime" was a "mighty thing," ask children to:

   a. Suggest tips for interviewing (i.e., reading background material
      about interviewing, scheduling a time to meet with the one you

want to interview, writing the questions to ask, asking about the person's birthplace and date, schooling, motivation, and so on, taking notes or using a tape recorder, and writing a brief introduction when writing about the interview).

b. Interview a resource person who is a leader (the mayor, the president of a school or community group, the school district superintendent or school principal, the pastor or preacher of a nearby church, the owner or manager of a business, the manager of a sports team, the librarian, or a teacher).

c. Ask about the person's "childtimes" and what it took for the person to get to where they are today and talk about the good and bad times they had. Ask children to write the interviews as a report for a class newsletter to send home to parents.

d. Write about a time and place in their own "childtime" and early life experience that they judge was a "mighty thing" (made an impression, changed their views, solved a problem, established an important friendship or relationship, created a better aspect of life) in their lives.

119 Grifalconi, Ann. *The Village of Round and Square Houses.* Ill. by the author. Boston: Little, Brown, 1986.

Tells why the men in Tos, a Cameroon village in central Africa, live in square houses while the women live in round houses. One night long ago, the old Naka volcano erupted and left only two houses standing in the village — one round and one square. To take care of the people while the village was being rebuilt, the village chief sent the men to live in the square house and the women to live in the round house.

The teller of this tale says that this arrangement is peaceful and continues to this day because people need a time to be apart as much as a time to be together. The women decided they enjoyed being together to talk, laugh, and sing in the round houses and the men became used to relaxing in their own place in the square houses. A read aloud. Folk literature. 4–6.

Target Activity: "Storytelling in Every Culture"

From stories of different cultures, introduce the storytelling beginnings. For stories related to an African heritage, discuss the beginning ("In the days of long, long ago") and ending ("And that is how our way came about and why it will continue. . .". Ask the students to retell the story to one another in pairs. Each one takes the turn of beginning the story with the beginning words "In the days of long, long ago," and then ending the story with, "And that is how our way came about and why it will continue." Have the student switch roles so all have a turn to say the storytelling beginning and endings.

120 Hamilton, Virginia. *M. C. Higgins, the Great.* New York: Macmillan, 1974.

Living on Sarah Mountain near the Ohio River, M. C. sees an enormous spoil heap left by stripminers. The heap is oozing slowly down the hill heading toward the house of his family. This place has been home to his family since 1854 when his great-grandmother Sarah, a runaway slave, found refuge on it. His father refuses to accept the danger of the landslide and M. C. realizes he must save the family. To divert the slide, M. C. builds a wall of earth reinforced with branches, old automobile fenders and a gravestone. Contemporary realism. Advanced 6 up.

Target Activity: "Every Culture Has 'Great' Ones"

With the girls and boys, discuss the meaning of the word "greatness" and its meaning in the story. Does greatness mean helping prevent a danger from occurring? Being physically strong? Knowing the right thing to do? Reaching out to make friends with those shunned by others? Realizing that what is inside is more important than what is outside? The teacher invites the students to reflect upon the thought, "I'm a great one, too" and record reasons privately in their journals as to why they should be considered great just as M. C. Higgins was thought to be in the story.

121 Hamilton, Virginia. *The Planet of Junior Brown.* New York: Macmillan, 1971.

Junior Brown, an eighth grader, is a talented pianist who weighs 262 pounds. His friend, big Buddy Clark, is brilliant in science and math, works part-time at a newsstand, and leads a group of homeless boys who live on their own "planet" in the basement of an abandoned house. Junior and Buddy spend their time with a janitor, Mr. Poole, formerly a math and astronomy teacher, in his basement room behind a false wall in the broom closet. Mr. Poole and Buddy show Junior a ten-planet solar system, lit up and revolving, with the tenth planet named Junior Brown. It is shaped in the "soft, round contours of Junior Brown's own face" and "glazed in beige and black." Neither Junior nor Buddy has attended classes at school for two and one-half months. Frustration after frustration affects Junior as he slips away from reality. Events during this story that cover one week of time include his music lessons with Miss Peebs who won't let Junior play her grand piano but makes him beat out the music on a chair, his playing at home on a piano whose wires have been removed because the sound bothers Junior's mother, his caring for his asthmatic mother, his painting of a huge figure of a Red Man with smaller figures of people living their lives inside of it, and its destruction by his mother who considers the painting a "terrible sick thing." During another music lesson with Miss Peebs, Junior realizes she is crazy as she insists she has a filth-diseased relative in her apartment. Leaving, Junior tells Miss Peebs he is taking the relative with him but talks to the imaginary relative on the bus back to the school. Mr. Poole takes Junior, Buddy, and the ten-planet solar system to the "planet" of the homeless boys which Buddy renames "the planet of Junior Brown." Buddy says, "We are together . . . because we have to learn to live for each other." Contemporary realism. 5–10.

Target Activity: "Every Culture Has Those Who Help Others"

The teacher asks the students to consider the idea: *What would you have done to help the boys if you had been there with them when:*

  a. the group of homeless boys went to their own "planet" in the basement of an abandoned house.
  b. Mr. Poole and Buddy showed Junior a ten-planet solar system.
  c. neither of the boys went to classes at school for two and one-half months.

122 Harris, Joel Chandler. *Jump! The Adventures of Br'er Rabbit.* Adapted by Van Dyke Parks and Malcolm Jones. Ill. by Barry Moser. New York: Harcourt Brace Jovanovich, 1986.

Five traditional black American slave tales set in Hominy Grove, where Br'er Rabbit's mischievous wit outsmarts more powerful animals. Universal themes are portrayed in diluted Gullah dialect. Music and lyrics from "Hominy Grove" and a storyteller's historical note are included. Folk literature. 4–6.

Target Activity: "Every Culture Has Trickster Tales"

Invite students to match the titles of the tales and what Br'er Rabbit did in the stories. Discuss what was identified and ask children to give reasons for their choices.

Trickster Behavior	Titles
_____	*The Comeuppance of Br'er Wolf*
_____	*Br'er Fox Goes Hunting But Br'er Rabbit Bags the Game*
_____	*Br'er Rabbit Finds His Match*
_____	*Br'er Rabbit Grossly Deceives Br'er Fox*
_____	*The Moon in the Millpond*

Optional Activity: "Notes from a Cultural Storyteller"

Discuss with students what can be learned from the author's note in the book: Malcolm Jones and Van Dyke Parks tell about the history of the tales as told by black slaves in the southern United States who had come to America against their will. The stories are examples of the pluckiness and cleverness of the small winning out over those with brute strength. In the late 1800s, a newspaperman in Georgia by the name of Joel Chandler Harris collected the tales. Harris presented the stories in the Gullah dialect of the nineteenth-century black storytellers and created an elderly black plantation slave, Uncle Remus, to tell the stories about Br'er Rabbit and his friends to a little white boy. Harris has been deeply criticized for this portrayal, but the lessons in the stories have universal themes that send a message: no one can be totally owned who does not wish to be.

123 Hooks, William H. *The Ballad of Belle Dorcas*. Ill. by Brian Pinkney. New York: Knopf, 1990.

This conjure tale of the Gullah people tells of brave Belle Dorcas who is what was known as a "free issue" person, or the child of a slave master and a slave woman. Though free issue people generally married other free issue persons in order to take advantage of the relative freedom of which they could partake, Belle Dorcas loved Joshua, a slave, and no one else would do. Pressured to marry one of the free issue young men, Belle goes on a hunger strike and lets her mother know that she would sooner starve than marry someone other than Joshua. Her mother soon relents and allows Belle to marry Joshua and they happily move into the slave quarters. When their old master dies, the new master cares only for money and decides to sell their strongest slave, Joshua. Belle frantically runs to Granny Lizard, known for her magical spells, to get help for Joshua. Granny Lizard asks Belle, "Can you give up Joshua to keep him?" Without thinking, Belle answers yes to the strange question. She is given a "conger" bag to place around Joshua's neck. On the night before Joshua is to be sold, Belle secretly slips the conger bag around Joshua's neck and he turns into a cedar tree. Belle flees back to Granny Lizard, who gives Belle yet another conger bag that changes the tree back into Joshua every night. The master searches for his slave, but to no avail. Belle Dorcas and Joshua spend every night together until they grow old and Belle dies. Folk literature. 4–6.

Target Activity: "Living as a Slave"

Have students recount the hardships that slaves had to endure, as portrayed in this story. Ask them to imagine they are Belle, happily married to Joshua, and then the greedy master decides to sell him. Ask children to write a persuasive letter to the master, trying to convince him to allow Joshua to stay with his wife.

124 Lester, Julius, reteller. *The Tales of Uncle Remus: The Adventures of Br'er Rabbit*. Ill. by Jerry Pinkney. Foreword by reteller. Introduction by Augusta Baker. New York: Dial, 1987.

Lester arranges forty-eight adventurous stories by themes (how the animals came to earth) and links them in opening paragraphs. In the tales, Br'er Rabbit shows different facets of his character: helplessness in "Br'er Rabbit Goes Back to Mr. Man's Garden"; playing tricks in "Br'er Rabbit and Br'er Lion"; and being gullible in "Br'er Rabbit and the Tar Baby." Each of the adventures is a complete story in itself. 4–6.

Target Activity: "People in Every Culture Understand Feelings of Others"

Encourage students to talk about experiences from their background that help them relate to the feelings of Br'er Rabbit during his different adventures. Questions for discussion:

   a. Feeling Helpless. Br'er Rabbit felt helpless in the garden. As you think about this situation, what might convince you that Br'er Rabbit's feeling of helplessness could be just about the same as a feeling of helplessness you have had?

   b. Feeling Like a Trickster. Why do you suppose that Br'er Rabbit felt he had to play tricks in "Br'er Rabbit and Br'er Lion"? Do you think the tricks were justified or unjustified?

   c. Feeling Gullible. Br'er Rabbit was gullible in "Br'er Rabbit and the Tar Baby." What situations can you think of where someone else was gullible? What example can you give that clearly tells us what being gullible is? being helpless? playing a trick?

125 Lester, Julius, reteller. *The Tales of Uncle Remus: Further Adventures of Br'er Rabbit, His Friends, Enemies, and Others.* Ill. by Jerry Pinkney. New York: Dial, 1988.

This, the second part of a two-part retelling of the African American folk tales collected by Joel Chandler Harris in the late nineteenth century, includes thirty-seven more folktales that did not appear in the earlier volume, the *Tales of Uncle Remus: The Adventures of Br'er Rabbit* (Dial, 1987). As with the first volume, the retellings remain faithful to the spirit of the originals but without the drawbacks of heavy dialect and a stereotypical narrator. Folk literature. 6.

Target Activity: "Read Trickster Tales from Other Cultures"

Select *Bo Rabbit Smart for True: Folktales from the Gullah* (Philomel, 1982) retold by Priscilla Jaquith and illustrated by Ed Young, for four tales from the islands off the Georgia coast.

In Julius Lester's *To Be a Slave* (Dial, 1988), there is an historical narrative from early nineteenth century slaves. Quotations, rewritten to conform to the literary standards of the time, were taken down from the American Antislavery Society and other abolition groups. The second half, recorded in the speech patterns and language of the ex-slaves, comes from the 1930s from a Federal Writers Project. The interviews are from ex-slaves. The quotations are organized into chapters related to life as a slave in North America, abduction from Africa, labor on the plantations, experiences with the Ku Klux Klan, and segregation in the post–Civil War years.

In these two narratives, the author presents ways ex-slaves showed their persistence, perseverance, and problem-solving abilities and states this is "a vivid picture of how the slaves felt about slavery." Historical fiction. 5 up.

Optional Activity: "The People Could Fly, Too"

It is enlightening to some students to read some of the traditional tales of American blacks that come to us from Africans who became slaves in North America. From the experiences told in these tales, the students realize the impact of slavery. Virginia Hamilton, in a book of folktales, *The People Could Fly* (Knopf, 1985), states that the slaves created tales in which various animals took on the characteristics of the people found in the new environment of the plantation (page x). For example, Br'er Rabbit, a trickster character, is small and helpless, but usually wins out over larger, more powerful animals. Slaves identified with Br'er Rabbit, the one who survived against cunning beasts, and told many stories about his experiences and achievements. Hamilton points out that slaves saw themselves as Br'er Rabbit and the slaveholders as Br'er Wolf and Br'er Fox in the stories. The best way for them to win was to be more clever than their captors.

With the idea that various animals took on the characteristics of the people found in the new environment of the planation, invite interested students to read and discuss some of the tales.

126 McDermott, Gerald. *Anansi the Spider: A Tale from the Ashanti.* Adapted and ill. by Gerald McDermott. New York: Holt, Rinehart & Winston, 1972.

Six wondrous deeds are performed by the sons of Anansi. Each of the sons of the spider-hero is an expert in some way. Their names tell the children of their expertise that is useful in solving problems: See Trouble, Road Builder, River Drinker, Game Skinner, Stone Thrower, and Cushion. Folk literature. 3–4.

Target Activity: "Pattern of Six Is Found in Folktales from Different Cultures"

Before the story is reread, the children decide on motions and movements for the characters for an audience participation story. The names of the sons will lead the young children quickly into ideas for movements. When a character's name is mentioned in the rereading, the teacher pauses and gives the audience time to respond with the movments that identify the character. To further expand the pattern of six into folktales from other cultures, a teacher or librarian may invite children to find other folktales and record the information they find in the tales:

Pattern of Six (or Five)   *Title of Tale*   *Country-Culture*

127 McKissack, Patricia C. *Mirandy and Brother Wind.* Ill. by Jerry Pinkney. New York: Knopf, 1988.

Mirandy was hoping to win her first cakewalk, a dance rooted in African American culture in which the pair of dancers with the most flamboyant dances take home a cake. The trouble is, Mirandy's most logical partner, Ezel, is much too clumsy to be a partner who could help her win. Mirandy decides to try to catch Brother Wind and have *him* be her partner. Everyone she speaks to tells her, "Can't nobody put shackles on Brother Wind . . . he be free." She tries to put black pepper on his footprints to make him sneeze so she can slip up behind him and throw a quilt over him. She tries to catch him in a crock bottle, but he escapes. Finally, Mirandy traps Brother Wind in the barn. At the cakewalk, when another girl makes fun of Ezel's clumsiness, Mirandy defends him and claims him as her partner. She immediately regrets having said such a "tomfool" thing; she has caught Brother Wind. She goes to Brother Wind and makes a wish. She and Ezel dance with grace and style and win the cakewalk. A beautifully illustrated book that portrays a young black girl as highly resourceful and clever, yet compassionate. 3–4.

Target Activity: "Pursuing a Goal"

Have children retell the story, paying special attention to the attempts Mirandy made to catch Brother Wind. Ask them why they feel she did not give up. Ask them to take a couple of minutes to remember a time they really wanted to do something that seemed impossible. What was their goal? What did other people tell them about the possibility of pursuing their goal? Have each child share their goal with a partner. Let the partner be the "other person" who gives them reasons why their goal is impossible. Tell them to try their best to offer arguments as to why they should continue pursuing their goal. Compare the goals of the boys and girls in the classroom.

128 McMullan, Kate. *The Story of Harriet Tubman, Conductor of the Underground Railroad.* Ill. by Steven James Petruccio. New York: Dell, 1991.

Born in Dorchester County, Maryland, Tubman as a young girl worked as a field hand. She escaped to the North and decided to help others to escape. She took trips over the Underground Railroad to slave territory and led slaves back to freedom. This earned her the name of "Moses." Tubman, an American antislavery leader, was one of the greatest fighters for freedom. She returned to the South again and again to help rescue over 300 slaves. 4–5.

Target Activity: "Every Culture Has a Messenger of Freedom"

With students, discuss the writing of a script for a brief scene using the character of Harriet Tubman. Working in groups, the students should consider the task. Research various books of children's literature to find messengers of freedom from different cultures. In your notes you will want to include important information about the people and events:

Culture	*Messenger of Freedom and Book*
African heritage	
Asian heritage	
European heritage	
Latino heritage	
Native American heritage	

129 Myers, Walter Dean. *The Mouse Rap.* Ill. New York: Harper, 1990.

Living in Harlem, fourteen-year-old quick-thinking, fast-talking Frederick Douglas is known as "The Mouse." "Ka-phoomp! Ka-phoomp! Da Doom Da Doom!/ Ka-phoomp! Ka-phoomp!/ Da Doom Da Dooom!/ You can call me Mouse, 'cause that's my tag/ I'm into it all, everything's my bag/" is a sample of his fast talking. He searches for a treasure hidden by Tiger Moran, a gangster of the '30s. Through a mock bank robbery, Mouse and other teenage friends (with the help of Sheri's grandfather and Sudden Sam, a cohort of Moran's), find the money in an abandoned building. Shows independence. Contemporary realism. 6–10.

Target Activity: "Are Your Feelings Like Mouse's Feelings?"

Related to Mouse's feelings about his estranged father, discuss with students different reasons they can think of to explain why some teenagers are convinced that their parents don't care about them.

   a. What do you think can happen rather suddenly that would make a teenager feel unwanted by a girlfriend? boyfriend? friend? parent?
   b. To make a visual display of Mouse's feelings, draw a large "paper grocery bag" in the center of a sheet of art paper and write the name Mouse.
   c. Draw lines outward from the "bag" and at the end of each line

draw smaller "bags." Inside the "bags," write these headings: Mouse felt happy when . . . ; Mouse felt afraid when . . . ; Mouse felt sad when . . . ; and Mouse felt angry when . . . .

d. Now, discuss the headings with others in a circle group and finish the sentences on your paper. Read what you wrote to others.

130 Page, Valerie King. *Pi Gal.* Ill. by Jacques Callaert. New York: Dodd, Mead, 1970.

Prince Williams is a young boy growing up on Cat Island, an outer island in the Bahamas. Like many other children on the island, he longs for a chance to live a more exciting life in exotic places far beyond the island. While searching for his lost dog, he comes upon two divers who have come to the island to salvage a lost barge. Prince soon learns to dive and the beautiful underwater life of the reef is revealed to him for the first time. After many frustrating attempts, Prince finds the barge they have been seeking and at the same time discovers he is a talented diver and decides to pursue diving as a career. Contemporary realism. 5–6.

Target Activity: "Meet Human Resources in Every Culture"

Invite students to consider the idea that their class is a bounty of human resources; there are many talents and abilities that each studnet has that perhaps the others do not know about. Explain that just as Prince Williams had to discover his talents, others must keep searching to find what makes them unique and special. Write on the chalkboard the following three sentence stems:

> Once I couldn't (*ride my bike*)
>
> But today I can (*do wheelies*)
>
> Soon I may learn to (*win races like Greg LeMonde*)

Fill in the lines as a group, allowing many students to contribute ideas for the blanks. Next, encourage students to write their own human resource poems, illustrating them if they so desire. Collect the poems and put them into a class "Human Resources Book." Put the book on display so that all can see what their classmates can do and someday hope to do.

131 Palmer, Leslie. *Lena Horne.* New York: Chelsea House Publishers, 1990.

One of the titles in the *Black Americans of Achievement* series, this biography tells of the life of a truly dynamic performer, Lena Horne. Born into a middle-class African American household in 1917, Lena made her professional debut as a chorus girl in an exotic cabaret in Harlem that featured only black performers. She was sixteen. In 1937, Lena left New York City to tour with the Noble Sissle's Society Orchestra as a featured vocalist. Three years later she joined a jazz band and then, in 1941, she launched her career as a solo nightclub performer. She became one of America's most popular entertainers due to her heartfelt renditions of songs such as "The Man I Love" and "Good for Nothin' Joe." Her rising fame was bolstered by her appearances in musicals such as *Stormy Weather* and *Cabin in the Sky*. Earning a reputation as a respectable and glamorous light-skinned black woman, Lena Horne was the first black singer to be heavily promoted by the movie industry. She was one of the first to break the color barrier and win acceptance in white society. Yet Lena Horne did not forget her roots: Throughout her career Lena has taken civil rights issues to heart in the same way that she developed her artistic skills. 5–8.

Target Activity: "Taking Civil Rights to Heart"

Lena Horne was talented and glamorous, therefore, with much hard work she was able to break through the barriers of racial discrimination when many others could not. She still had compassion for her black sisters and brothers who were not so fortunate, and she fought hard for civil rights. Ask the students to identify a civil rights issue that does not directly apply to *their* own ethnic or racial heritage (e.g., an African American child might identify the problems of Native Americans living on reservation lands). Encourage the students to find current articles in the newspaper or magazines that concern their identified issue. Invite them to write a letter to the editor of the local newspaper about the issue, or write a letter to their local congresswoman or man, outlining their feelings about the unfairness of the problem.

132 Schroeder, Alan. *Ragtime Tumpie.* Ill. by Bernie Fuchs. New York: Joy Street/Little, 1989.

Showing an urban black community, this fictional biography tells the life of Josephine Baker, a dancer famous in Europe early in the twentieth century. As a young girl, Josephine (Tumpie) picks fruit from the yards and gathers coal fallen off the hopper cars at the railroad tracks. At night, she goes with her mother to hear ragtime music and to dance to the drums in the honky-tonks. One day, she wins a dance contest sponsored by a traveling peddler and receives a shiny silver dollar. This shows how dance enriches one's life. 4–5.

Target Activity: "Every Culture Has Dancers and Entertainers"

First, develop lists of ways dancers and entertainers are supposed to act. Using magazines, newspapers and tradebooks, have students explore entertainers and dancers from other cultures.

Culture	Dancer-Entertainer and Book
European American heritage	Zola, Meguido. *Karen Kain: Born to Dance*. New York: Franklin Watts, 1983.

Others:

Make a list of these dancers, singers, and other entertainers. Bring in videotapes of performances of entertainers from various ethnic backgrounds. Encourage children to discuss who their favorites are and why.

133 Stanley, Diane, and Peter Vennema. *Shaka: King of the Zulus*. Ill. by Diane Stanley. New York: Morrow Junior Books, 1988.

With illustrations full of details, here is a story of a boy with a vision of his own destiny and the determination to carry it out. Shaka, who has no help in the making of his nation, becomes known as a fighter, is made ruler of his clan, and trains them as a vast army. Information on pronunciation of Zulu words is given along with information about where Zulus live. Background on this nineteenth century ruler is provided. Biography. 4–6.

Target Activity: "Every Culture Has Strong Leaders"

Begin a *Record Book of Lists* and add entries as they are found by students. Here are some lists to start with:

African Leaders
African Americans Who Made a Difference
Asian American Who Speak Out
Hispanic Leaders

134 Steptoe, John. *Mufaro's Beautiful Daughters: An African Tale*. Ill. by the author. New York: Lothrop, Lee and Shepard, 1987.

From G. M. Theal's *Kaffir Folktales* (1895) comes this tale told by people living near Zimbabwe ruins, a former site of a great trade city of Africa. The father, Mufaro, is happy, for all agree that his two daughters are beautiful. Nyahsa is beautiful and kind, and Manyara is beautiful but has a bad temper and is selfish and somewhat spoiled. When the king decides to take a wife all the most "Worthy and Beautiful Daughters in the Land" are called to appear before him. To make certain that she is chosen, Manyara leaves before the others to get to the king. Along the way, she has three challenges: to feed a hungry boy (she tells him to get out of the way); to listen to the old woman in the woods (she tells her to stand aside); to not laugh at the grove of laughing trees (she laughs out loud at them). When Nyasha meets the same three challenges, she feeds the boy her lunch, she gives the woman sunflower seeds, and she does not laugh at the trees. At the king's city, she finds her sobbing sister who says the king is a "great monster, a snake with five heads." When Nyasha sees the king, she sees only the little garden snake, her friend. The snake transforms into the king, Nyoka, who asks her to be his wife, the queen. Manyara becomes a servant in the queen's household. Folk literature. 4–6.

Target Activity: "Every Culture Has Its Fables"

Label two or more columns (one each to represent a culture) on the board or on overhead transparencies. Ask the students to dictate or to write down words or phrases that tell the characteristics of fables they have found from different cultures. After discussing the fables, use the visual display of the stories to write paragraphs about a favorite tale.

135 Wepman, Dennis. *Jomo Kenyatta.* New York: Chelsea House, 1985.

This biography is one of a series documenting one hundred leaders from ancient times to the present. Jomo Kenyatta was born in East Africa in a time when white people ruled and their word was the law. Faced with the injustices of racism and colonialism, Kenyatta vowed that he would one day lead the Kenyan people out of the abject poverty and exploitation to which the British white man had subjected them. After learning to speak English and becoming literate with the help of British missionaries, Kenyatta made his way to London, where he furthered his political education and began to understand the oppressors who had considered their civilization for all people. Upon his return to Kenya, Jomo Kenyatta put his training and experience to the test. Under his leadership, the Kenyan tribes united in the quest for independence while the British responded with curfews and concentration camps. Even after being imprisoned by the British, Kenyatta remained the leader of Kenyan nationalism. Finally, in 1961, Kenyatta regained his freedom and went on to become one of the most widely respected leaders in the Third World—the man who led Kenya out of slavery and into the twentieth century. 5–8.

Target Activity: "Jomo's Journal"

Discuss with students the meaning of colonialism. Allow students to share their knowledge of countries other than Kenya that suffered under colonial rule. Why did powerful countries such as England feel justified in ruling a country so far away? Help the students to internalize the outrage of colonialized people by keeping a journal that Jomo Kenyatta might have written in times of deep frustration. Have them choose to create entries based upon the following events:

    a. Running away from his village so that he could learn to speak English with the help of the missionaries who patronized him.

b. Arriving in London and experiencing extreme culture shock.
c. Being imprisoned for years as a result of his quests for Kenyan independence.
d. Other.

ASIAN AMERICAN HERITAGE

136 Clark, Ann Nolan. *To Stand Against the Wind.* New York: Viking, 1978.

In this emotional story, eleven-year-old Elm, a refugee living now in America, is helping his grandmother, older sister, and uncle prepare for the traditional Day of the Ancestors and his family is ready to honor and remember those who have recently died. As the head of his family, Elm's responsibility is to write the family history and tell the descendants about a country they may never know. To do this, his thoughts return to Vietnam and the beautiful country in the Mekong Delta that was his family's home for hundreds of years. He compares his memories of prewar and war times when the buildings in his village were burned and its dikes destroyed. 5 up.

Target Activity: "Children in All Cultures Can 'Stand Against the Wind'"

With students, discuss what Elm remembers about his life in Vietnam: his father, who loved the land, and the American reporter who often visited them to learn more about the people in the village. As Elm remembers more about the war, he recalls some of the members of his family going off to fight, the fall of Saigon, and the day when his village was bombed. After this, he finds his mother, father, and other family members dead. With students, discuss Elm's journey to America where he (and the remaining members of his family) are sponsored by a church group.

After discussing the meaning of the book's title and Elm's father's words: "It takes a strong man to stand against the wind" (see p. 132), invite the students to suggest other stories where both women and men (and girls and boys) from different cultures could "stand against the wind" and list the book titles on a chart for a suggested reading list:

"Children in All Cultures Can 'Stand Against the Wind'"

African heritage
books:

Asian heritage
books:

Latino heritage
  books:

European heritage
  books:

Native American heritage
  books:

137 De Jong, Meindert. *The House of Sixty Fathers.* Ill. by
  Maurice Sendak. New York: Harper, 1956.
  This historical fiction book tells of Small Tien Pao, who was swept
by a storm into Japanese-occupied territory. Walking back home through
the mountains toward Hengyang, he helps a wounded American airman.
Both are found by Chinese guerrillas who care for the airman and take Tien
back to Hengyang—where the Japanese are fighting in the city. Tien left
the city hidden in a deep basket with his pig, Glory of the Republic. The
basket rolls out the open door of the train. Unhurt, Tien is found sleeping
by American soldiers who take him to the barracks where sixty men belong
to a bomber squadron. This is the base of Lieutenant Hamsun, the airman
he helped. The sixty men help him look for his family. 4–8.
  Target Activity: "Children in All Cultures Face Their Problems"
  With the students, the teacher may review the story and discuss what
Tien Pao needed to survive the problems he faced. The teacher invites the
recall of the sequence of events:

  a. Tien Pao is swept by a storm into Japanese-occupied territory.
  b. Tien Pao walks back home through the mountains toward Hen-
     gyang, finds a wounded American airman and helps him.
  c. Both are discovered by Chinese guerrillas who care for the airman
     and take Tien back to Hengyang.
  d. Leaving the city hidden in a deep basket with his pig, Glory of the
     Republic, Tien and the basket roll out the open door of the train.
  e. Unhurt, Tien is found sleeping by American soldiers who take him
     to the barracks where sixty men belong to a bomber squadron.
     This turns out to be the base of Lieutenant Hamsun, the airman
     he helped.
  f. The sixty men help him look for his family.

  Review the events again and engage the students in contributing their
ideas to the question, "What would you have done if you had been in this
situation?"

138 De Roin, Nancy. *Jataka Tales: Fables from the Buddha.*
  Ill. Houghton Mifflin, 1975.
  This book has thirty fables from India that teach a moral lesson, and

in some cases, include Buddha as a noble example, a connection to the Indian culture. 4–5.

Target Activity: "One's True Nature"

With students, discuss a fable that indicates the moral that, "one always reveals his/her true nature." For a comparison story, introduce Marcia Brown's *The Blue Jackal* (Scribner, 1977). In this tale, a jackal, colored with indigo dye, rules the animals until he reveals his true nature.

In connection with the fables they have read, students may create their own newspaper headlines about the characters in fables they have read, write them on the board, and ask others to relate the headlines to fables. To begin the activity, invite the students to guess the following headlines for fables: Jackal Reveals True Nature; Mouse Calls for Peace, Not Fear; Tortoise Is Slow Winner; and Boy Learns About Crying Wolf.

139 Friese, Kai. *Tenzin Gyatso, the Dalai Lama.* Ill. Boston: Chelsea House, 1989.

In Tibet, a two-year-old peasant boy was named the fourteenth reincarnation of the Dalai Lama, the supreme ruler of Tibet. He was the head of Tibet until the Chinese Communists invaded his country. He is thought to be the reborn soul of the man who ruled before him and was born at exactly the moment the former Dalai Lama died. The wise men of the country look for his appearance on the surface of the holy lake and then search among the children born at the right moment for a face to match the one seen in the lake. He comes to the throne very young and in a colorful ceremony and jeweled splendor of a fairy-book prince. This book tells of his unique education, his efforts to keep the culture alive, his life in exile and his Nobel Peace Prize. Useful reference tools include black and white photographs with captions, quotes, bibliography, chronology, and index. 5 up.

Target Activity: "Keeping the Culture Alive"

With the students, discuss the idea of "keeping the culture alive" and its meaning for those in the classroom. In what ways could a group's culture die? What meaning does this have for you if your group's culture dies? Stays alive?

140 Garland, Sherry. *Song of the Buffalo Boy.* Harcourt Brace Jovanovich, 1992.

Loi, a modern-day Cinderella, works for her uncle's family and is kept from school. Only Khai, a buffalo boy, sees her worth. When Loi is promised in marriage against her wishes, she runs away with Khai but finds herself all alone in Ho Chi Minh City. She finds a godfather in the form of a Vietnam veteran who offers to sponsor her back in the United States. 7–8.

Target Activity: "What Did I Learn About the War Years in Vietnam?"

With the students, review what was learned about the war years in Vietnam from the story. For examples, the students may mention the devastating effects of war on people and discuss families whose members were torn apart, families whose members fought one another, and the effects on families of the defoliant used in battles. From this conflict, ask students to consider what change came about. Emphasize the conflict-and-change (a cause-and-effect approach) theme with the situations they describe:

> *Conflict*   *Change*

1.

2.

141 Humble, Richard. *The Travels of Marco Polo.* Ill. by Richard Hook. Watts, 1990.

Born in Venice, Marco Polo journeys to serve the Great Khan, the Mongolian ruler. The book discusses the politics and religion of the time period and refers to the Polo family and Marco Polo's completion of his book, *Description of the World,* also known as *Travels* (1299). Includes a time chart, glossary and index. 4–6.

Target Activity: "Marco Polo's Time Period"

With the students, discuss evidence from the book that provides information about the culture in Asia during this time period.

142 Lamb, Harold. *Genghis Khan and the Mongol Horde.* Ill. by Elton Fax. Reprint, 1954; reprinted Linnet, 1990.

This portrays the life of a successful military leader and his boyhood on the plains of the Yakka Mongols. He became chief of his tribe at thirteen. This book tells of his accomplishments and claims to vast territories in the East including northern early China, Korea, Mongolia, Siberia, Turkestan, Afghanistan, and the Soviet Union. His grandson was Kublai Khan and was described by Marco Polo in his *Travels.* 5 up.

Target Activity: "Life of a Military Leader"

With the students, discuss the title and the meaning of the word horde, and what message it sends about the author's point of view. Ask students for events they found interesting in the life of Genghis Khan, a boy who became chief at age thirteen. Record the events in an idea association web on the board:

Boyhood   Chief of the Tribe

Life of a Military Leader

Manhood and Military Events   Old Age

143 Lord, Bette Lao. *In the Year of the Board and Jackie Robinson.* Ill. by Marc Simont. Harper & Row, 1984.

In 1947, a Chinese girl, Bandit Wong, discovers that she likes baseball, the Brooklyn Dodgers and Jackie Robinson. Bandit and her mother join her father in New York City. The refrigerators and washing machines are strange things to the ten-year-old but she enjoys bubble gum and roller skating. When school starts, she calls herself Shirley Temple Wong and has a difficult time being accepted by her fifth-grade classmates until she shows she can really hit a baseball. After the hit, she is called "Jackie Robinson" and she finds that she can accept this part of the new culture and still maintains ties to her family and her Chinese culture. Developing a love for baseball helps a Chinese girl make friends in America. 4 up.

Target Activity: "Finding Something a Newcomer Excels In"

With students, discuss the idea that is the group's responsibility to accept newcomers and talk about ways that can be done in the classroom and on the playground and in the neighborhood. Accept the students' ideas and write them on the board:

	Accepting Newcomers	
in the classroom	on the playground	in the community

Ask the students to pair up and find something the other excels in and to give one another "likeable" nicknames. Return to the group and introduce one another to the rest of the class by telling what the student excels in and announcing the new nickname. Distribute name tags and let the students write their nicknames on the tags and use them in the classroom.

Optional Activity: "Bonds to America's Culture and a Native Culture"

With students, discuss the question that many immigrants to America face: Do I have to lose my native culture to become an American? Are "hyphenated Americans" doubly blessed because they can choose the best of both cultures?

144 Lyttle, Richard B. *Land Beyond the River: Europe in the Age of Migration.* Ill. by the author. New York: Atheneum, 1986.

Anglos, Goths, Huns, Muslims, Mongols, Saxons, Vandals, Vikings, and such figures of the time period as Alfred the Great, Attila, Genghis Khan, and Mohammed are presented in this history of Europe, 2nd through 9th century. Bibliography and index are included. 4 up.

Target Activity: "Cross Checking Facts About Cultural Leaders"

To students, read aloud excerpts about Genghis Khan and invite interested students to suggest facts about the Khan and write their ideas on the board. With copies of other books about Genghis Khan, ask students to crosscheck the facts on the board and look for evidence in the other books that do or do not support the facts.

145 Masani, Shakuntala. *Gandhi's Story.* Ill. by the author. New York: Henry Z. Walck, 1950.

The life of India's great leader is told here in a simple, direct style that makes wonderful reading. Young people who are not ready for more adult biographies will find this account of one of the greatest peace-loving figures in history a compelling introduction to this life. The shy but lively boy, living in a small Indian town, then studying in England, grows up to become a crusader for human rights in South Africa and finally a revered pacifist leader in India. The author, Shakuntala Masani, knew Gandhi well and writes of him with the highest personal reverance and affection. Gandhi's whole life was a testament to the idea of change through peaceful resistance and his life story is an inspiration for children who want to know how to effect change peacefully. 4–5.

Target Activity: "Satyagraha"

Gandhi's method of resisting one's opponents peacefully was called Satyagraha (p. 38). *Satya* means "truth" and *graha* means "firmness," and the two words together, suggest that the most peaceful way to resolve a conflict is to tenaciously adhere to the truth. Have students think of a time that they were engaged in an argument with a friend or sibling and knew that they were right, or were telling the truth, when the person with whom they were arguing was not. Invite children to reflect orally upon how this argument might have been carried out more peacefully using Gandhi's concept of "satyagraha."

146 Mikerji, Shan Gopal. *Rama, the Hero of India.* Dutton, 1930.

This is a story from *The Ramayana,* a major epic of India that describes the devotion of Rama, the god-hero and his wife Sita, who is faithful to him in spite of years of separation and travail. 4 up.

Target Activity: "Heroes and Heroines of Different Cultures"

With a discussion of this tale, the students can develop an understanding of the epic as a literary form that is found in several cultures. Discuss the following: How did Rama become a hero? How did other people you know about become heroes? If you were to tell us a short story about a hero or heroine you know about, what would you say? Who is one of your heroes (or heroines) today? Why?

147 Namioka, Lensey. *The Coming of the Bear*. San Francisco: HarperCollins, 1992.

In Japan in the 1600s, two young samurai, Senta and Matsuzo, flee to a strange island and discover the Ainu people. There is increasing tension between the Ainu and the Japanese colonists who are trying to settle on the island. Part of this tension is caused by a bear who keeps attacking the Japanese settlement during the winter. The two samurai realize that winter is when the bear should hibernate and they set out to solve the mystery. Solving the mystery stops the impending war between the Ainu and the settlers. 5–9.

Target Activity: "Learning About Ainu Life"

With the students, discuss the information in the story that gives details about Ainu life in the 1600s. Write the facts in a list on the board and ask students to label all facts that related to Ainu food with the letter A, facts that related to medicine with B, related to hunting with C, and about self-defense with D. Show students a way to collect all the facts labeled A into an A paragraph, a way to collect all the facts labeled B into a B paragraph, and so on for C and D. Show the students how the facts turned into paragraphs can become an outline that looks like this:

Aimu Life

A. Ainu Food

_____ (write A paragraph)

B. Ainu Medicine

_____ (write B paragraph)

B. Ainu Hunting

_____ (write C paragraph)

B. Ainu Self-Defense

_____ (write D paragraph)

Ask students to team up and write a brief report (with A, B, C, and D paragraphs) about what they have learned about Ainu life. Ask teams to meet and listen to one another's reports and suggest improvements in the writing. Give students time to make revisions, draw illustrations, and write revised copies. Display in a class book for independent reading.

148 Namioka, Lensey. *Yang the Youngest and His Terrible Ear*. New York: Little, Brown, 1992.

This story explores cultural and individual differences and the problems a newcomer faces in a new environment. A recent immigrant from China to America, nine-year-old Yang Yingtao is tone deaf but is supposed to play in the family's string quartet. His father is a violinist in the Seattle Symphony and his performance will attest to his father's skill as a music teacher and bring honor to the family. Additionally, his father needs more music students to add to the family's income. 4–6.

Target Activity: "Individual Differences"

With the students, discuss Yang's friendship with curly-haired Matthew and their reversed situations:

a. Matthew's family wants him to practice baseball, but in contrast, Matthew wants to play the violin.

b. Yang's family wants him to excel at playing the violin but he discovers his natural affinity for baseball.

Ask the students to discuss the idea of individual differences and talk about why everyone needs to recognize this important feature of humans and their abilities.

149 Nhuong, Huynh Quang. *The Land I Lost: Adventures of a Boy in Vietnam.* Ill. by Vo-Dinh Mai. Harper & Row, 1982.

This is a portrayal of the author's boyhood experiences in Vietnam. It begins in prewar days of Vietnam and recounts the family and village life. The traditions and beliefs of the family are shown. 4 up.

Target Activity: "Traditions and Beliefs"

With students, select some traditions that they observe in the story and write a list on the board. Ask them to team up with partners, select the entries on the list to discuss and write comparative traditions they observe here in America.

150 Rappaport, Doreen. *The Journey of Meng.* Ill. by Yang Ming-Yi. New York: Dial, 1991.

Based on an ancient Chinese myth, this story tells of the superhuman efforts of a dutiful wife, Meng, to locate her husband, who has been forced to work on the building of the Great Wall of China. At first, her efforts are determined, but unrealistic and almost futile. When the crows teach her to fly, she can overcome the distance, but not the fact that her beloved husband has already died. Determined to honor him, she bargains with the Emperor for a funeral ceremony and national mourning. He complies in order to have Meng for his own wife. When the ceremonies are completed, she spurns him and jumps into the sea. This spunky woman is an antidote to many of the traditional fairy tales where the young woman always does as she is told and accepts her lot in life without question. 4–5.

Target Activity: "Taking Control of One's Life"

After reading this folktale, read the story of *Cinderella* to the children. Then place two column headings on the writing board, "Control" and "No Control." Have the children retell first the story of The Journey of Meng and then Cinderella, discussing whether each action shows that the female character has control over her own life or is merely controlled by the events. When children clearly see Meng as a strong character and Cinderella as more of a romantic victim, ask them to tell which character they would rather be, and why.

151 Takashima, Shizuye. *Child in Prison Camp.* Montreal: Tundra Books, 1971.

This is a first person account by a Japanese-Canadian artist of the impact of the war in the Americas. Citizens of Japanese descent in Canada were treated to unjust internment. The reader experiences the anti–Japanese feeling on the Pacific Coast and the blamelessness of those interned. 6 up.

Target Activity: "Experiencing Anti-Your-Culture Feelings"

With students, point out the universality of how one feels when faced with words and actions that are against his or her culture or ethnic group. Discuss the meaning of the words, unjust treatment, and elicit examples from the students. Write their ideas on the board, overhead transparency, or a classroom chart. Elicit ways people feel when they are caught up in these unjust situations and develop a word of feelings for the students to copy and place in their journals.

Feelings in Unjust Situations

152 Yagawa, Sumiko. *The Crane Wife.* Ill. by Suekichi Akabas. Morrow, 1981.

In this traditional Japanese tale about greed and failure to heed good advice, a poor peasant man goes out into the winter snow and sees a crane dragging its wing. He removes the arrow from the crane and dresses the wound. Later that night, a beautiful woman appears at his door and asks to be his wife. The peasant agrees and the woman offers to weave cloth to help provide food for them. Each time she weaves she warns the man never to look in on her. After weaving, she appears exhausted and frail. However, the cloth she weaves is beautiful and brings a high fee. The peasant becomes curious, looks in on the weaving, and sees a crane plucking feathers from her own breast to weave the beautiful fabric. Now seen, the crane, who is a shape shifter, cannot stay as a human and away she flies. 4 up.

Target Activity: "Heed Good Advice"

With the students, discuss the value of listening to good advice from others. Ask the students to look for traditional tales with the theme of heeding advice from other cultures. Write their suggestions in a list on a chart for a class reference. Show the theme as the center of an association chart:

European culture

Latino culture

Theme: Heeding Good Advice

Native American culture

Asian culture

African culture

153 Yee, Paul. *Roses Sing on New Snow: A Delicious Tale.* Ill. by Harvey Chan. New York: Macmillan, 1992.

Totally engrossing from the first page, this story, set in the late nineteenth century in a generic, nonspecific New World Chinatown, is delicately told with a feminist flourish. Maylin is the primary cook in her father's restaurant, but receives no recognition; indeed, her lazy brothers are reported to be the geniuses behind the restaurant's most delicious dishes. When a government official asks for a particular dish to be prepared in the man's presence, the truth comes out. The tale offers a realistic slice of life from early immigrant Chinese history that could have taken place in either Canada or the United States. The pictures, full of expression and vigor, are equally helpful in describing the characters and action in the story. Realistic fiction. 4–5.

Target Activity: "Who Gets the Credit?"

After reading the story aloud to students, discuss the feelings of all the characters when it finally came out that Maylin was the prized cook in her father's restaurant. What were the reactions of: Maylin? her brothers? the government official? her father?

Have the students share a time in their life when, similar to Maylin, they did something significant for which someone else received the credit. Have them write a paragraph about that time, or ask them to create an event similar to the one in the story.

Optional Activity: "Renaming the Foods"

Chinese foods are often named to remind the partakers of a beautiful image in nature. Ask them to make a list of their favorite foods and then select several for which to brainstorm new, more visual names (e.g., a jelly sandwich on whole wheat might be renamed "cloud of strawberries on wheat field").

154 Yep, Laurence. *Child of the Owl*. New York: Harper & Row, 1977.

A Chinese American girl finds herself and her roots when she goes to live with Paw Paw her grandmother in San Francisco's Chinatown. When Barney, Casey's gambling father, winds up in the hospital after being beaten and robbed of his one big win, he first sends Casey to live with her Uncle Phil and his family in suburbia. Casey does not get along with Uncle Phil's family and they are horrified by her, so she is sent to Chinatown. At first, Casey does not like the narrow streets and alleys or the Chinese school, but Paw Paw tells her about Jeanie, the mother Casey never knew, about her true Chinese name, and the story of the family's own charm. Gradually, she comes to like it all and to realize that this place is her home just as it is home to Paw Paw, her father and her mother. Casey learns to respect her heritage and to look deep inside herself.

Target Activity: "Knowing My Heritage Brings Pride"

Invite students to meet in small groups where each member of the group reads a part of a selected book. Each will report back to the small group about what was learned related to the idea that "knowing one's heritage brings pride." Then, invite the small groups to gather into a whole group situation. Ask the students to discuss the big idea and contribute what was learned from the different stories that were read. Examples of books with characters from different cultural backgrounds are:

   a. for African American heritage: read *Zeely* (Macmillan, 1967) by Virginia Hamilton
   b. for Asian American heritage: read *Angel Child, Dragon Child* (Raintree, 1982) by Michell Maria Surat
   c. for European American heritage: *Rose Blanche* (Creative Education, 1985) by Roberto Innocenti
   d. for Latino heritage: read *Secret of the Andes* (Viking, 1980) by Ann Nolan Clark
   e. for Native American heritage: read *To Live in Two Worlds: American Indian Youth Today* (Dodd Mead, 1984) by Brent Ashbranner or *The Potlatch Family* (Atheneum, 1976) by Evelyn Sibley Lampman

In the group, focus on the theme and write examples related to the knowing one's heritage-pride relationship in an idea association web for the students to add to during their independent reading:

European American heritage   Latino heritage
           heritage-pride relationship
                    Native American heritage
Asian American heritage   African American heritage

155 Yep, Laurence. *Dragonwings.* Ill. by David Wiesner. New York: Harper & Row, 1975.

In 1903 in San Francisco, eight-year-old Moon Shadow is determined to help his father build a flying machine. Motivated by the work of Orville and Wilbur Wright, the father builds an airplane, called Dragonwings, and sails off the hills at San Francisco Bay. Moon Shadow modifies his views of the cultural stereotypes of the white people and learns that his ideas are not always accurate. He finds an Anglo-Saxon woman friendly and considerate and gains respect for her. His father maintains some differences in the cultures with, "We see the same thing and yet find different truths."

Target Activity: "Children in All Cultures Have Dreams of Success"

Divide the students into small groups to read a book in a class period about characters from different cultures who have dreams of success. To read the book in a short period of time, the students select different chapters to read and then tell about the part they read to the others so all can become familiar with the entire story:

group #1: African American heritage: read *How Many Miles to Babylon?* (Bradbury Press, 1980) by Paula Fox

group #2: Asian American heritage: read *Dragonwings* (Harper & Row, 1975) or *Sea Glass* (Harper & Row, 1979) by Laurence Yep

group #3: European American heritage: read *The Glorious Flight Across the Channel with Louis Bierot, July 25, 1909* (Viking, 1983) by Alice and Martin Provensen

group #4: Latino heritage: read *And Now, Miguel* (Crowell, 1953) by Joseph Krumgold

group #5: Native American heritage: read *High Elk's Treasure* (Holiday House, 1972) by Virginia Driving Hawk Sneve

In the group, engage the students in focusing on the theme of reading "a book in a class period." Discuss the idea that girls and boys and men and women in all cultures have dreams of success. Write the dreams of success from the stories on the board:

Children in All Cultures Have Dreams of Success

African	Asian	Latino	European	Native American

156 Yep, Laurence. *The Rainbow People.* Ill. by David Wiesner. New York: Harper & Row, 1989.

The story mentioned in the title is the tale of a wanderer who plays his flute and walks up the path of a magical mountain ruled by a powerful wizard. Facing the wizard, he is given a warning that he could lose "something in the very act of saving it." Returning to the oppressed farmers on the mountain, he finds they have been replaced with golden dragons leaping into the sea. In return for saving the farmers from their oppression by facing the wizard, the flute player finds he has lost the girl he loves. The other tales are stories of a superior mouse, a wise woman, and a colorful snake. 4 up.

Target Activity: "Learning About a Culture from Its Folktales"

With students, point out the background for these tales: during the 1930s, the workers in a WPA project in the Oakland Chinatown would gather after work and tell the folktales related to their heritage. Invite the students to meet in small groups and ask each to select a tale to learn to tell the others. Write their selections in a list on the board.

>   *selections*   *student names*

In the whole group, ask students to gather together in a scene similar to that of the workers who gathered around to tell and to listen to stories.

157 Yep, Laurence. *Sea Glass*. New York: Harper & Row, 1979.

Craig deals with the unhappy experience of leaving Chinatown and learning to live in a non–Chinese community. Craig faces problems as he tries to make his father understand his desires.

Target Activity: "Accepting a Newcomer in Your Community"

With students, brainstorm ways the girls and boys can accept a newcomer as their friend, classmate, and as a member of the community. Write a list of their ideas on the writing board. Ask them to team up with partners and take the roles of newcomer and resident implementing some of the ideas on the list. Students should change roles and repeat acting out the ideas.

158 Yep, Laurence. *The Serpent People*. New York: Harper & Row, 1984.

In the 1900s, the time of China's battles with Manchu and British dominance, a young girl finds the strength to protect her family.

Target Activity: "Cultural Stereotypes Are Incorrect"

With students, discuss some of the many stereotypes about people from different cultures that are incorrect. Invite the students to find evidence about traditions and

>   a. *the respect people feel for the aged and the dead*
>
>   *African*
>
>   *Asian*

Latino

European

Native American

b. *the value placed on honor*

African

Asian

Latino

European

Native American

c. *the support given to others in times of adversity*

African

Asian

Latino

European

Native American

d. *the prejudice they experience*

African

Asian

Latino

European

Native American

EUROPEAN AMERICAN HERITAGE

159 *Aesop's Fables.* "The Town Mouse and the Country Mouse." Sel. and ill. by Heidi Holder. New York: Viking, 1981.

A country mouse invited his cousin, the Town Mouse, to dinner and gave him the best food. The Town Mouse disliked the food and said, "How can you stand such food? Why don't you go home with me? When they arrived in the city, the Town Mouse gave him nuts, dates, cake and fruit. But a huge creature dashed into the room with a terrible roar. The Country Mouse made up his mind to go home and said, "I'd rather have common food in safety than dates and nuts in the midst of danger." Folk literature. All ages.

Target Activity: "A Different Perspective from Different Cultures"

With students, a teacher discusses the idea of reading this fable (and others) from versions from different cultures. In a whole group, the students may discuss: What is the effect of the story/fable on an audience when they hear a version that has a culture/geographic change of the story? After the discussion of some of the stories that follow, students may join with a partner and write their thoughts about the effect of the changes from their points of view:

a. Asian American heritage: Fables from *Golds Gloom, Tales from the Panchatantra* (University of Chicago Press, 1925) edited by Arthur Ryder, can also be introduced in this manner: A female crow in "The Crow and the Partridge" leads children to the moral, "Be yourself if you want to be your best."

b. Eastern American heritage: Fables from *Eastern Stories and Legends* (Dutton, 1920) by Marie L. Shedlock may be selected: A man who enters a wheat field that can be changed to another setting in "A Persian Fable: The Seeds and the Wheat." Discuss the moral: "How should she/he who did not sow have any right to the wheat that grew from it?"

c. European American heritage: The shepherd boy becomes a shepherdess in "The Shepherd's Boy and the Wolf" leads listeners to the big idea that, "Liars are not believed, even when they tell the truth." Other fables from *The Fables of La Fontaine* (Viking, 1954) by Marianne Moore, translator, are a source for discussion. The setting can be changed to another culture with the role of a dairy maid in "The Dairy Maid and Her Pot" with the moral: "Don't count your chickens before they are hatched."

d. Latino American heritage: Bierhorst, John, ed. *Dr. Coyote: A Native American Aesop's Fables* (Macmillan, 1987). A traditional fable from the Indians of Mexico. 4 up.

160 Bawden, Nina. *The Robbers.* New York: Lippincott, 1975.

New in London, nine-year-old Philip's life becomes difficult because the children at school tease him about his fine manners. His outlook changes when he makes friends with Darcy, whose crippled father is a canal worker. Darcy is an active female character who makes friends with Philip after he is teased and attacked by children at his new school. As a street child, Darcy lacks fine manners but is independent and competent in her unprotected world. In contrast to Darcy's life, Philip has a find lifestyle in his grandmother's apartment. Darcy and Philip develop a friendship and Philip matures with the realization that not everyone lives in a protected environment. Contemporary realism. 6 up.

Target Activity: "Manners Are for Everyone"

Ask students why they think other children teased Philip, and discuss the meaning of "elegant," and his elegant manners. Have students close their eyes and lead them through a visualization of a world where people have no manners: no one says "please" or "thank you" but just grabs whatever they want; no one says "excuse me" but just knocks each other down; no one is ever introduced to anyone or is greeted by anyone. Ask students to enumerate some problems that would be caused by everyone behaving like this. Invite the students to share some ways they may know in which manners differ across cultures (e.g., in the Arabic world it is considered rude to display the bottoms of one's shoes).

161 Bergman, Tamar. *The Boy from Over There.* Translated from Hebrew by Hillel Halkin. Boston: Houghton Mifflin, 1988.

On a kibbutz in a children's house in 1947, several wait for their families. Rami's father returns with Arvamik, the boy from "over there," but Rina's father is never among the returnees. Other children misunderstand Arvamik and make fun of him. When Arvamik becomes a hero during the first Arab-Israeli war, the others begin to accept him. Contemporary realism. 4–6.

Target Activity: "Arvamik's Feelings"

After this book is read, help the students discuss his feelings when:

a. During the first Arab-Israeli War, Arvamik, a young Arab boy, returns with Rami's father.
b. Teased by the Israeli children, he perseveres.
c. His heroic actions cause them to accept him for his bravery.

With the students, develop a visual organizer with the title of the book in the middle of a page and then a space to write names of brave book characters from other cultures at the end of lines radiating outward from the title.

162 Birrer, Cynthia, and William Birrer. *Song to Demeter.* New York: Lothrop, Lee & Shepard, 1987.

This is the story of Demeter (Greek for Ceres), the goddess of agriculture (including grain, harvest, fruits, flowers, and fertility of the earth). She was greatly grieved when her daughter Persephone was abducted by Hades, god of the underworld. The story tells of seasonal changes.

In this Greek myth, Hades carries Persephone off to his land to be his bride. Her mother, Demeter, mourns for her daughter and asks Zeus to do something. She is told Persephone can return if she has eaten nothing in Hades. However, since she ate pomegranate seeds, she has to return for four months every year. Demeter attempts to solve the problem facing her when her daughter, Persephone, is abducted. Folk literature. 4–6.

Target Activity: "Different Cultures Explain Why Seasons Change"

With the students, the teacher discusses the way that an artist and author tell a culture's story explaining why seasons change.

Introduce students to other versions of this story for a "what's similar?/what's different?" discussion. Study Margaret Hodges' *Persephone and the Springtime: A Greek Myth* (Little, Brown, 1973); Gerald McDermott's *Daughter of Earth: A Roman Myth* (Delacorte, 1984); Penelope Proddow's *Demeter and Persephone* (Doubleday, 1972); and Sarah Tomaino's *Persephone, Bringer of Spring* (Crowell, 1971).

163 Brett, Jan, reteller. *Beauty and the Beast*. Ill. New York: Clarion, 1989.

Threatened with death by an angry beast, a merchant promises the beast that one of his daughters will come willingly to save his life. Beauty returns to the beast and refuses his offer of marriage and dreams of a handsome prince who says, "Do not trust too much to your eyes." Visiting her father and delaying her return, she dreams of the beast dying and wishes herself back at the beast's palace. She searches for him and finds him near death. When she sprinkles water over his face, he revives and Beauty says, "Oh, Beast, how you frightened me! I never knew how much I loved you until just now, when I feared I was too late to save your life." He asks her to marry him and she says, "Yes, dear Beast." In Beast's place stands her long-loved prince of her dreams and Beauty and the prince live happily ever after. 4 up.

Target Activity: "Seeing One's True Nature"

Beauty is able to see the true nature of Beast—she knows he is really gentle in spite of his ferocious looks and his dreadful voice. Beast says, "I cannot refuse you anything you ask, even though it should cost me my life. But remember your promise and come back when the two months are over, for if you do not come in good time you will find your faithful Beast dead." She realizes the importance of keeping one's promises. Folk literature. 4–6.

Optional Activity: "Characters from Different Cultures Are Sensitive to Others"

To show that the characters in folktales from different cultures are sensitive to one another, a teacher may ask the students, working with partners, to identify excerpts about *Beauty and the Beast* from different versions and compare the words and illustrations from such titles as:

Partnership #1: de Beaumont, Madame. *Beauty and the Beast*. Translated and ill. by Diane Goode. Bradbury, 1978. 4–6.

Partnership #2: Hutton, Warwick, reteller. *Beauty and the Beast*. Atheneum, 1985. 4–6.

Partnership #3: Lang, Andrew. "Beauty and the Beast" in *The Blue Fairy Book*. Longmans, Green, 1948.

Partnership #4: Other folktales that are found by students.

164 Cain, Michael. *Mary Cassatt*. Ill. New York: Chelsea House, 1989.

This biography, one of fifty titles in the American Women of Achievement series, describes the career of Mary Cassatt, generally regarded as one of the finest painters of the Impressionist era. Although her father — and society in general — strongly discouraged women of her time and class from pursuing a career, Mary Cassatt persevered. She studied at a highly regarded Pennsylvania art school and eventually left for Europe, where she studied the masters. Edward Degas, ten years her elder and an established artist, saw her work and realized she was a kindred spirit. He asked her to join a defiant group of artists who were breaking away from the way art was executed at the time. Risking her career, she joined these rebels and continued to experiment with Japanese-inspired prints and portraits of mothers and children. By the time she died in 1926, she was considered a critical and commercial success for her vivid colors and textures. Through her prolific career she had changed society's views about art and women. Biography. 4–6.

Target Activity: "Living in a Different Culture"

Mary Cassatt spent much time living in France when she was a young woman. Have children close their eyes and take them through a visualization activity of how Mary must have felt when she first arrived in France, all alone. How would it feel to not know the language and not be able to understand what people were saying? How must it feel when the food tastes different, the customs are different, and people know you are from another country? Ask children to then brainstorm some ways people around her might have helped Mary's adjustment to the new culture.

Optional Activity: "All Cultures Have Artists"

For those interested further in this subject, invite a librarian in to talk to the students about ways to locate a book that was published about artists from different cultures. Present some diversified role models and their accomplishments. Encourage research by the students into artists' contributions and achievements:

Diverse Role Models	*Contributions and Achievements*
Edmonia Lewis	a talented African American sculptor who created busts of people who fought against slavery (i.e., John Brown, Charles Sumner and William Story).

Others:

165 Crofford, Emily. *Healing Warrior: A Story About Sister Elizabeth Kenny.* Ill. by Steve Michaels. Minneapolis: Carolrhoda, 1989.

Kenny was an Australian nurse who developed the "Sister Kenny" method of treatment for infantile paralysis (polio). During World War I, Kenny was in the Australian army and set up a clinic in Townsville, Queensland. Receiving funds, she set up the Elizabeth Kenny Institute in Minneapolis, Minnesota. Kenny's adventures in the Australian outback are mentioned along with her outstanding qualifications and some of her medical successes. Personal interviews are also sources for some of the information. Notice the bibliography which clearly labels primary and secondary sources.

Concerned with the treatment of students who had polio, Sister Kenny found that the immediate application of hot packs to relieve the muscle spasms, and then gentle massage and exercise, usually kept the child from becoming crippled. 4–5.

Target Activity: "All Cultures Have Healers"

For those interested further in this subject, Kenny wrote her autobiography titled *And They Shall Walk* (Prior, 1952). Invite a librarian to talk to the students about ways to locate a book that was published long ago. If Kenny's book is available in one of the collections of a state's library, read some of the excerpts from Kenny's own words.

For those interested further in events important to women and girls, present these diversified role models and their accomplishments. Encourage research by the students into female role models' contributions and achievements:

Diverse Role Models	*Contributions and Achievements*
Elizabeth Blackwell	First woman doctor in the United States, born February 3, 1821, in England.
Clara Barton	A Civil War nurse and the founder of the American Red Cross.

Others:

166 De Angeli, Marguerite. *The Door in the Wall.* New York: Doubleday, 1949.

Robin, a young boy, is crippled by a strange disease and he goes to live with some monks when the Black Plague hits London. With perseverance and the help of the monks, he learns to become independent and develops his abilities and is able to save the town where his parents live. Historical fiction. 4–6.

Target Activity: "Understanding the Culture of London"

To identify and understand Robin and his traits, present a character display to the students with the name of Robin displayed. To draw the character display on the board, draw a large circle and print the name Robin in the center. Draw lines outward from the circle and at the end of each line draw smaller circles. Write the words the students contribute in the smaller circles and add more circles as needed. Through discussion with the students, create the display with adjectives and descriptive words that the students have contributed. Then focus the discussion on the way the author has developed the character of Robin to show his perseverance. Reread the parts that show Robin's actions to help the listeners gain a better understanding of perseverance. Finally, help students prepare a British/English dictionary of words and phrases that differ in the two countries, even though English is the official language of both.

167 Emmerich, Elsbeth. *My Childhood in Nazi Germany.* New York: Watts, 1992.

This is a memoir of a non–Jewish middle class German family during World War II. Five-year-old Elsbeth knew that the war took her father away, knew her grandfather was periodically arrested for his socialist activities, and knew her mother lost her coaching job because she refused to join the Nazi party. 4–8.

Target Activity: "Individual Decisions Need to Be Made"

With older students, discuss the devices of propaganda and censorship in the story. Discuss the fact that Elsbeth discovered that sometimes people lie and that she could not take on faith what she heard or read during this time of war. Ask the students to pair up with others in teams of two and discuss times from their experiences when they discovered that people sometimes lied or when they realized they could not believe something they had heard or read. In the whole group, invite the partners to tell others some of the examples they discussed.

168 Frank, Anne. *Anne Frank: The Diary of a Young Girl.* New York: Doubleday, 1952.

An autobiography and account of the changes in the lives of eight people who hid for two years in a secret annex of an office building in Amsterdam and were finally found and imprisoned by the Nazis. After the war, the diary was found by Anne's father, the only one of the eight to survive. Biography. 6 up.

Target Activity: "Tributes to the Human Spirit in Different Cultures"

Other books are tributes to the amazing spirit shown by children in true accounts of their survival. Ask students to contribute titles as they participate in independent reading through the year and add the titles to a bulletin board display:

African American Heritage　　　　　　　Asian American Heritage

"Tributes to the Human Spirit in Different Cultures"

European American Heritage

Latino Heritage　　　　　　　　　Native American Heritage

169 Hurwitz, Johanna. *Anne Frank: Life in Hiding.* Ill. by Vera Rosenberry. Philadelphia: Jewish Publication Society, 1989.

This book tells of Anne's life before she went into hiding as well as her days in hiding. With Anne, seven other people hid for two years in a secret annex of an office building in Amsterdam but were eventually found and imprisoned by the Nazis. The book ends with an explanation of her death, for none who lived in the annex survived the war except Anne's father. This is appropriate for students who are not yet able to read Anne's diary. Includes a time line, map and list of related books. For two years, Anne persevered and lived in an attic with seven other people. During this time, she wrote her diary, a lasting tribute to her spirit of perseverance. Autobiography. 6 up.

Target Activity: "Anne Frank Remembered"

After the students listen to or read this book (less difficult than the diary), engage them in listening to another point of view, that of the Dutch woman who helped hide the Frank family. To supplement the Anne Frank story, read selections from Miep Gies' book, *Anne Frank Remembered* (Simon and Schuster, 1987, grade 6 and older), to show life in Amsterdam during the Nazi occupation and to present more characterizations.

170 Hurwitz, Johanna. *The Rabbi's Girls.* Ill. by Pamela Johnson. New York: Morrow, 1982.

Carrie is one of six daughters of Rabbi Levin in a story that is a rich account of a stressful year in the life of the family, as told through Carrie's eyes. When her youngest sister is born, many of the women in the neighborhood worry that her father will be disappointed that his sixth child is not a son, but Carrie notices the Rabbi's huge smile when told he has another daughter and realizes he thinks girls are just as important as boys. She learns resilience from her father when the baby becomes gravely ill. "If God is good," Carrie asks him, "why does he make bad things like sickness and people getting angry at one another?" Gently and wisely, her father explains that life is both bitter and good. In both happy and sad times, the Rabbi's wisdom and strength are shared with Carrie as she must face prejudice and hard times in the early times of the twentieth century. The story is important for Carrie's courage, but also for the sensitive and tender way the Rabbi raises his six daughters. 5–6.

Target Activity: "Daughters in Other Cultures"

Ask students why they think Carrie's neighbors thought the Rabbi would be disappointed with another daughter. Encourage them to share stories that they have heard in their own family about the birth of sons and daughters. Divide students into research groups. Have them select a country such as China, India, or Saudi Arabia and investigate how families in that country feel about the birth of girl and boy babies. Have them hypothesize some reasons why boys may be favored over girls. Discuss whether the reasons were valid and if they think such preferences persist today.

171 Hutton, Warwick, reteller. *Theseus and the Minotaur.* Ill. by reteller. New York: McElderly Books/Macmillan, 1989.

This book takes the reader into the somber and human world of the myth and introduces Theseus, one of the early Athenian kings who was the son of Aegeus. This tells of one of his exploits that shows him as a flawed hero and it includes the death of Aegeus, his father, who kills himself when he believes Theseus has lost his life on the mission to kill the minotaur. It includes the abandonment of Ariadne, daughter of King Minos of Crete. Ariadne, with a ball of thread, helps Theseus to find his way out of the labyrinth where he has been confined to be devoured by the minotaur. She falls in love with him and marries him, but is deserted by him on the Aegean island of Naxos.

Sent on a mission to kill the minotaur, Theseus shows his resiliency but needs the help of Ariadne. The minotaur was a monster creature born of Pasiphae, the wife of Minos II, and a magnificent white bull called the Cretan or the Marathonian bull. The minotaur had the body of a man and the head of a bull and was housed in the labyrinth built by the architect Daedalus. Folk literature. 4–6.

Target Activity: "Heroes from Different Cultures Journey on Quests"

With the students, the teacher asks the girls and boys to locate the setting of this Greek hero on a world map. The events in the story are reviewed and the students trace the travels of Theseus on the map. A wipe-off marker allows a student volunteer to draw lines to indicate his journeys. They talk about the details in the illustration that give them more information about his ship and his weapons. Then, with the teacher serving as a facilitator, the students review the events in this tale and select events they want to dramatize in brief scenes for others to see. As they contribute their ideas, the events are written in a list form:

Adventures of Theseus

a. Theseus, a young hero, travels to Athens and destroys the monsters and highwaymen he meets along the road. King Aegeus proclaims Theseus as the heir to the throne of Athens and Theseus decides to travel to Crete to put an end to the minotaur.
b. Ariadne, with a ball of thread, helps Theseus find his way from the labyrinth where he has been confined to be devoured by the minotaur. After his defeat of the minotaur, Theseus becomes the greatest king Athens ever had.
c. Theseus and his friend, Pirithous, defeat the wild centaurs who abducted the bride of Pirithous at the wedding feast.
d. Theseus and his friend, Pirithous, are tricked by Hades into sitting on a magic bench from which no human could rise. Theseus is rescued by Heracles.

Following a review of the reading related to their assigned events, the students roleplay one or two scenes related to the events. Then they can divide into study groups and identify another monster against which the hero, Theseus, can test his resiliency. With a new monster as the villain in the story, the group members can create an original myth about Theseus and his heroism.

172 Innocenti, Roberto. *Rose Blanche.* Mankato, Minn.: Creative Education, Inc., 1985.

Rose Blanche is probably one of the most poignant and courageous characters in historical fiction. An ordinary-looking young blonde German girl, she wants to know what is happening to the students who have been taken off the streets and transported away by the soldiers. She follows the Jeeps to a concentration camp outside of town and comes face to face with the reality of the Holocaust. Though so many ignored what was happening, Rose Blanche confiscates food from home and brings it to the camp, sneaking out of school early every day. The Allied forces finally come into the town. There is much uproar and confusion. Rose Blanche heads for the concentration camp to see the students she has been feeding and, in the haze of the shadows and fog, she is shot. Historical fiction. 5–6.

Target Activity: "Heroines and Heroes from Different Cultures"

Write the words heroine and hero on the writing board. Ask students to define the words and then give examples of what one would have to do to be given this title. Use a word map to help the discussion:

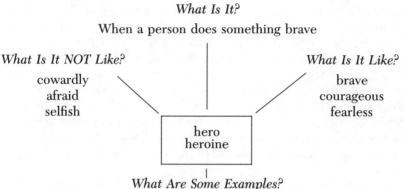

What Is It?

When a person does something brave

What Is It NOT Like?
cowardly
afraid
selfish

What Is It Like?
brave
courageous
fearless

hero
heroine

What Are Some Examples?

Rose Blanche   Martin Luther King   firefighters

Tell students you are going to play a game called heroines. On 3″ × 5″ cards, put the names of famous women who have done brave things and could be considered heroines, one per card. Tape one card to each child's back. By asking questions that could only be answered by "yes" or "no," have students try to determine the identity of the heroine on their card. Some possible heroines include:

Elizabeth Kenny	Indira Gandhi	Golda Meir
Sally Ride	Anne Frank	Harriet Tubman
Susan B. Anthony	Marie Curie	Barbara Jordan
Barbara Bush	Corazon Aquino	Margaret Thatcher
Mother Theresa	Eleanor Roosevelt	Other Heroines

Allow students to do research about the heroines with which they are unfamiliar.

173 Kherdian, David. *The Road from Home: The Story of an Armenian Girl.* New York: Morrow, 1979.

Veron Dumehjian (the author's mother) is the center of this life story told in first person. Author's note, a map showing Veron's travels, and two quotations open the book. In one opening quotation dated September 16, 1916, the reader finds that the Turkish government has decided to destroy completely all the Armenians living in Turkey. "An end must be put to their existence, however criminal the measures taken may be, and no regard must be paid to either age or sex nor to conscientious scruples." In a second quotation, the reader finds an order given by Hitler in 1939 which orders the extermination "without mercy or pity, [of] men, women, and children belonging to the Polish-speaking race . . ."

While Veron's first seven years were happy ones, it was in the eighth year that there was a deportation of Armenians living in Turkey (1915). Within three days, Veron and her family (her parents, sister, brothers, grandfather, and uncles) left their home in western Turkey in a horse-drawn wagon. By 1919, Veron's family was dead and she returned from her four-year exile. During a Greek attack on Turkey, Veron was injured and hospitalized. Recovering, she traveled to her Aunt Lousapere in the city of Smyrna. In 1922 the Greeks evacuated the city, taking Armenians considered enemies of the Turks. In Greece, Veron lived with other Armenian refugees until the announcement of her engagement by her fiancé's family in 1924. She traveled with his family to America and married Melkon Kherdian.

Though her exile was filled with hardships, sorrow, and frightening experiences, Veron always tried to find good in everything, had some happy memories, and made friends in the Aleppo school for orphans she attended. Historical fiction. Advanced 6 up.

Target Activity: "Early Life Stories from Different Cultures Can Be Happy Ones"

Veron's first seven years were happy ones and could be recorded as a brief early life story. Engage students in reflecting on pleasant early life experiences for a writing experience for their journals. Invite representatives from other cultures who live in your community to come into the classroom and share their early life stories with the students.

174 Kimmel, Eric. *Herschel and the Hanukkah Goblins.* Ill. by Trina Schart Hyman. New York: Holiday House, 1985.

Herschel of Ostropol is looking forward to reaching the next village on his journey so that he may celebrate Hanukkah with the villagers. He is disappointed to find that they are *not* celebrating Hanukkah because they are afraid of a band of goblins that haunt the synagogue at the top of the hill overlooking their village. Herschel comes up with several tricks to outwit the goblins and the spirit of Hanukkah triumphs.

Much is learned along the way, by the reader, of the rituals connected with Hanukkah, and an extension is included that explains even more about the history of, and the symbols associated with, Hanukkah. Fanciful fiction. 4–5.

Target Activity: "Miracles"
After reading the story to students, share the following background information with them:

> When Israel was ruled by Syrians, the Jews were not allowed to worship as they wished. But in 164 B.C., Jewish soldiers defeated the Syrian army. The Jews were free to celebrate Hanukkah. When they went to light the menorah, however, they found there was only a tiny trace of oil. The oil somehow burned for eight days—which the Jewish people considered a "miracle."

Then ask the students to discuss the meaning of "a miracle." Invite them to share miracles that they know of or have heard about that were said to have occurred in their religion(s).

Optional Activity: "Dreidel"
Make a dreidel out of wood or tagboard for the students to see and use. A dreidel is a square-shaped top with one of four Hebrew letters on each side. Jewish children play a game with pennies, raisins, or nuts. To play, each player puts one item in the center of the table and then another spins the dreidel. If the Hebrew word "gimmel" comes up, the spinner takes the pot; if the word "nun" comes up, the spinner gets nothing; if the word "hay" comes up, the spinner takes half; and if the spinner goes "shin," (s)he adds a nut (or a raisin or penny) to the center. Let students take turns playing this game.

In the story, this game is played between Herschel and a goblin. Ask the students to name some of the games they know that are similar to this game.

175 Lewis, Naomi, reteller. *Stories from the Arabian Nights.* Ill. by Anton Pieck. New York: Henry Holt, 1987.

This is a long novel of tales, some with humor. It is Sheherazade's scheme to keep her head on her shoulders and to please a mad king. At first her stories focus on "rare and curious" objects that can be desired or destroyed. Other stories are about real devotion and lasting love, and still others contain magical objects with which the characters solve their problems. Consider some of the characters: 1) a flying ebony horse; 2) a tortoise who is a gourmet chef; 3) a Magnetic Mountain that smashes ships; 4) a Jinni who becomes a flea in order to wake a sleeping princess; and 5) a young merchant "as beautiful as a moonlit night" who rescues a bejeweled maiden buried alive. Folk literature. 4 up.

Target Activity: "Cinderella's Cousins Are Found in Different Cultures"

The teacher discusses some of the versions of Cinderella to compare with a story in this book. Use Lewis' version in a brief story talk: a poor youngest sister puts on borrowed finery and visits the royal harem. When she slips away, her diamond anklet falls into the water trough to be discovered the next day by the prince. The students will guess the rest of the story. For other comparisons, the girls and boys may talk about: how the story changes with a male Cinderella (Prince Cinders); how the story changes with a resourceful, competent Cinderella (Sheherazade, Ashpet, Princess Furball); and how these characters compare with the original, passive Cinderella. Selections are:

Cole, Babette. *Prince Cinders*. New York: Putnam, 1988. (male Cinderella)
d'Aulaire, Ingri and Edgar. "Karl Woodenskirt": In *East of the Sun and West of the Moon,* New York: Macmillan, 1938. (male Cinderella)
Davenport Films, Rte. 1, Box 527, Delaplane, VA 22025. *Ashpet: An American Cinderella* (video), 1990. (Southern United States)
Huck, Charlotte. *Princess Furball*. Ill. by Anita Lobel. New York: Greenwillow, 1989.
Martin, Rafe. *The Rough-Faced Girl*. Ill. by David Shannon. New York: Putnam, 1992. (Algonquin tale)
San Souci, Robert D. *The Talking Eggs*. Ill. by Jerry Pinkney. New York: Dial, 1989. (Southern United States)

176 Lowry, Lois. *Number the Stars*. Boston: Houghton Mifflin, 1989.

By 1943, ten-year-old Annemarie Johansen is accustomed to the Nazi soldiers who have been on every corner of Copenhagen for three years as she walked to school with her little sister and her best friend, Ellen Rosen. Like the lack of meat and butter, the soldiers have been a nuisance of the war. However, all that changes when Annemarie's Lutheran family learns the Nazis are about to relocate Denmark's 7,000 Jews, including the Rosens, who live in the same apartment building. Annemarie discovers what courage is and that she has it. Suddenly one night Ellen comes to live with her as a sister and the older Rosens are hidden by the Resistance. Late that night, Nazi soldiers awaken them and demand to know where their friends the Rosens are. Before the girls get out of bed, Annemarie breaks Ellen's gold chain and hides her Star of David. After searching the apartment, the Nazis ask why one daughter has dark hair. Quickly the father goes to the family picture album and rips out three baby pictures, carefully obscuring the dates of birth. Annemarie's older sister, who is dead, was born with dark hair. With this invasion into their home, the girls realize the Nazis are no longer just a nuisance.

The next morning, Annemarie's mother takes the three girls on the train to her brother's house at the sea. Uncle Henrik, a bachelor fisherman, is a member of the Resistance. After a carefree day at the beach, a hearse arrives with a casket and strangers come to mourn a dead great aunt. Annemarie suspects there was no such aunt and questions her uncle privately in the barn.

Target Activity: "People in All Cultures Are Brave in the Face of War" Point out to students that the destructive force of war has been with humans in all time periods where there has been war and that humans have persevered. To emphasize this idea with books showing similar situations but in different time periods, a teacher takes students back in time to discover the destructive force of war and its effect on people from other time periods. To balance this negative force, call attention to the heroes and heroines who also emerge from such desolate eras. Have students scour newspapers and magazines for stories of exceptional valor that men and women have shown in wartime, such as the bravery of those selfless persons who helped the Jews escape in World War II.

177 McCurdy, Michael, reteller. *The Devils Who Learned to Be Good.* Ill. Boston: Little, Brown, 1987.

In this Russian folktale, an old soldier on a pension gives all of his bread to two beggars he meets and says, "God will provide." In return, one of the beggars rewards him with a magical deck of cards and tells him that he can never lose a game with the cards; the other beggar gives him a magical sack which will climb anything the old soldier commands. Returning to his village, the old soldier discovers an abandoned palace and is told that the Tsar built it but cannot live there because of the band of devils who inhabit it. The soldier goes to the Tsar and asks permission to spend one night in the palace and rid it of the devils. Folk literature. 4–5.

Target Activity: "People in All Cultures Can Help Improve the Lives of Others"
With the students, the teacher discusses the objects (the magical deck of cards and the magical sack) and invites the students to think of ways they would use the objects if they took the place of the old soldier in this old Russian tale. Without the use of these objects, in what ways could they convince others to be good and to improve the lives of others less fortunate?

178 Mark, Jan. *Handles.* New York: Atheneum, 1985.

Eleven-year-old Erica Timperley loves motorcycles and, on a trip to the country, she meets the owner of a motorcycle repair shop, Elsie Wainwright. Elsie has a sense of humor and gives people nicknames. Erica wishes for a nickname of her own. 4 up.

Target Activity: "Language by People Outside Our Country"

With students, discuss the meaning of the words slang, dialect, and idioms. Write the words as headings for three columns across the board and ask students to dictate examples of each kind. Then, discuss some of the British slang, dialect and idioms in the story. Ask the students to make "S-I-D (slang, idioms, dialect) Sheets" and to list the British slang, regional dialect and idioms. They should write the meanings in their own words.

179 Mark, Jan. *Thunder and Lightnings.* New York: Atheneum, 1985.

Two British boys, Andrew and Victor, are friends. Andrew is a newcomer and works with Victor in class to research a report on Lightnings, a type of aircraft that Victor likes. Through Victor's interest in planes, Andrew learns about different kinds of planes and begins to notice the ones taking off and landing at the nearby airfield.

Target Activity: "Everyone Needs to Care and Be Cared About"

With students, discuss what can be done by the girls and boys to welcome a newcomer to class each day.

180 Matas, Carol. *Lisa's War.* New York: Scribner's, 1987.

This story is based on true experiences with a setting in Copenhagen. Lisa and her brother, Stefan, were Jewish teenagers who fought against Jews' being sent to camps with the organized Resistance movement. Lisa and Stefan warned friends and neighbors to flee to coastal towns to escape to neutral Sweden in the fall of 1943 before a roundup of Danish Jews by the Nazis. In Denmark, Lisa persevered and helped the Resistance movement. She "dropped" anti–Nazi literature on streetcars, and with her friend, Suzanne, took on life-threatening jobs for the Resistance. Contemporary realism. 6 up.

Target Activity: "People in All Cultures Can Save Others from Danger"

With this book, a reader needs maturity to understand that sometimes acts of violence are needed to save oneself or others from danger. The story emphasizes heroics of battling against enemies, the tragedy of war, life-threatening situations, and severe problems people have during wartime. Since these acts are not unique to any one war but to all wars, other books discuss these happenings in other time periods. Related to saving others from danger, consider reading short excerpts aloud from *Across Five Aprils* by Irene Hunt (Follett, 1964; Civil War era) or from *Johnny Tremain* by Esther Forbes (Houghton Mifflin, 1943; Revolutionary War days). With information from the excerpts, students can record the happenings during times of war:

Saving Others from Danger

In Revolutionary War	In Civil War	In World War II

Students can also record the heroic people who saved themselves from life-threatening situations.

181 Meltzer, Milton. *Rescue: The Story of How Gentiles Saved Jews in the Holocaust.* New York: Harper & Row, 1988.
Gentiles risked their lives to save Jews in Europe from death. From archives of the Yad Vashem and other libraries in New York, Meltzer gathers his facts about the humanitarian acts by individuals and Gentiles in different countries. Exciting and true stories of the heroic and compassionate people who sought to rescue Jews from the Nazi captors create a tribute to their courage. In spite of differences in their beliefs, Gentiles (at great danger to themselves) helped Jewish families persevere and escape from Nazi persecution in Europe. Historical fiction. 6 up.

Target Activity: "Compassionate Heroes/Heroines Are Found in Every Culture"
With the students, the teacher discusses the meaning of compassion and heroes (heroines). Students dictate words related to compassion and heroes/heroines and the teacher lists words on the board. Words are grouped into categories to show relationships. Words in the categories are then rewritten in a word web with "Compassionate Heroes/Heroines Are Found in Every Culture" as the center of the diagramming:

African Background
1. *Martin Luther King* (Archway, 1968) by Ed Clayton
2. Others:

Asian Background
1. *The Adventures of Rama* (Little, 1954) by Joseph Gaer (India)
2. Others:

**Compassionate Heroes/Heroines
Are Found in Every Culture**

European Background
1. *Myths of Ancient Greece* (Putna, 1981) by William Wise (Greece)
2. Others:

Latino Background
1. *Black Rainbow* (Farrar, 1976) edited by John Bierhorst (Incas, Peru)
2. Others:

Native American Background
1. *The Surprising Things Maui
   Did* (Four Winds, 1979) by Jay
   Williams (Hawaii)
2. Others:

182 Neimark, Anne E. *One Man's Valor: Leo Baeck and the
     Holocaust.* Ill. with photographs. New York: Lodestar,
     1986.
     After Hitler's rise to power, Leo Baeck, the chief rabbi of Berlin,
helped many Jews, especially the children, to escape from Germany. He
continued to defy Nazi tyranny while imprisoned in the Theresienstadt
concentration camp, an ordeal he miraculously survived. This book is one
of several in Lodestar's Jewish Biography series. Bibliography for further
reading and index. Historical fiction. Advanced 6 up.
     Target Activity: "Struggles for Freedom in Different Cultures"
     With older students, a teacher may discuss some of the struggles for
freedom by women and men like Baeck that are continuing today and point
out evidence of this that is found in current news articles. A teacher should
invite the students to participate in a newspaper search to find all the examples they can about people's causes and struggles for freedom. They can
be stories about one individual or about a group. After many articles have
been found, discuss the following: In a free country, how is it possible that
so many people (from the news articles) find that they have to go to great
lengths (sometimes the Supreme Court) to get the freedom that they are
after? Record what they find about struggles for freedom by those in
different cultures.

183 Price, Susan. *The Ghost Drum: A Cat's Tale.* Ill. New
     York: Farrar, Straus & Giroux, 1987.
     In a magical place there is a cat, and this is the tale she tells:

     In a northern land where winter is a cold half-year of darkness,
     Chingis, a Woman of Power, is a most gifted shaman who lives in a
     house what runs on the legs of a chicken. Safa, the Czar's son, has
     spent his entire life in a windowless room (imprisoned by his father)
     and knows nothing of sky or trees or even the world of humans.

     In one of the emotional scenes in the book, Chingas leads Safa, the
adult, from his windowless prison out into the sunlit world and they form
a partnership to fight against the problems caused by their most feared
enemies. A read aloud. Folk literature. 4–8.

Target Activity: "Common Folklore Themes Are Found in Different Cultures"

The teacher points out how the author puts several common folklore themes into the original story that is both new, and yet, old. To study this idea further, a teacher may engage the students in discussing some of the common folklore themes they know about: motifs of magic (fairy folk, shape-changing, wise women, wizards, giants, fairy animals); magical objects; enchanted people. They also can discuss some universal ethics from the tales: the humble and good shall be exalted; love suffers long and is kind; and that which you have promised you must perform.

184 Schur, Maxine. *Hannah Szenes: A Song of Light.* Ill. by Donna Ruff. New York: Jewish Publication Society, 1990.

As a teenager, Hannah Szenes leaves the stifling anti–Semitism of Hungary in 1939 for a new life in Palestine. In 1943, she parachutes back into Nazi-occupied Yugoslavia to save the lives of Jews. Captured and tortured, she defies the Nazis only to be executed in the closing days of the war. An inspirational story of a young woman's bravery. Historical fiction. Advanced 6 up.

Target Activity: "All Cultures Have People Who Try to Save Others"

For those students (advanced 6 up) interested further in the subject, there is Albert Marrin's book *Hitler* (Viking, 1987). Hitler's life is inseparable from Hitler's war so it is not surprising that, after describing the dictator's childhood and youth in Austria, Marrin describes the campaigns of World War II. Through the history of events, however, he points to the influence of Hitler as a dictator, his racial policies, and his responsibility for major military decisions. The book emphasizes facts that young readers should know about the impact of Hitler's policies on the lives of people, the controls he exercised, and the horrors of the Second World War. In addition to its insight into the nature of totalitarianism, the book's maps, photographs, bibliography, and index make it a valuable addition to a collection on the subject.

Optional Activity: "Parachuting to Save Lives"

To help students internalize the bravery of Hannah Szenes, take them through a visualization exercise. Have them close their eyes and verbally lead them through donning their parachutes, jumping from a plane, and landing in a forest in Yugoslavia. Have them imagine conversations between Hannah and the Jews she is trying to save. Allow them to vicariously experience how Hannah must have felt when she was captured by the Nazis. Finally, invite students to now open their eyes and share their reactions to the visualization.

185 Sevela, Ephraim. *We Were Not Like Other People.* New York: Harper & Row, 1989.

In 1937, a nine-year-old boy loses his Red Army Commander father to Stalin's purge. The following six years are retold in first person in vignettes that begin and end abruptly. The boy is resilient and at the end of the war is reunited with his family. The resilient boy perseveres and survives the loss of his father and the devastation of the war. Helping him to overcome obstacles, "good" people assist him during his times of great deprivation. Historical fiction. Advanced 6 up.

Target Activity: "In Every Culture, Good People Assist Those in Need"

Before discussing the story with the students, discuss the concept of vignettes or episodes. To show these visually on a graphic organizer, draw four rectangles side by side on the board and label them vignette 1, vignette 2, vignette 3, and so on. As each episode is discussed, add information from the discussion about characters, setting, and the problem under the appropriate vignette heading. If space and class time allow, add information about the action taken to solve the problem and the final resolution. For those students interested further in this subject, suggest that they compare this story with *The Wild Children* (Scribner's, 1983) by Felice Holman.

What *We Were Not Like Other People* Says	What *The Wild Children* Says

186 Staples, Suzanne Fisher. *Shabanu.* New York: Knopf, 1989.

Eleven-year-old Shabanu lives in contemporary Pakistan with her nomadic family in the desert. Her parents betroth her to a middle-aged man and she faces the dilemma of obeying her family or obeying her desire for her own well-being. Shabanu faces her inner turmoil, is courageous, and finds signs of caring and warmth in her family. Historical fiction. 6 up.

Target Activity: "Marriage in Other Cultures"

Have groups of students select a culture with which they are unfamiliar. Encourage them to research courtship and marriage rituals and customs in that culture. Additionally, ask them to try to find the reasons why these customs differ from American customs. Ask them if they can think of some reasons why the customs prevail.

187 Vogel, Ilse-Margaret. *My Twin Sister Erika.* New York: Harper & Row, 1976.

This book, one of a series about a young German girl, Inge, and her twin sister, Erika, is a must—not only for twins, but for all young girls who must fight for their identities. Told through Inge's point of view, the story powerfully relays the sisters' struggle with friends and family who constantly compare them or confuse them with each other. Inge shares her feelings about identical clothing, cherished items and deep secrets. Just when they seem to be developing their separate identities, Erika dies. The death is handled in a sensitive, poignant way that allows the reader to vicariously experience Inge's feelings of loss and her courage in confronting her pain. Inge begins to discover a new place for herself and a new importance in her mother's life; the bond helps her to overcome her grief. Contemporary realism. 3–6.

Target Activity: "Older Siblings"

Ask students for a show of hands as to how many have older brothers and sisters. Ask these students to share if they have ever felt they were being compared with these older siblings. How does it make them feel? Ask students to divide a piece of paper into two columns, and at the top of one column, have them write "I am . . ." and at the top of the other column have them write "My sister/brother is. . ." Encourage them to think of as many similarities and differences as they can between themselves and their siblings. Urge them to confine their list to personality traits and qualities, rather than physical features. Note: For those students who have no older siblings, have them choose a younger sibling, cousin or friend of the family with whom they have been compared. Finally, have students discuss whether they think that the fight for identity between twins and or siblings would be markedly different in other cultures. Why or why not?

188 Yolen, Jane. *The Devil's Arithmetic.* New York: Viking/Kestrel, 1988.

In a story of transformation, Hannah, weary of hearing her Jewish relatives tell of the Holocaust, wishes to be somewhere else. Her wish is granted when she steps out into the building hallway and into a small village in Nazi-occupied Poland—she has become the villager, Chaya, whose name means "Life." Chaya experiences the Holocaust. On a cattle car with her family and friends, she is branded, stripped, and shaved at the concentration camp. When Hannah finds herself again at her family's apartment, she appreciates her relatives for who they are and what they know. Historical fiction. Advanced 6 up.

Target Activity: "Hannah Appreciates Her Family"

With the girls and boys in small groups, the teacher asks them to think of their family members, what they do, and what they know. The information is discussed in the small groups. The students should discuss the ways they can show their appreciation for their family members for who they are and what they know.

LATINO AMERICAN HERITAGE

189 Beatty, Patricia. *Lupita Manana.* New York: Morrow, 1981.

This story is a moving and close-up view of the illegal immigrant situation in the United States. When her father suddenly dies, thirteen-year-old Lupita emigrates illegally from Mexico into the United States. In slum alleyways, under the cover of night, in freight cars, and across the desert, gritty Lupita—dressed as a boy—learns the meaning of courage. The immigration police, who are forever on her trail, haunt her thoughts day and night. This book effectively portrays the plight of the illegal alien, but also describes in realistic detail the hope and heartbreak of poor families all over the United States. Moreover, the text is a poignant tribute to the courage and determination of young Lupita. Contemporary realism. 4–8.

Target Activity: "Empathize with People from Other Cultures"

As this harrowing tale of an illegal immigrant's plight is told in the third person, children will gain a better appreciation into the main character's fear and exhilaration by trying to empathize with those feelings. Reread different excerpts from the text to children, such as the part where she is traveling by freight car when she is alone and very, very thirsty in the desert. Brainstorm some of the thoughts that might be going through her head at these times. Invite students to select three events that took place in Lupita's life and write diary entries as Lupita might have written them. Encourage them to select one of their entries to read to the rest of the class.

190 Bouchard, Lois. *The Boy Who Wouldn't Talk.* New York: Doubleday, 1969.

In New York City, Carlos and his family are newcomers from Puerto Rico and he is frustrated with the language problem so he decides to stop talking in English and speak only in Spanish. When he meets Ricky Hernandez, a blind boy who asks for directions to get home, he finds that Ricky cannot see signs needed for his movement in the neighborhood and Carlos reads for him. 4 up.

Target Activity: "Language Problems Can Be Overcome"

To students, show other books with the theme that language problems can be overcome when moving to a new country: *Go Up the Road* (Atheneum, 1973) by Evelyn Sibley Lampman; and *Blue Willow* (Viking, 1940) by Doris Gates.

191 Buff, Mary, and Conrad Buff. *Magic Maize*. Ill. by the
authors. Boston: Houghton Mifflin, 1954.

When Fabian's brother Quin, a peddler, visits him, Quin gives him
twenty kernels of corn that will (he promises) produce so much more than
the old that it is really "magic" maize. Quin gets the seed from "gringos"
(whom Father distrusts) and so Fabian plants the seeds in secret in an ancient Mayan ruin, the City Up Yonder. Later, when Father sees the plants,
he is convinced of the superiority of the new seed and changes his opinion
of the white men because of the treatment they show his sons. They convince Father that Fabian should go to school and pay Father well for the
jade earplug Fabian finds in the ruins. In this Newbery book, elements of
the old ways of life in the '50s in Guatemala are shown along with included
history and folklore. Historical fiction. 4–6.

Target Activity: "Everybody Likes Corn"

Encourage students to look for information in recent books that brings
additional information about the people of different cultures and their
reliance on corn as a crop. Discuss various ways corn is used in people's
lives today.

192 Clark, Ann Nolan. *Secret of the Andes*. Ill. by Jean
Charlot. New York: Viking, 1952.

In Peru, Cusi leaves Hidden Valley up in the Andes and goes down
to the lowlands in search of another way of life. When his search fails, he
realizes he wants to remain with old Chuto, care for the herd of llamas, and
carry on his work when Chuto is gone. Chuto tells Cusi of his heritage (he
is descended from Inca nobility). He says the golden earplugs he wears are
proof. Contemporary realism. 5–8.

Target Activity: "Know Your Cultural Links to the Past"

According to a legend told by Chuto, the llamas they tend have a
special relationship, too, to the time of the Incas. The Spanish captured a
"mighty Inca" and "the Indians sent ten thousand llamas, carrying bags of
gold dust to ransom their king." The Spanish, however, feared the wrath
of their king if they set the Inca free, and so killed him. "And the ten thousand llamas marching down the trails of the Andes vanished from the land,
and with them vanished the gold dust, ransom for the King." Chuto takes
Cusi to Sunrise Rock to show him a secret cave containing the bags of gold
dust. It seems the llamas they tend are descended from those of long ago.
Cusi vows to keep the secret of the cave forever. Encourage students to
explore the links of their heritage to the past by asking adults in the family
to tell them stories of their history. Invite students to tell their stories to
others in the class. If interested, students may record the stories into a class
book.

193 De Trevino, Elizabeth Borton. *I, Juan de Pareja.* New York: Farrar, Straus & Giroux, 1965.

De Pareja tells his own story. Early in the seventeenth century, Juan de Pareja was born the son of a black slave and a Spaniard. At twelve, Juan became the property of the painter, Don Diego Rodreguez de Silva y Velasquez of Madrid, later the court painter to King Philip IV. Juan taught himself to paint and Velasquez learned of his skill, gave Juan his freedom, and made him his assistant. Juan was instructed in the grinding and mixing of colors and in all matters related to painting. Juan was not permitted to practice painting. Juan taught himself to paint by watching Velasquez at his work. Historical fiction. 5–8.

Target Activity: "Some People in All Cultures Have Taught Themselves"

With the students, the teacher discusses the idea of teaching yourself to do something. The teacher engages the girls and boys in discussion to identify which hobby or talent each is interested in accomplishing and to determine their ability to plan ahead as each thinks of ways to learn to accomplish a goal. Invite a member from the community from a different culture or ethnic group to talk to the students about a skill that the person taught him/herself.

194 Dewey, Ariane. *The Thunder God's Son: A Peruvian Folktale.* New York: Greenwillow, 1981.

Thirteen-year-old Acuri, son of the thunder god, is disguised as a beggar and sent down to earth to learn about the people. Acuri learns the meaning of dishonesty in the thefts of golden rings, vanity in the contests of drinking chicha, dancing, house building, and stone throwing, and recognizes greed in the house with the feathered roof. Under the powerful eye of his father, who is never far away from Acuri, he learns to punish and to reward. With this education over, he returns to the heavens as a much wiser young god. In a beggar's disguise but with a feeling of autonomy and sense of control over his life, the thunder god's son, Acuri, gains the attention of the family in the house with the feathered roof. Sustaining a positive vision of life, Acuri learns to reward (and punish) people on earth and returns to the thunder god's heavens much wiser. Folk literature. 2–3.

Target Activity: "Time to Brag"

With the whole group, a teacher may ask students to write wonderful and exaggerated statements about themselves to emphasize their positive attributes.

195 Duran, Gloria. *Malinche, Slave Princess of Cortez.* Linnet/Shoe String Press, 1992.

This is a biography of the Aztec princess who was given in slavery to Cortez. Malinche also was an interpreter during the Spanish conquest of Mexico. Advanced 6 up.

Target Activity: "Set the Scene in a Culture with Facts from Library Books"

With students in groups, engage them in choosing a topic related to the life and times of Malinche. Sample topics and suggested books could include the following:

Group studying tales and creation myths about the culture during the conquest: read John Bierhorst's *The Hungry Women: Myths and Legends of the Aztecs.* Morrow, 1984.

Group studying area now Los Angeles, California: read Penina Keen Spinka's *White Hare's Horses* (Atheneum, 1991).

Group studying eyewitness account of Cortez and the reconquest of the Aztecs and the conquest of Mexico by the Spaniards in 1521: read B. G. Herzog's *Cortez and the Conquest of Mexico by the Spaniards in 1521: An Eyewitness Narrative by Bernal Diaz Del Castillo.* Repr. 1942. Linnet, 1988.

196 Foreman, Michael, and Richard Seaver. *The Boy Who Sailed with Columbus.* New York: Arcade, 1992.

Because of his good character and singing talent, Leif is selected by Columbus to be a ship's boy and he sails on the *Santa Maria.* Sailing along the coast of land, Leif is at the wheel when the ship runs aground and Columbus leaves him on land when the ships set sail for Spain. Leif is captured by the native people and is trained to help an elderly wise man who is blind. The wise man teaches Leif to be a medicine man. When he is named Morning Star, Leif travels, increases his healing knowledge, marries, and has children and grandchildren. Years later, he sees ships off the shore and he takes his family away toward the West for he remembers how Columbus captured the native people to take them back to Spain. 4–5.

Target Activity: "Accepted by Others"

With the students, discuss the events where Leif is accepted by the native people as he is taught to be a medicine man and receives a native name, Morning Star. Invite the girls and boys to get together in groups of two and discuss times when they were accepted by others and the way this made them feel.

197 George, Jean. *Shark Beneath the Reef.* New York: Harper & Row, 1989.

Tomas Torres, a young Mexican Indian, loves his life as a fisherfolk in the waters off of the Baja coast. Changing times that include government interference are destroying the life as Tomas and his family have known it in the past. The changes bring choices for the family: whether to continue to fish and try to cling to the old familiar way of life or go to school and work toward a new way. The boy's emotional struggle and his physical fight with a huge shark are portrayed with a compromise in the ending. Contemporary realism. 5–6.

Target Activity: "People in All Cultures Have Resiliency"

With the students, discuss: One of the ways for a student to experience what it is like to be resilient in times of stress is to read books about students from other cultures the same age as the reader who have faced stress by being resilient. What are some stories that the students have read and can suggest for a class display?

198 Lattimore, Deborah Nourse. *The Flame of Peace: A Tale of the Aztecs.* Ill. New York: Harper & Row, 1987.

In a story that borrows from and extends Aztec mythology, young Two Flint honors his father's death by going on a quest to bring a new flame of peace from the hill of Lord Morning Star. Along the way he outwits nine demons, including Lord Smoking Mirror, with his cloak of forgetfulness, and the chattering bones of Lord and Lady Death. He is rewarded by Lord Morning Star with a "feathery touch" of New Fire, which he delivers to the temple in Tenochtitlan. There he glows "bright and true" to mark an end to the war and fighting. Folk literature. All ages.

Target Activity: "More About the Aztecs"

To further appreciate this tale, have students research the Aztec culture paying special attention to the religion, customs, and rituals they employed. Have older girls and boys research the Mayan cultures and compare and contrast the two in terms of religion, customs, and rituals.

Optional Activity: "Tyrant or Liberator?"

To further develop awareness of people's struggles for change in another time period, read excerpts from a biography of Fidel Castro, Cuba's head of state since 1959. *Fidel Castro* (Chelsea House, 1986) by John J. Vail is one of a series called *World Leaders Past and Present.* Castro was born into a wealthy Cuban family in 1926 and became active in revolutionary politics while still in college. In 1954, he and a band of followers attempted a national uprising against the current Cuban dictator, Fulgencio Batista. Although the raid failed, the attempt was the beginning of a rebellion that eventually ousted Batista and established Fidel Castro as Cuba's leader. In 1961, Castro shocked the world by announcing that Cuba had become a communist state. While Castro's new government got rid of much of the corruption that had previously plagued the nation, his regime also put an end to freedom of the press and thousands of his opponents were jailed. Castro's policies alienated the United States, but allowed him to align himself more closely with the Soviet Union and some Third World nations. Fidel Castro has always been surrounded by controversy, as this biography documents. Hailed as a spellbinding orator and one who freed his country from a series of social injustices, Castro has also been regarded as a tyrant who betrayed the promise of the Cuban revolution. In either case, Fidel Castro has been a key player in modern world history.

After students have heard (read) excerpts about Fidel Castro, ask them if they can think of any leaders they know of that are "good" and "bad" at the same time. Discuss their opinions about these leaders. Then put two columns on the writing board or overhead, one saying "tyrant" and the other "liberator." Ask the students to document instances from the book that describe things Castro did that would cause him to be considered one or the other. Invite students to find more articles and books on Castro in the school or public library and add to the list. Finally, encourage children to interview any Cuban Americans they might know and ask them which characteristic they think best describes Castro and why. Discuss why different people may have differing points of view about this leader.

199 Wolf, Bernard. *This Proud Land: The Story of a Mexican American Family.* Photographs. New York: Lippincott, 1978.

Traveling from the Rio Grande valley to Minnesota to find work, the proud Hernandez family is shown through its relationships at work and at play as they create a better life for themselves in difficult times. Wolf, the author, focuses on the "many Americas" in this proud land and writes: "There is an America of inequality and racial prejudice. There is an America of grave poverty, despair, and tragic human waste. And yet because of people like the Hernandez family, there is also an America of simple courage, strength, and hope" (p. 95). 6 up.

Target Activity: "Many Americans with Courage, Strength, and Hope"

Invite students to discuss some of the literary elements in this biography or in another of their choice:

Literary Elements	*Discussion*
theme:	"What theme does the title of the biography reflect?"
plot:	"What problems were presented in the biography?"
purpose:	"What was the biographer's purpose in writing?"
writing style:	"Find example(s) of ways the biographer caught your interest."

Literary Elements	Discussion
character:	"What evidence can you find for the biographical character's ability to show "courage, strength and hope" and triumph over obstacles? If you were to draw an illustration of the biographical character, what information did you find to help you make a drawing?"
setting:	"Find the specific locations mentioned in the biography and locate these places on a map or globe. If you were to draw the setting, what information did you find to help you make the drawing?"
background:	"In what ways can you check the accuracy of dates and happenings in other informational sources?"

200 Yolen, Jane. *Encounter*. Ill. by David Shannon. New York: Harcourt Brace Jovanovich, 1992.

This story is about an imagined first encounter between the Tainos, the people of San Salvador, and Columbus, and is told by an unnamed narrator, a young Taino boy. The boy has been warned in a dream that the strange people are a threat and may bring trouble to the Tainos. His concerns are ignored by the others who greet the strangers with a feast and gifts. However, the young boy and the other young people are abducted. When the boy escapes and warns those he meets, they still refuse to believe him. 4–5.

Target Activity: "First Encounters"

With the students, discuss the idea that this story is "how things might have been." Point out the friendly reception given by the Tainos to the Spanish sailors. Invite students to discuss what the adults in their home do to greet strangers in a friendly manner. Ask students to tell why it could be important to greet strangers in a friendly way.

NATIVE AMERICAN HERITAGE

201 Bierhorst, John, reteller. *Doctor Coyote: Native American Aesop's Fables*. Ill. by Wendy Watson. New York: Macmillan, 1987.

In this book, cultures take on new ideas by incorporating them into what is familiar. For instance, in the sixteenth century the Aztec Indians found a book of fables from a Spanish ship. With these trickster tales, the Aztecs retold them and they were translated into Aztec language by a scribe, who made the familiar Indian trickster figure, Coyote, the main character. This book has twenty tales retold from that Aztec manuscript. Coyote is in the stories along with Puma, Wolf, and other indigenous animals. There are native figures of speech such as "his mind was nowhere." These give the stories new flavor. Details in illustrations are humorous and look for a repetition of shapes and patterns. Folk literature. 4 up.

Target Activity: "Trickster Tales in All Cultures"

The teacher may discuss with the children in a prereading activity: Try to think back to a time when you were younger than you are now and you had an animal companion which you talked to and played with. What did you do together? How did your parents feel about your pretending things with your companion? When did your animal companion cause trouble for you? When did this companion help you the most and make you the happiest? To extend this further, a teacher may ask the children to write numerals in front of each animal's name listed below. Children may write numerals from 1 to 3 to identify their choices for their own personal animal companions from the fables they know. They should be encouraged to add any animals that don't appear on the list.

_____Coyote

_____Puma

_____Wolf

Further, each child may tell someone in the class a favorite fable(s) and which fables have the animals on the list as characters. To point out the culture of origin of the tale, a child may choose a tale and discuss the setting of the tale.

Option: "This Fable Is from _____ Report"

After reading one of the fables, fill out the report that follows:

This Fable Is from _____ Report

Date_____

Name_____

1. What were clues that told you about the place of this fable's origin?

2. Where did the action take place?

3. From what you read or saw in the illustrations, what did you learn about the country of origin for this fable?

202 Bierhorst, John, editor. *The Naked Bear: Folktales of the Iroquois.* Ill. by Dirk Zimmer. New York: Morrow, 1987.

This collection has an excellent introduction to the Five Nations of the Iroquois, the place storytelling has in this culture, the manner in which Iroquois folktales were collected, and the traditional characters that were in them. Don't miss the story of the Moose Wife who warned her husband with the prediction: "If you marry another woman your hunting power will vanish and your new wife will soon be sucking her moccasin from hunger." These tales of heroes, giants, and monster bears focus on solving problems with humor. Folk literature. 4 up.

Target Activity: "Similar Motifs in Tales from Different Cultures"

Bierhorst has included tales that are considered typical of the New York Indians. In these tales, the teacher asks the students to look for recurring motifs (patterns) that they have found in other tales. For instance, one story contains the motif of the clever turtle that will remind one of stories from African folklore and Br'er Rabbit fame. Start an informational chart for the classroom about motifs. Invite students to add information to the chart as they find motifs in the tales that remind them of other stories.

Motifs	Name of Tale	Culture-Country
1. Overflowing kettle	*Strega Nona*	Italy
2. Clever turtle		
Other:		

203 Blair, David Nelson. *Fear the Condor.* New York: Lodestar, 1992.

This book presents a vignette from Central American history in the 1930s. In Bolivia, the Aymara-speaking Masuru people are sharecroppers and the Spanish-speaking patron conscripts the men to fight for Bolivia. Ten-year-old Bartolina sees her father leave, and with the others, works twice as hard without the men. She sees her ancient society move toward a contemporary one as she learns inkweaving (reading and writing), sees labor unions form, and supports her people who stand up for the right to own their land. 5–8.

Target Activity: "Best of Two Societies"

Invite the students, in partnerships, to discuss the societal conflicts and resulting changes that are portrayed in the story. Ask them to make a conflict-and-change list from their discussion:

Conflict   *Change*

1. The conflict of _____   led to _____

Invite the students back to a whole group situation and ask them to read aloud some of the entries from the conflict-and-change list for a class discussion.

204 Bryant, Martha F. *Sacajawea: A Native American Heroine.* Billings, Montana: Council for Indian Education, 1989.

This is the thrilling story of the life of Sacajawea, the Shoshone Indian girl best known for her part in guiding the Lewis and Clark expedition. The story documents her remarkable life from childhood to her later years. Like most historical fiction, it combines biography, myth, and legend with validated events in her life. As an Indian woman living in a society mostly dominated by men, both red and white, most of the details of her life were not considered worthy of recording, and the legends surrounding her life do not always agree. The author has taken what is known and woven it together into the most accurate account of Sacajawea's life, appropriate for both children and adults. The author's research includes an impressive array of old letters, diaries, textbooks, as well as the journals of Lewis and Clark. 4–8 and up.

Target Activity: "Two Different Points of View"

This book is one of the few pioneer expedition documents to offer the events from the point of view of a Native American. Introduce students to *The Journals of Lewis and Clark* (Riverside Press, 1969) edited by Bernard Devoto. Have students discuss the differences in the points of view between Captain Lewis and Clark and compare their views with Sacajawea's on:

 a. motivation for the expedition
 b. feeling about the land
 c. sensitivity toward animals
 d. spiritual awareness

205 Curry, Jane Louise, reteller. *Back in the Beforetime: Tales of the California Indians.* Ill. by James Watts. New York: Macmillan, 1987.

Curry portrays the beforetime, a time when the world was newly made by Old Man Above and when animals lived together as people. The stories are told as a chronicle and trace the world from its creation to Coyote stealing the sun, to his first making of man, and then to the awakening of the first man.

When man awoke, great changes came to the world, and a warning was given to the animals. The Old Man Above warned:

For in the aftertime to come, no longer will
any of you be shape-shifters and workers of magic.
You will be animals only,
and only Man will have the powers of speech and spirit.
Coyote has made Man worthy to rule, so rule he will.

Folk literature. 4–6.

Target Activity: "Changes Came to the World"

The teacher encourages all in the group to think of some "changes that came to the world" from the point of view of this author. In study groups, each student may print his/her thoughts on a paper and pass it to the right (or left) to the person next to him or her. Receiving the paper, each student in turn writes something more about "changes that could come." Finally each student receives his or her own original "changes" sheet to keep and use as a resource during a class discussion.

206 George, Jean Craighead. *Julie of the Wolves.* Ill. New York: Harper & Row, 1972.

Thirteen-year-old Julie-Miyax, an Eskimo girl, leaves her father-selected husband, Daniel, to cross the tundra toward Point Hope where she plans to leave for San Francisco to find a California pen pal, Amy. Lost, Julie survives because of her knowledge of Eskimo lore (setting her course by migrating birds and the North Star) and her friendship with Amaroq, the leader of a wolf pack. This story shows the coming together of two cultures as Julie lives like the traditional Eskimo did as well as returning to her father, Kapugen, and accepting the fact that he has abandoned his former way of life, married a white woman (a gussak) and began hunting from a plane for sport rather than for food. Contemporary realism. 6–10.

Target Activity: "The Coming Together of Two Cultures"

Considering the way that students live today, they should have no use for many of the items that are listed below. The teacher asks the girls and boys to imagine that they are caught in a snowstorm in the tundra, lose their way, and feel lost and become marooned on the ice and snow. There are no other human inhabitants. Ask the students to prioritize the following items in terms of necessity for survival.

Items for Survival

_____bow and arrow		_____clothes
_____a dogsled		_____dishes
_____fence		_____firewood
_____fishhook and line		_____flintstone
_____food and water		_____hut, cabin (a shelter)
_____knife or spear		_____pet
_____signal device (flashlight)		_____showshoes

207 Goble, Paul, reteller. *Beyond the Ridge.* Ill. by reteller. New York: Bradbury Press, 1989.

An old woman goes from her deathbed to the world beyond the ridge, pulls back to the world where her family mourns her, and then goes forward to where she is reunited with all of her loved ones who have gone before her. This living-dying story includes Native chants and prayers. In the illustrations, notice the contrast of the sorrow and pain of the grieving family and the joy of the elderly grandmother as she travels beyond the ridge. The Plains Indians' perception of passing from life to death—only a change of worlds—presents a positive vision of life's cycle. Folk literature. 4 up.

Target Activity: "People in All Cultures Have Perceptions of Passing from Life to Death"

With the students, the teacher may discuss this selection of folk literature and the strength of the elderly Native American grandmother. Read some of the Native American poetic chants and prayers in this living-dying story and discuss the words or phrases that point to the need for a person from any culture to be strong.

With interested students, the teacher may compare this selection of folk literature with realistic fiction, *A Ring of Endless Light* by Madeleine L'Engle. Goble refers to a change of worlds (from life to death) and L'Engle refers to the wholeness of life as including death. Discuss these two selections with a point-by-point comparison of the story elements of: setting, characters, plot, goal, resolution. What similarities could the phrases "beyond the ridge" and "a ring of endless light" have in common? How do these two phrases portray a positive vision of life from the author's point of view?

208 Goble, Paul, reteller. *The Girl Who Loved Wild Horses.* Ill. by the reteller. New York: Bradbury Press, 1978.

A girl goes down to the river at sunrise to watch the wild horses. She rests in a meadow and then sleeps. A thunderstorm rumbles and the girl joins the horses as they run away from a lightning flash and the gathering storm. She finally goes to live with them.

Once students understand the point of view that many Indian tales are handed down from a time when the distinctions between animals and humans were blurred, they should realize that in the early beginnings of these tales, listeners accepted that animals and humans could understand one another or "speak the same language." Thus, there is no distinction between animals and humans interacting in some of the ancient Native American tales, or in this one, a story of an Indian girl's attachment to horses. The girls and boys need to realize that certain features from the early beginnings of these tales still exist in the stories. In this story, the animal character is very sensitive and caring toward a human character. 5–6.

Target Activity: "Animals and Humans in Early Tales Were as One People and Both Were Sensitive and Caring"

Before reading the story to the students or before their independent reading, the teacher should remind students that in many of the Native American tales the distinctions between animals and humans were not clear, and that in some tales, the animals and humans were as one people and could speak the same language and understand one another. Thus, it is no surprise when a human goes to live with or marries an animal in some of the ancient Indian tales. Remind the students of the Indians' belief in the beforetime, when the world was newly made by Old Man Above and when animals lived together as people. Discuss the point of view shown by this story and the ways it may differ in the points of view held by some children in the class.

Next, read another story to show that distinctions between animals and humans were not made in these early tales; read *Buffalo Woman* (Macmillan, 1984) by Paul Goble. In this tale, a young hunter marries a female buffalo in the form of a beautiful maiden. When his people reject her, he must pass several tests before he is allowed to join the Buffalo nation so that he can be with her. Discuss the vocabulary of *buffalo, Calf-boy, Chief of the Buffalo Nation, tipi,* and *Straight-up-person.*

209 Highwater, Jamake. *Anpao: An American Indian Odyssey.* Ill. by Fritz Scholder. Philadelphia: J. B. Lippincott, 1977.

In this Blackfeet legend of Scarface, scarred Anpao (whose name means Dawn) goes on a Ulysses-type quest to obtain the permission of the sun to marry beautiful Ko-ko-mik-e-is. Befriending Morning Star on his trip through a terrible desert, Anpao saves Morning Star (whose parents are the Sun and Moon) from monster birds. In return, the Sun removes the scars from Anpao and recognizes Anpao as a long-lost son of the mighty sun and an earth woman. On his return trip, Anpao meets Smallpox who tells Anpao that sooner or later everyone will come to know Smallpox and that all the people he visits will die (a reflection on the Blackfeet's experience with the white man). Carrying beautiful gifts from the Sun, Moon, and Morning Star, Anpao returns to Ko-ko-mik-e-is and marries her, and they live happily in a village below a great water. Anpao goes on a quest and survives his journey through the debilitating desert, overcomes the monster birds, rescues Morning Star, and returns to marry Ko-ko-mik-e-is. Folk literature. 6 up.

Target Activity: "A Mural of a Hero's Quest"

After discussing the events in Highwater's story and recording them in sequence with the students, the teacher invites the students to make a picture of the long quest and to draw the events in order on butcher paper. The paper will make a mural for the classroom. Two students are assigned to each event and to a section of the paper. The students are encouraged to consult the story as needed to get information for their drawings. After the mural is completed, the two students will write a narrative together to explain their event and place the paragraph(s) beneath their section of the mural for others to read.

210 Levitt, Paul M., and Elissa S. Guralnick. *The Stolen Appaloosa and Other Indian Stories*. Ill. by Carolyn Roche. New York: Bookmakers Guild, 1988.

This book has five tales from the Pacific Northwest Indian tribes. In "The Story of Hot and Cold," mythic characters tell the story of how seasons come to change. In another, a woman prefers a dog to a human suitor (there is no clear distinction between animals and humans in the ancient tales) and is reunited with her people only when her offspring prove to be the hunters that save the village during a difficult winter. In "The Stolen Appaloosa," two magicians battle over the beautiful horse in a contest of will and power. One story tells how the Indians used their magic to defeat an attempt by the white "face" to steal their home. Still another tells of the ability of the people to outwit the evil bush-tailed rat man and win back their families, their livelihood, and their dignity. Folk literature. 4–6.

Target Activity: "All Cultures Have Tales Explaining How Seasons Change"

Bring children together to discuss "The Story of Hot and Cold" and ask them if they know of similar stories about the reasons seasons change. Read the story of "Demeter and Persephone" and discuss the similarities between the two stories. Build a chart of information that compares stories from different cultures and display it so that children can add information to it as they find additional stories.

Tales Found	*Culture-Country of Origin*
1. "The Story of Hot and Cold"	
2.	
3.	

211 Lipsyte, Robert. *The Brave*. New York: HarperCollins, 1991.

In this sequel to *The Contender* (HarperCollins, 1986), Lipsyte follows Sonny Bear, a young man with a raging anger which makes him a ferocious boxer. The offspring of a white father and an Indian mother, Sonny Bear spends his early childhood being dragged from city to city by his mother and then returned to his Uncle Jake and the Moscondaga reservation every time she runs out of money. After fighting in some local matches, Sonny leaves the reservation for New York City, longing to be a heavyweight boxer. Within a few minutes, he is picked up by a couple of hustlers, his wallet is stolen, and in the process he inadvertently knocks out a police officer. When he is picked up the next day for doing a drug run, the chief officer tries to help him but Sonny will not cooperate. He is sent to prison where he is badly knifed in a fight. He is finally sent back to the reservation to train with his Uncle Jake for a boxing career. Sonny begins a series of fights leading to the Gotham Globes title and the potential of becoming a heavyweight champion one day. When he is disqualified because someone tips off the boxing commission that he was paid for fighting earlier in his career, Sonny has, at that time, finally grown able to control the rage inside him so that he can pick himself up and start all over again in his boxing career. Realistic fiction. 6–8.

Target Activity: "Dealing with Anger"

Discuss with the students the positive and negative ways that Sonny dealt with his rage as described in the story. Point out that being angry itself is not wrong; it is how one deals with it that can be constructive or destructive. Ask the students to write a paragraph telling how they deal with their anger, ending with a self-reflective statement of whether the behavior is constructive or destructive and why they think so.

212 Martin, Rafe. *The Rough-Faced Girl.* Ill. by David Shannon. Putnam, 1992.

In this Algonquin folktale, the youngest of three sisters has to keep the fire going. The heat scars and burns her face and hair. Like her sisters, she wants to marry the "invisible being" who lives in the large wigwam across the village. Her sisters falsely claim to see the "being" but she is the only one who truly sees him and can answer the being's sister's questions correctly. Folk literature. 3 up.

Target Activity: "The Rough-Faced Girl Story Is Found in Other Cinderella-type Stories"

A teacher may suggest other versions of a "Cinderella-type" story and ask students to read several versions and tell others what they found.

213 Monroe, Jean Guard, and Ray A. Williamson. *They Dance in the Sky: Native American Star Myths.* Ill. by Edgar Stewart. Boston: Houghton Mifflin, 1987.

In the first two chapters, there are stories from many tribes about the Seven Sisters (the Pleiades) and the Big Dipper. The remaining chapters are divided by regions and tell different stories from the tribes of the regions. There are informative introductions to each story about the tribe and symbolic significance is explained. There are pictures of constellations framed with branches shaped into circles and decorated with feathers and beads. Other small Indian designs separate the stories. The book is decorated with black and white drawings of a variety of Indian symbols, of the constellations, and of animals and people, which lend additional meaning to the pages. A read aloud. Folk literature. 4–8.

Target Activity: "Reading Aloud Tales Explaining Sky Origins from Different Cultures"

With the students, the teacher discusses the tellings and the style of the oral tradition in which these stories were originally passed along to others. The teacher may decide to save this one for the end of the school year as students begin to talk about going to day camp or away to camp in the country. After reading some of the other selections with their origins in other cultures, a teacher can encourage the students to take a favorite story along (checked out from the library) to summer camp.

214 O'Dell, Scott. *Island of the Blue Dolphins.* Boston: Houghton Mifflin, 1960.

On the island of San Nicolas off the California coast near Los Angeles, Karena survives alone for eighteen years (1835–1853) before a ship takes her to the California mainland. In her struggles for survival, Karena and her six-year-old brother Ramo are left behind when their people are being removed by ship from their home island. Many of the men have been slain by Aleutian hunters. Ramo is soon killed by wild dogs and the book tells Karena's story of survival. Karena makes a fenced-in house and a cave dwelling. Karena's story is based on an actual incident. Karena's story is a survival story, a story of a human's need to love and be loved, and a story of the importance of the way a human reacts to a disaster. Karena is an active and interesting female with positive personality characteristics. She is intelligent, independent, brave, strong and competent. She portrays a positive female role and her story deals thoughtfully with the problem of friendships with others.

Target Activity: "Understanding a Universal Character"

With students, the teacher may discuss:

a. Karena observes nature with sentences such as "The sea . . . is a flat stone." What else does she refer to in nature through metaphors?

b. What is it like to be lonely? How do you describe Karena's need to love and be loved?

c. The episode on the island where Karena made the change from her present world "where everything lived only to be exploited, to a new and more meaningful world." With students, a teacher may discuss ways Karena learned that humans could be islands secure unto themselves and yet part of humanity where all could "transgress our limits in reverence for all life."

d. After listening to an excerpt from Scott O'Dell's acceptance speech for the Newbery Medal for *Island of the Blue Dolphins* (Kingman, 1965), the students may discuss what they think he meant when he said that through the character of Karena, he "wanted to say to children and to all those who will listen that we have a chance to come into a new relationship to the things around us."

e. Why do you agree/disagree that coming into a "new relationship" with the things around us would include the forgiveness of our enemies?

215 O'Dell, Scott, and Elizabeth Hall. *Thunder Rolling in the Mountains.* New York: Houghton Mifflin, 1992.

Based heavily on eyewitness accounts and recollections of survivors, this sad tale of displacements tells the story of the horrible winter of 1877, when the Nez Perce nation of the Wallowa valley in Oregon fled the U.S. Army troops who were forcing them to move to a reservation in Montana. Sound of Running Feet, a Nez Perce Indian, describes the hardships in the journey, the deaths of her loved ones, and her decision to leave her father and escape to Canada rather than surrender to the Army. The situations described are compelling and reminiscent of the more frequently told story of the Cherokee people. The strongly pacifist chief of the Nez Perce chooses to lead his people in flight rather than to defend their land: "The people waited for my father to say more. When he was silent, they wandered off to the lodge. I heard no cries and no weeping. They had swallowed their tears" (see p. 61). 6–8.

Target Activity: "Choosing to Be Pacifist"

Discuss with students the meaning of the term pacifist. Ask students why they think the chief of the Nez Perce chose to lead his people in flight rather than to defend their land. Ask students to do research on the philosophies of two other famous pacifists, Martin Luther King, Jr., and Mahatma Gandhi. From their research, have them make a presentation to the class on why the person that they chose embraced a pacifist ideology. Finally, hold a general discussion with students in which they brainstorm situations where they feel it would be better to take a pacifist stance than to fight.

216 Pitseolak, Peter. *Peter Pitseolak's Escape from Death.* Introduced and edited by Dorothy Eber. New York: Delacorte Press/Seymour Lawrence, 1977.

On a walrus hunt in his canoe with his son, Peter Pitseolak, an Eskimo artist of Baffin Island, finds himself stranded in a huge ice field that is moving swiftly out to sea. After two nights on the ice, a bluebird appears to Peter in a strange dream. The dream gives Peter courage and hope that they will find a path through the ice field and return to safety. The wind that Peter had once feared drives their canoe back toward Baffin Island. Peter notes in this retrospective story, "There is nothing in the world that is not good. I understood this then." 4–6.

Target Activity: "Obstacle or Challenge?"

Write on the chalkboard the following sentence from *Peter Pitseolak's Escape from Death*: "There is nothing in the world that is not good." Ask children to share what they think Peter meant by this statement in the context of his harrowing experience and his culture. Bring out the idea that some very difficult situations that we go through seem overwhelming and unfair at the time, but they often bring us new understandings about ourselves and the world, new friends, or in some other ways turn out to have been positive challenges. Write on the chalkboard, "Obstacle or Challenge?" and invite children to share some past event they have experienced that first seemed like an obstacle, but later, in retrospect, they can view as a challenge, because it turned out to have had positive benefits. After all who wish to have shared orally, ask students to select one event to describe in essay format using the title, "Obstacle or Challenge?"

217 Roop, Peter, and Connie Roop. *Ahyoka and the Talking Leaves.* New York: Lothrop, 1992.

Ahyoka, the daughter of Sequoyah, helps her father create a written Cherokee language in the early 1800s. When he is accused of magic and ostracized from the tribe, she leaves home to go with him. She discovers that letters relate to sounds, which is the key to beginning the syllabic alphabet. 4–5.

Target Activity: "Talking Leaves"

With the students, discuss the problems that Sequoyah and Ahyoka faced as they tried to record the sounds of the Cherokee language. To develop insight into the difficulty of this, ask the students if they have ever talked in the popular children's language called Pig Latin in which the first sound of a word is moved to the end of the word and "ay" is added. Thus, hello becomes ello-hay. Invite the students to practice talking in this "ay" language to partners and then ask them to return to the whole group to suggest ideas for recording the sounds of the "ay" language into letters, thus making their own "talking leaves." Write the suggestions in a list on the board. Invite the students to work together and create "new" letters to record this language. Ask the partners to return to the whole group at the end of the activity time and report what was accomplished in trying to record the sounds of this language.

218 Salisbury, Graham. *Blue Skin of the Sea.* New York: Delacorte, 1992.

On Hawaii, in the village of Kailua-Kona, Sonny Mendoza and his father face the sea and their natural enemies. Sonny's difficulties in growing up are portrayed in short stories that focus on Sonny's childhood, facing a sixth-grade bully, his teenage years and a confrontation over a beautiful girl, and finally his search for his identity when his father's fishing boat fails to return to port on time and Sonny fears he has lost him. 7 up.

Target Activity: "Sonny's Feelings"

With students, discuss the family ties and some of the difficulties Sonny faced as he grew up. Draw parallels from the students' offered experiences. Mention the support Sonny's father gave him at different times. With the students' dictated suggestions, begin a feelings web on the board.

About Family Ties ⟍   ⟋ About His Childhood

Sonny's Feelings

About His Teenage Years ⟋   ⟍ About His Search for Identity

219 Speare, Elizabeth George. *The Sign of the Beaver.* Boston: Houghton Mifflin, 1983.

Although thirteen-year-old Matt faced his responsibility bravely, he was more than a little apprehensive when his father left him alone to guard their newly built cabin in the wilderness. When a white stranger stole his gun, Matt knew he would no longer be able to hunt, nor would he be able to protect himself. It was only after meeting a proud and resourceful Native American boy that Matt began to discover new ways to survive in the forest. In getting to know his new friend, Matt also began to appreciate the heritage and way of life of the Beaver Clan and their growing problem with the white people and the changing frontier. This is an exceptionally compelling survival story filled with wonderful detail about living in the wilderness. It provides the reader with insights into the complex relationship between the Native Americans and white settlers in the 1700s. Realistic fiction. 5 up.

Target Activity: "Learning from Each Other"

At the beginning of this book, it is clear that Matt was raised not only to fear the Indians, but to believe that his ways and customs were superior to theirs. Forced into a situation where he was dependent upon these people, he came to trust them and finally to understand the relative merits of their way of life.

Have small groups of students select a group of people who live in their community. Have each group research the contributions the group has made to American culture. Ask each group to select a spokesperson to present their findings to the rest of the class.

Extended
Activity Unit:
Grades K–3

AFRICAN AMERICAN HERITAGE

220 Patricia McKissack. *Flossie and the Fox.* Ill. by Rachel Isadora. New York: Dial, 1986.

Theme: A spunky young black girl outwits a troublesome fox with aplomb—a trait also found in characters from other cultural backgrounds.

Overview: A young girl, Flossie Finley, is sent to take eggs to "Miz Viola at the McCutchin Place" and is warned about a dangerous fox; Flossie has never seen a fox and doesn't know what one looks like. 2–3.

New Vocabulary: aine, August, ceremony, creature, critter, curtsy, disremember, generation, particular, proof, rascal, recollect, slickster, smokehouse, Tennessee, terrified, tucked

Materials: drawing paper, pencils, crayons, pictures of fox

Motivation (linking prior knowledge; "into" the reading activities):
1. Ask students to think of a way they would describe a fox if, like Flossie, they had never seen one. Have them quickly sketch their idea of a fox on paper. In small groups, ask them to tell their classmates why they drew their sketches the way they did.
2. Show students the picture of the fox in the book. Cluster their words to describe the fox on the chalkboard or overhead.
3. Ask children to think if they have ever changed their minds about a person/animal after getting to know them. Encourage them to share incidents that made them change their minds about the person/animal.
4. Write the word "scary" on the board. Have students turn to a partner and discuss, "One thing that I thought was scary was when..."

Purpose for reading or listening: "You are going to read (hear) a story about a young girl named Flossie Finley who has never seen a fox before. She meets one when she takes eggs to Miz Viola at McCutchin's cabin. Read (listen) to find out how Flossie outwits the fox when he meets her in the woods."

Discussion Questions ("through" the reading activities):
1. What stories had Big Mama told Flossie about the fox?
2. Describe what you think Flossie thought when she saw the fox.
3. How do you think Flossie felt when she saw the animal sitting beside the road "like he was expectin' somebody"? What might *you* have said or done?
4. How did Flossie introduce herself to the fox? How did the fox introduce himself to Flossie?
5. How did Flossie try to get the fox to prove he was a fox?
6. When Flossie said, "I don't believe you a fox, that's what," what were Flossie's feelings? How would you have felt?

7. What would *you* mean if you said to someone, ". . . you sho' think a heap of yo'self"?

8. What do you think Flossie meant when she said to the fox, "You just an ol' confidencer"?

9. When Flossie and the fox came out of the woods, how did Flossie get him to turn back to the woods?

Retelling ("through" the reading activities): With partners, engage students in a roleplay of the story, taking turns being Flossie and the fox.

Extended Activities ("beyond" the reading activities):

1. Taking the role of Flossie, have the children tell to Big Mama how the fox tried to frighten her and how she outwitted him.

2. Have girls and boys retell the story with their name and personality substituted for Flossie, with the words, "Suddenly, there I was looking at the fox and . . ." Encourage them to see how the story changes as their personality makes choices different from Flossie's.

3. Have children rewrite the story from Flossie's point of view. Help them to imagine that Flossie knew the fox was afraid of Mr. J. W. McCutchin's sharp-toothed hound.

4. Let one child roleplay Flossie. Have the girls and boys interview her by saying, "What was your trip through the woods like?"

5. With children roleplaying Miz Viola, engage them in writing a note asking for eggs and another note to thank Flossie for delivering the eggs to her house.

Interdisciplinary Ideas

Social Studies: Children may discuss the idea that Flossie was a problem-solver in this story. For example, the problem of thinking of a way to get the "best" of the fox (or any other dangerous wild animal) may be discussed. Talk about alternatives that girls and boys in the class might have tried in facing a similar problem. Discuss how these alternative ideas might have influenced Flossie and changed her actions in the story. Discuss the relief the little girl must have felt when she reached the cabin and the frustration the fox must have felt when he failed to get the eggs.

Further, discuss some of the strengths Flossie showed in the story and record them for the students to see.

1. "Why come Mr. J.W. can't catch the fox with his dogs?" Flossie asked, putting a peach in her apron pocket to eat later (p. 5, unpaged).
   Strength:

2. "What if I come upon a fox?" thought Flossie. "Oh well, a fox be just a fox. That aine so scary" (p. 7, unpaged).
   Strength:

3. Flossie skipped right up to him and nodded a greeting the way she'd been taught to do. "Top of the morning to you, Little Missy," the critter replied, "and what is your name?" "I be Flossie Finley," she answered with a proper curtsy" (p. 9, unpaged).
Strength:

4. Flossie rocked back on her heels then up on her toes, back and forward, back and forward . . . carefully studying the creature who was claiming to be a fox. "Nope," she said at last. "I just purely don't believe it" (p. 10, unpaged).
Strength:

5. "So, why should I be scared of you and I don't even-now know you a real fox for a fact?" Fox pulled himself tall. He cleared his throat. "Are you saying I must offer proof that I am a fox before you will be frightened of me?" "That's just what I'm saying" (p. 11, unpaged).
Strength:

6. "I have the proof," he said. "See, I have thick, luxurious fur. Feel for yourself." Fox leaned over for Flossie to rub his back. "Ummm. Feels like rabbit fur to me," she said to Fox. "Shucks! You aine no fox. You a rabbit, all the time trying to fool me" (p. 14, un- paged).
Strength:

7. "You know," she finally said, smiling, "it don't make much difference what I think anymore." "What?" Fox asked. "Why?" "Cause there's one of Mr. J. W. McCutchin's hounds behind you. He's got sharp teeth and can run fast, too. And, by the way that hound's lookin', it's all over for you!" (p. 25, unpaged).
Strength:

Have children find books in the library that tell how others have been strong when they met "troublesome" animals in folk literature. As one example, the children may hear/read *The Gunniwolf* (Dutton, 1967) by Wilhemina Harper.

Science: Investigate foxes (i.e., their habitat, etc.).

Art: Ask the girls and boys to draw scenes of Flossie's walk in the woods.

Math: Chart the number one favorite animal in stories of all the children in the class. Discuss if there are differences between the choices of the girls and boys.

Music: Refer back to the girl's words for her song in Harper's *The Gunniwolf* and ask students to suggest musical tones for the words:
> "Kum-kwa, khi-wa,
> kum-kwa, khi-wa."

Recreational Reading: Invite children to look for other stories about troublesome animals.

221 Patricia C. McKissack. *Mirandy and Brother Wind.* Ill. by Jerry Pinkney. New York: Knopf, 1988.

Theme: Mirandy is anything but the stereotypical "passive" little girl character. She actively solves problems in her own way and refuses to give up.

Overview: Mirandy is determined to catch the wind to be her partner in the cakewalk, a traditional southern dance rooted in African American culture. She tries a variety of strategies and finally succeeds. 3–4.

New Vocabulary: cakewalk, commenced, conjure, whitewashed, sassy, guarantee, moping, hedges, gait, flickering

Materials: map or globe, writing board, or chalkboard and chalk

Motivation (linking prior knowledge; "into" the reading activities):

1. Write the word wind in a box in the center of the board. Ask children to free-associate all the things that come to their mind when they hear this word. Example:

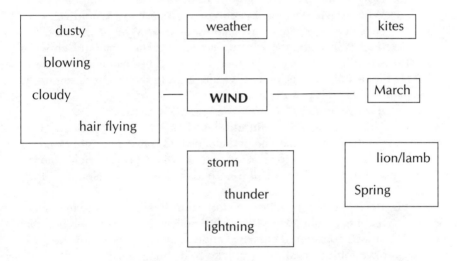

2. Ask children if it is possible to catch the wind. Why or why not? What ways might they think of to try and catch the wind?
3. The illustrations in Mirandy and Brother Wind are rich, eye-catching watercolors for which the illustrator received a Caldecott Honor Award. Show children the illustrations page by page and ask them to construct what they think is happening in each one.

Purpose for Reading or Listening: "You are about to hear the story of a remarkable young girl who wanted very badly to win a dance contest. Read (listen) to find out how she did not give up and managed to reach her goal."

Discussion Questions ("through" the reading activities):

1. Why did Mirandy think Brother Wind would be an ideal partner for the cakewalk?
2. What were the answers that were given to Mirandy as she tried to find out how to catch the wind?
3. Why did Ezel tell Mirandy he was going to ask Orlinda to be his partner?
4. Why did Mirandy decide to dance with Ezel after all?
5. What made Mirandy win the cakewalk?
6. What evidence do you have that Mirandy was a very determined young girl?
7. What did Grandmama Beasely mean when she said "Them chillin' is dancing with the wind"?
8. How did the conjure woman, Miz Poinsettia, help Mirandy?
9. How do you think the other little girls felt when they saw "clumsy" Ezel winning the cakewalk?
10. How would *you* have gotten yourself ready for the cakewalk? Who (or what) would you choose for a partner? Would you have consulted the conjure woman for advice? Why or why not?

Retelling ("through" the reading activities): Have pairs of children take turns reading a page of text to each other. The "listener" then summarizes the text of the page and the reader adds to the listener's summary. The pairs switch roles on every page.

Extended Activities ("beyond" the reading activities):

1. This story is written in obsolete Southern black dialect. Have children read each line of dialogue and translate it into standard English. Explain to children that this dialect is very rich, colorful and expressive. Ask children to identify a bit of dialect that they particularly like.
2. Have children rewrite the story from Ezel's point of view. Help them to emphathize with the little boy who was rejected because he was considered clumsy. Guide them to imagine how he must have felt when Mirandy stuck up for him.
3. Ask children to pretend they are newspaper reporters who have been assigned to cover the cakewalk. Have them write a newspaper article that contains the essential elements of who, what, why, where, when. Let them read their newspaper articles to the class.
4. Have children roleplay this story, choosing children to reenact scenes such as: Mirandy asking Grandmama Beasely, Ezel, Mr. Jessup, and the conjure woman how to catch the wind; Mirandy chasing the wind into the barn; the cakewalk.
5. Write an acceptance speech that Mirandy might have written as she graciously accepted her triple-decker cake award.

Interdisciplinary Ideas

Social Studies: Have children investigate the African American culture in the early 1900s, when this story takes place. Specifically have them search for information about the flamboyant cakewalks.

Science: Have children research the meteorologic phenomenon of "wind." Why is it generally more windy in the spring? Before a storm? By a body of water?

Art: Using watercolors, invite children to paint their concepts of what "Brother Wind" would look like.

Math/Social Studies: Have children ask their parents (or adults in the home) what other states they have lived in during their lives. Make a list of the Southern states. Chart the number of those who have lived in any of these states. Find these states on a map or globe.

ASIAN AMERICAN HERITAGE

---

222 Ellen Levine. *I Hate English!*. Ill. by Steve Bjorkman. New York: Scholastic, 1989.

Theme: Mei Mei is determined not to learn English; a caring teacher helps Mei Mei feel comfortable about learning English at a Chinese Learning Center.

Overview: A young girl who loved to speak Chinese lived in Chinatown in New York and attended school where everything was done in English. Mei Mei hated English and wouldn't speak it because she thought English was a lonely language where each letter stood alone and made its own noise. She felt it was different from Chinese where there were fast strokes, short strokes, and long strokes in writing and Mei Mei could make the brush fly in her hand. 2–3.

New Vocabulary: California, covered wagon, Chinese, Director, dragon dances, English, Hong Kong, Shek, Yee Fong

Materials: paper, pencils, pens, illustrations from the book, chalk, chalkboard, supplementary reading books

Motivation (linking prior knowledge; "into" the reading activities):

1. Ask the girls and boys to close their eyes and visualize one thing that they dislike. Have them quickly sketch the object of their dislike on paper. In small groups, ask them to tell their classmates why they dislike the item and how it makes them feel.

2. Show the children some of the illustrations of Mei Mei which show her dislike of English: her stubborn look (p. 3, unpaged); her lack

of participation in class (p. 8, unpaged); her thoughts about the post office in New York (p. 11, unpaged); and her thoughts about the happening of a "terrible thing" (p. 17, unpaged). Cluster the children's reactions to Mei Mei's attitude on the writing board or on a transparency. Solicit possible reactions why many children might hate English.

3. Ask the boys and girls if they have ever hated learning words in another language. Encourage them to share incidents that made them change their minds about the language.

Purpose for Reading or Listening: "You are going to read (hear) a story about a young girl from Hong Kong named Mei Mei who was determined not to speak English. Read (listen) to find out how Mei Mei became a friend of the teacher's and how the teacher, Nancy, helped her to overcome her objections to English."

Discussion Questions ("through" the reading activities):
Ask the children:

1. What reasons did Mei Mei have to dislike English? Would you agree/disagree with the reasons? Why did Mei Mei call English a lonely language?

2. Describe what you think a day in Mei Mei's life must have been like when she did not understand English. What sort of problems, if any, could Mei Mei have had during a day at school? How could you have helped Mei Mei if you had been there?

3. Why did her cousin Bing take her to the Chinatown Learning Center for help? How do you think Mei Mei felt when she decided not to work in English?

4. Why did Mei Mei help others with arithmetic?

5. How did Mei Mei address her letters to friends in Hong Kong?

6. What were Mei Mei's feelings about English by the end of the story?

7. What would you do if you discovered someone like Mei Mei who did not want to speak the language of the country in which she/he was living? How could you help the student?

8. What are some ways you can become a friend to a student who does not speak English?

Retelling ("through" the reading activities): Ask the children to:

1. Retell this story again using some cue words to show sequencing: first, second, third, finally.

2. Retell the story and mention the name of the main character, what the character wanted, what got in the way to keep the character from getting what was wanted, and the way the problem was resolved.

3. Retell the story through group participation. The teacher asks the

students in one group to find information that tells about the character and to write it down; a second group finds facts about what the character wanted to do and writes it; a third group finds sentences that tell what got in the way of the character's goal and writes them; a fourth group finds sentences that tell how the problem was resolved and writes them. The teacher collects the informational sheets and redistributes them to the groups. Working together and discussing the information, the members determine which of the story parts they have (character, goal, conflict, resolution) and report on the story parts in order to keep the sequence of the retelling. The members can add more information about their part.

Extended Activities ("beyond" the reading activities):

1. Participating as an audience, have the girls and boys give a refrain in the background during an oral rereading. As a group, the children should decide on the refrain they want to say when Mei Mei's name is heard during a read aloud (perhaps Mei Mei's feeling of "I love Chinese! I love Chinese!"); when the teacher, Nancy, is mentioned (Forever talking English! Forever talking English!)

2. Have children rewrite the story with their names substituted for Mei Mei. Encourage them to see how some of the events in the story will differ as each one's character makes choices different from those of Mei Mei.

3. Ask the boys and girls to rewrite the story from the teacher's point of view. Help them to imagine the teacher's concern for Mei Mei.

4. Have children interview a friend who has had to learn a second language in addition to his/her own. Listen as he or she points out comparisons of the first language and second language. Are there any words in one language for which there are no words in the other language?

5. Playing the role of Mei Mei, engage the children in writing a thank-you note to Nancy and tell the teacher at the Chinatown Learning Center how Mei Mei feels one year later as she thinks back to the day when the teacher engaged her in speaking English.

Interdisciplinary Ideas

Social Studies: "Sensitivity to Mei Mei and Other Newcomers." Engage the children in watching as many television programs (or listening to radio programs) as they can after school during a week to pay special attention to any newcomers and the way they are portrayed in the media. Engage the children in doing "research" about each program they watch (hear) with a research form similar to the one that follows:

Research from Radio and TV Programs

_____   _____

name   date

_____   _____

name of media program   channel and date and time

1. Traditions and customs of newcomer presented:

_____

Observed/heard in a media program _____
Did not observe/hear in a media program _____

Discuss what portions of the program appeared to show the strengths of the newcomers and their contributions. Talk about what appeared to be accurate or inaccurate.

Recreational Reading: Have the girls and boys look for and read folk literature for Mei Mei's cultural group.

Science: What examples of contributions from science are found in the illustrations of the story? List and discuss.

Art: Ask children to make a different type of book — a "regular" picture book or a "concertina" book — about the teacher and Mei Mei. To make a "concertina" book, the children fold or tape together the pages concertina style. To complete the book, the students draw illustrations to show the title page that says *Mei Mei's Story,* and on succeeding pages, the events that happened in Mei Mei's life before and after she met the teacher at the Chinese Learning Center.

Math: Tally the responses related to what was observed (or not observed) in a media program from the research activity suggested earlier.

223 Leo Politi. *Mr. Fong's Toy Shop.* Ill. by the author. New York: Charles Scribner's Sons, 1978.

Theme: This story gives new appreciation to the festivals and customs of China as seen through the eyes of an elderly Chinese man.

Overview: Mr. Fong, a toymaker, and his young friends prepare a shadow puppet play for the Moon Festival in Chinatown in Los Angeles.

New Vocabulary: bamboo, originated, contortions, transparent, mimicked, oppressors, procession, ferocious, dramatize

Materials: set of children's encyclopedias, cardboard, popsicle sticks, overhead projector, picture of the moon, scissors

Motivation (linking prior knowledge; "into" the reading activities):
1. Show children a picture of a full moon. Solicit responses as to what tales children have heard about what the moon is made of. Brainstorm what children actually know about the moon from astronauts' explorations.
2. Show the children the front cover of the book. Judging from the picture and the title, invite children to speculate about what they think might be in Mr. Fong's toy shop (e.g., types of toys, tools for repair work, etc.).
3. Write the word "festival" on the writing board or overhead transparency. Ask children if they have ever been to a festival. List on the board the different kinds of festivals with which the children are familiar.

Purpose for Reading or Listening: "You are going to read (listen to) a story about a Chinese man who lives in Chinatown in Los Angeles. Read (listen) to find out how he helps his young friends participate in the Moon Festival."

Retelling: Have children recite the two stories-within-the-story, the legend of Chang-O and the legend of how the shadow puppets originated.

Discussion Questions ("through" the reading activities):
1. Why did the children come to Mr. Fong's store?
2. Name some things the children learned how to do from Mr. Fong.
3. Do you think the children believed the legend of Chang-O was true today? Why or why not?
4. Explain the reason for the Lantern Parade. What does it look like to observers?
5. How did Mr. Fong tell the children that he was proud of their performance?
6. What was Mr. Fong's "reward" as he made his way home? Why were the poems important to him?
7. How did Mr. Fong respond to the poems?
8. What kind of a man would you say Mr. Fong was? Would you like to meet him? Why or why not?
9. How do you think the children would describe Mr. Fong to their other friends?
10. Why do you think Mr. Fong was so kind and helpful to the children?

Extended Activities ("beyond" the reading activities):
1. Show children the pen and ink black-and-white illustrations in the story. Why do they think the illustrator chose not to use any color for this story? Do they think the illustrations would have been more effective with color? Why or why not?
2. The beginning of the story shows the children entering Mr. Fong's

toy shop saying, "Good morning, Mr. Fong" very politely as they enter one by one. Have children reenact this scene, with the cordial greetings and a customary Chinese bow.

3. The poems written by the children made Mr. Fong smile. Share the poems with the children, pointing out that each one contained four lines with an A, A, B, B pattern. Invite children to write one poem together as a group using this pattern. Finally, ask interested children to write their own poems using this pattern. Brainstorm some reactions to the moon to be used in the poems.

Interdisciplinary Ideas

Science: On the writing board or overhead transparency, make three columns with headings: What We Know, What We Would Like to Know, and What We Found Out. Solicit information about the moon from children and enter it in the column titled "What We Know." Then invite suggestions from children as to what they would like to know about the moon and enter these in the "What We Would Like to Know" column. Using tradebooks and children's encyclopedias, help children to find new information in answer to their self-initiated questions. When they have finished their exploration, complete the "What We Found Out" column with their new information and answered questions.

Art: Using cardboard, scissors, and popsicle sticks, help children to make birds and tigers, tracing the ones in the book. With the overhead projector, children can now do a shadow puppet play, in pairs, like the one in the story.

Social Studies: Using a children's encyclopedia, read children a couple of paragraphs about the Yuan Dynasty when the Mongol oppressors were defeated by the Chinese people, as mentioned in the story.

Music: Introduce children to the Moonlight Song in this story. Invite them, as a group, to compose a second verse for the song.

Recreational Reading: Leo Politi has created many well-loved stories to describe the tradition and folklore of the Chinese, Hispanic, and Italian people living in California. For children interested in such stories, introduce *Lito and the Clown, Song of the Swallows, Moy Moy,* and *Pedro, the Angel of Olvera Street,* all by Politi.

EUROPEAN AMERICAN HERITAGE

224 Cynthia Rylant. *Miss Maggie.* Ill. by Thomas di Dirazia. New York: E. P. Dutton, 1983.

Theme: A young boy sensitive to the needs of an elderly woman; relationship with caring "other" person; positive vision of life.

Overview: Nat, a young boy, has heard stories about the old lady who lives in the log hut on his family's property. A big black snake is rumored to live with her. Nat initially fears Miss Maggie but overcomes his fear when she is in trouble. He develops a special relationship with her. 2–3.

New Vocabulary: trembled, rafters, cupboards, Guernsey, wrinkled, starling

Materials: live snake, picture of black snake or plastic snake, drawing paper, pencils, shoeboxes, pipe cleaners, art paper

Motivation (linking prior knowledge; "into" the reading activities):

1. Ask students to close their eyes and visualize one thing that makes them afraid. Have them quickly sketch the object of their fear on paper. In small groups, ask them to tell their classmates why they are afraid of the object and how it makes them feel.
2. Show students the snake. Cluster their reactions to the snake on chalkboard or overhead. Solicit possible reasons why many people fear snakes.
3. Ask children if they have ever been afraid of a person prior to getting to know them. Encourage them to share incidents that made them change their minds about the person.
4. Write the word "loneliness" on the board. Have students turn to a partner and discuss, "One thing that made me feel lonely was when . . ."

Purpose for Reading or Listening: "You are going to read (hear) a story about a young boy named Nat who was very afraid of an old woman named Miss Maggie who lived alone in a little hut near his house. Read (listen) to find out how Nat became Miss Maggie's friend and how Nat helped her to overcome her loneliness."

Discussion Questions ("through" the reading activities):

1. What stories had Nat heard about Miss Maggie and her hut? Were they true? Why did people tell these stories?
2. Describe how you think a day in Miss Maggie's life must have been before she became Nat's friend.
3. Why was Miss Maggie clutching the dead bird? How do you think she was feeling?
4. How do you think Nat felt when he saw Miss Maggie clutching the dead bird? What might *you* have said or done?
5. When was Nat no longer afraid of Miss Maggie? How did he lose his fear?
6. How did Nat and Miss Maggie become friends?
7. What were Nat's feelings about Miss Maggie by the end of the story?

8. How do you think Miss Maggie felt about Nat?
9. What would *you* do if you discovered someone like Miss Maggie living all alone without food or heat?
10. What are some of the ways you can become a friend to an older person?

Retelling ("through" the reading activities): Pairs of students roleplay the story. They should take turns portraying Nat or Miss Maggie.

Extended Activities ("beyond" the reading activities):

1. Taking the role of Nat, have children write a letter to Miss Maggie telling her how she used to frighten them and why. Have the children explain what they learned about her and how much they care about her now.
2. Have children rewrite the story with their name and persona substituted for Nat's. Encourage them to see how the ending to the story differs as their character makes choices different from Nat's.
3. Have children rewrite the story from Miss Maggie's point of view. Help them to imagine that Miss Maggie is afraid of the little boy who is constantly peering in the windows.
4. Have children interview a grandparent or an elderly person living in a nearby nursing home. Questions can include, "Are you ever lonely? What is a day in your life like?" Help them to compare their lives with that of an elderly person.
5. Have children write a thank-you note to Nat from Miss Maggie telling Nat how she felt when he visited and found her alone holding the starling.

Interdisciplinary Ideas

Social Studies: Have children find books in the library that tell how elderly people are respected and treated in other cultures.

Recreational Reading: Have children look for folklore about snakes. Discuss how snakes are considered in these legends. Why do they suppose this is so?

Science: Investigate the habits of nonpoisonous snakes. Have children make a poster explaining why these creatures have been unfairly maligned.

Art: Have children construct a diorama of Miss Maggie's log house in the middle of the pasture.

Math: Chart the number one fear of all the children in the class. Discuss if there are differences between the fears of the girls and boys. Brainstorm ways to overcome these fears.

225 Elsa Beskow. *Pelle's New Suit.* Ill. New York: Harper, 1929.

Theme: Pelle is a sensitive young boy who has a relationship with caring "other" persons.

Overview: In Sweden, Pelle shears a lamb's wool, pulls the weeds in Grandmother's garden while she cards the wool, tends his other grandmother's cows while she spins the yarn, goes to the store to buy some dye and dyes the wool. He takes care of his little sister while his mother weaves the yarn into cloth. He rakes hay, brings in wood, and feeds the tailor's pigs while the tailor makes Pelle's suit. Pelle is considerate of others and says "please" when making requests of his relatives and the tailor. He doesn't object or argue when Mother says, "Take care of your little sister for me." K–1.

New Vocabulary: shears, lamb's wool, cards the wool, dye, weaves, tailor

Materials: remnant of blue wool, pictures of people spinning, carding, weaving; art paper and markers or crayons or colored pencils

Motivation (linking prior knowledge; "into" the reading activities):

1. Ask students to close their eyes and visualize one time when they were helped by others to acquire something they wanted. Have them quickly sketch the object they wanted on paper. In small groups, ask them to tell their classmates what they wanted, who helped them, and how they felt when they acquired the object.

2. Engage the children in observing and touching the piece of blue wool. Cluster their reactions to the material on the board or overhead transparency. Solicit ideas of possible jobs that had to be done to make the piece of blue wool.

3. Ask children to think if they have ever helped another person acquire something she/he wanted. Encourage them to share incidents from their experience.

4. Write the word "Pelle" on the board and show Pelle's picture from the book. Have students begin a sentence and discuss, "One thing that I think of when I see Pelle is . . ."

Purpose for Reading or Listening: "You are going to read (hear) a story about a young boy named Pelle who wanted a new suit. Since Pelle lived in a time and place where there were no stores to buy a new suit, read (listen) to find out how Pelle got his new suit."

Discussion Questions ("through" the reading activities):

1. What are some of the things that Pelle did to acquire his suit? Were they helpful to others? Why did he do these things?

2. Describe how you think a day in Pelle's life must have been after he got his new suit.

3. What were some of the things Pelle did to shear a lamb's wool? How do you think he learned to do this?

4. How do you think Pelle felt when he tended his grandmother's cows while she spun the yarn for the suit?
5. How do you think Pelle felt when he tended his little sister while his mother wove the yarn into cloth?
6. How did Pelle help the tailor while the tailor made his suit?
7. What were the ways Pelle showed he was polite and considerate?
8. How do you think Pelle felt about his new suit?
9. What would *you* do if you had to get a new suit the way Pelle did?
10. What are some ways you can be polite and considerate to others?

Retelling ("through" the reading activities): Pairs of students roleplay the story taking turns being Pelle and the other characters.

Extended Activities ("beyond" the reading activities):

1. Taking the role of Pelle, have children review the illustrations and act out his motions in pantomime.
2. Have the girls and boys rewrite the story with their names and to-day's setting to tell how they would acquire a new suit/dress. Encourage them to see how their story differs as their character is in a different time and place from Pelle's.
3. Have children discuss and dictate the story from another point of view—the mother's view, the little sister's view, the tailor's view.
4. Have the girls and boys discuss and dictate the story by switching the male character to female.
5. Have children interview a tailor. Questions can include, "How do you make a suit?" "What do you need to do?" "What tools do you use?" Help them to compare what the tailor says with what Pelle had to do.
6. Have the girls and boys design a poster (mural) to show the steps that one has to do to make a suit from lamb's wool as Pelle did.

Interdisciplinary Ideas

Social Studies: Have children find books in the library that tell how clothing is made. Display Tomie de Paola's *Charlie Needs a Cloak* (Prentice-Hall, 1974) and Lauren Mills' *The Rag Coat*.

Science: Investigate the characteristics of dye (use food coloring or egg coloring). Have children experiment with drops of food coloring in water in a glass container.

Art: Have girls and boys cut out paper shapes of "new suits" and "dresses."

Math: Chart the number one wish for an article of clothing of all the children in the class. Discuss if there are differences between the wishes of the girls and boys.

Language Arts: Engage the boys and girls in an activity called "Please do this for me." With questions such as the ones that follow, encourage children to roleplay making requests of others and showing they can be polite as well as "give something back."

Discuss with children:

1. *Describing words.* After looking at the illustration where Pelle shears the lamb, how many different describing words can you use to tell about what you see in the illustration? In the illustration that shows Pelle pulling weeds in Grandmother's carrot patch while she cards the wool? Children may participate in roleplay in various scenes.

2. *Roleplay.* Consider roleplay for the following and introduce a simple form of a play in three acts:

   Act 1: Scene 1: Pelle asks his other grandmother to spin the wool into yarn. Grandmother says she will if he will tend the cows for her. *Scene 2:* Pelle asks his neighbor to give him some paint to color the yarn. Pelle learns he has to row to the store to buy some dye.

   Act 2: Scene 1: Pelle dyes the wool himself until it is blue. *Scene 2:* Pelle asks his mother to weave the yarn into cloth for him. Mother says she will if Pelle will take care of his little sister for her.

   Act 3: Scene 1: Pelle asks the tailor to make a suit for him out of the cloth. The tailor says he will if Pelle will rake the hay, bring in the wood, and feed the pigs. *Scene 2:* Pelle puts on his new suit and visits his lamb to say, "Thank you very much for my new suit, little lamb." The lamb replies, "Ba-a-ah."

Recreational Reading: Have children look for other stories with a setting in a country other than the United States.

LATINO AMERICAN HERITAGE

226 Leo Politi. *The Nicest Gift.* Ill. by the author. New York: Charles Scribner's Sons, 1973.

Theme: The book acquaints children with the customs and flavor of Mexican American life for a family who lives in the barrio in East Los Angeles.

Overview: Blanco, Carlito's dog, has disappeared while his family is busy with the festivities of the Christmas season. Carlito finds the animal near the nativity scene and realizes this is the nicest gift he has ever received. K–3.

New Vocabulary: confusion, somersaults, nudges, jolly, merchandise, acrobatic, aisle

Motivation (linking prior knowledge; "into" the reading activities):

1. Have children close their eyes and imagine they are in a favorite toy store one week before Christmas. What toys especially catch their eye? Which toys would they love to have? Are there any toys they have wished for for Christmas and actually received? What is their favorite toy? Have children open their eyes and share with a neighbor what they "saw."

2. Have children write a brief paragraph beginning with the sentence stem, "The nicest gift I ever got was _____." Ask them to tell why the gift was the nicest. Invite children to share their paragraphs in small groups.

3. Show children the cover for *The Nicest Gift*. Based upon the cover, ask children to make predictions as to what they think this story will be about.

4. Write the following words on the board or overhead transparency:

Carlitos	clown
Mother	lost
market	sad
dog	Christmas Day

5. Ask children to read the words out loud. Based upon these words, have them tell the story of what they think happens to Carlitos and his dog.

Purpose for Reading or Listening: "You are about to read (listen to) a story about a little boy named Carlitos who lives in East Los Angeles with his family and his dog. Read (listen) to find out what turns out to be the nicest gift Carlitos has ever received for Christmas.

Discussion Questions:

1. What was the nicest gift that Carlitos had ever received?

2. Why do you think Carlitos felt that it was the nicest gift he had ever received?

3. How is Carlitos' Christmas celebration different from or the same as yours?

4. Why did Carlitos lose Blanco? Do you think he would do that again? Why or why not?

5. What did the author mean when he said, "Carlitos loves his dog Blanco so much that he wouldn't know what to do with him"?

6. Why didn't Leandro recognize Blanco?

7. Do you think Carlitos ever gave up on the idea that he would find Blanco? Why or why not?

8. How do you think Blanco found his way to the church? Why might he curl up near the nativity scene?

9. What do you think was the reaction of the other people in the church when Blanco came running to Carlitos?

10. What advice do you think Carlitos' parents gave him after finding Blanco? Were they as happy as he was?

Retelling ("through" the reading activities):

1. Put children in groups of three or four. Select one child to play the part of Carlitos as a grown man. Ask the remaining children in the group to play the part of Carlitos' children. Have Carlitos, the grown-up man and father, tell his "children" about the time he lost his dog and found him again on Christmas making it the best Christmas gift ever.

2. Have small groups of children act out the following scenes using appropriate dialogue:

   a. Carlitos just realizes he has lost Blanco. He tries to find him and then tearfully tells his mother and father that the dog is lost.

   b. Carlitos wakes up sad on Christmas morning. He and his mother and father walk to church, but Carlitos' mind is on his lost dog.

   c. Carlitos and his parents are in church and they see a dog who looks like Blanco. They discuss it, and then realize it is Blanco.

   d. Carlitos plays joyfully with Blanco all the rest of Christmas Day.

3. As a group, write a want ad as Carlitos might have written it to try to get his lost dog back. Brainstorm what the reward might be for his return.

Interdisciplinary Ideas

Social Studies: Help children recall the festivities in this story that help make Christmas special for some people in the Hispanic culture. If there are Hispanic children in the class, invite them to compare and contrast their Christmas traditions with those of Carlitos' family. Bring in several members of the community from diverse cultures who celebrate Christmas or another religious holiday in other ways.

Math: Find a recipe for tamales or churros as described in the story. Ask interested parent volunteers to bring in ingredients for the food. Using the recipe, help children measure the ingredients as they are needed. Have other children time the cooking of the food. Have still others divide the food so that all can have equal portions.

Spanish Language: Call children's attention to the following Spanish words that are introduced and defined in the text:

caballito	little horse
blanco	white
mercado	market
balones	balloons
cacahuatitos	peanuts
bueñas dias	good morning
payaso	clown
Como está?	How are you?
bien	fine

Allow children to practice pronouncing these words. Ask them to use them in an original skit about further adventures of Carlitos and Blanco.

Recreational Reading: Point out to children that the author of this book has written many outstanding books for children that use the diverse people of Los Angeles as their subjects. Introduce interested children to *Juanita; Pedro, the Angel of Olvera Street;* and the *Song of the Swallows.*

227 Ariane Dewey. *The Thunder God's Son: A Peruvian Folktale.* New York: Greenwillow, 1981.

Theme: This is a story of the son of the thunder god who was sent to earth to learn about the people's ways.

Overview: Thirteen-year-old Acuri, son of the thunder god, is disguised as a beggar and sent down to earth to learn about the people. Acuri learns the meaning of dishonesty in the thefts of golden rings, vanity in the contests of drinking chicha, dancing, house building, and stone throwing, and recognizes greed in the house with the feathered roof. Under the powerful eye of his father, who is never far away from Acuri, he learns to punish and to reward. With this education over, he returns to the heavens as a much wiser young god. Folk literature. 2–3.

New Vocabulary: Acuri, Thunder God, beggar, chicha, feathered roof

Materials: drawing paper, pencils, crayons, pictures of the folktale

Motivation (linking prior knowledge; "into" the reading activities): A teacher may ask students to write/sketch their interpretation of the title.

Purpose for Reading or Listening: "You are about to hear the story of young Acuri who is sent down to Earth to learn the people's ways. Read (listen) to find out how he learned to punish the evil and reward the good."

Discussion Questions:

1. The questions/activities that follow are examples of the types which teachers and librarians can ask to encourage children to talk about how they feel about some of the ideas related to the book before it is read or heard:

    a. Why do some people have folktales from early times about their gods (and goddesses)?

b. Without using the words "thunder god," talk about what the title means to you.

Retelling ("through" the reading activities):

Working in groups, suggest that students roleplay scenes from the tale:

1. Scene between thirteen-year-old Acuri and his father, Paricaca, the thunder god, who sends him to Earth disguised as a beggar to "learn more than you know."
2. Scene in which Acuri overhears two foxes talking about a selfish rich man.
3. Scene at the rich man's house in which Acuri makes the man promise to share his wealth with the rest of the village.
4. Scene in which the wife of the rich man promises never to steal again.
5. Scene in which the couple's son challenges Acuri to a contest of best costume, best drinker of chicha and best dancer.
6. Scene in which the thunder god transforms the rich man's family into deer.

Extended Activities ("beyond" the reading activities):

1. Create a "thunder" research project. Make a list of words that best describe thunder. Make a list of things that are related to thunder. Tell how you recognize thunder.
2. After reading or listening to the story, the students may be asked to think back to the final event and then write their impressions about what Acuri learned about the ways of people. Take time to discuss the children's work and point out similar examples in stories from other cultures.
3. With the children, a teacher or librarian may read some of the sentences about what Acuri experienced in the story. After hearing each sentence, invite the students to "tell how you think Acuri felt and more about what he did" and "As Acuri was feeling this way, tell how you think the other person felt."

Interdisciplinary Ideas

Social Studies: With children, review the episode in the story where the couple's son, Rupay, suggests another contest to see who can build the best house the fastest. Have children find books in the library that tell how characters from other cultures have been challenged to contests.

Science: After reading about the ending episode where Acuri leads the llamas to the mountain pasture to graze and gives the animals to the villagers so that all could share in the riches their wool would bring to their economy, the children may be interested in a way to test a fiber to determine if it is wool or another type of fiber. With adult supervision and the directions for "Testing Fibers" in *Chemically Active* (Lippincott, 1985) by Vicki Cobb, students can determine what kind of fabric is found in a remnant by observing what happens when an adult holds a small square of sample fabric with metal tongs into a small flame and by observing what the ash looks like when placed in a metal pan. For example, a sample of wool fabric will sizzle and burn slowly in a flame, smell like burnt hair, and have a hollow ash that looks like a fragile bead. In contrast, a sample of cotton fabric will burn rapidly with a yellow flame, smell like burning paper, and have a fine gray ash.

Art: Have girls and boys look at such Peruvian folk art themes as a roof of red and yellow feathers, a red puma costume, and others, that are included in the book's illustrations.

Math: Survey the children to determine their favorite episode in the story and chart the results:

Episode	Girls	Boys
Acuri rids the rich man's house of a fever-inducing two-headed toad.		
Acuri gets rid of two serpents hovering over the house.		
Acuri dances to the rhythm of a magic flute.		
Acuri is helped by animals and builds a fine house in one night.		
Acuri gives the llamas as a gift to the villagers.		

Language Arts: Engage the boys and girls in talking about ways birds are recognized in this Peruvian tale: the feathered shape of the thunder god; the feathered head covering of Acuri; the red and yellow feathered roof of the rich man's house; the feathered shape of the thunder god fighting the serpents; the feathers in the headdress of the couple's son; the wife of the rich man wearing a dress trimmed with feathers; and the birds and other animals who helped Acuri build the "best" house.

Recreational Reading: Have children look for other folktales about contests with a setting in a country other than the United States.

NATIVE AMERICAN HERITAGE

228 William Sleator. *The Angry Moon.* Ill. by Blair Lent. Boston: Little, Brown/Atlantic Monthly Press, 1970.

Theme: This is a story of a rescue — a quest also accomplished by characters from other cultural backgrounds.

Overview: A rainbow appears and takes Lapowinsa to the sky when she angers the moon. To retrieve the girl, Lupan shoots his arrows toward the moon. He notices a chain of arrows forms a ladder on which he climbs into the sky. Reaching the top, he is taken by a small boy to his grandmother's house, where Lupan receives four objects to aid in the rescue of Lapowinsa. Lupan follows the sobs of Lapowinsa to the moon's home, substitutes a pine cone in her place in a smoke hole and they begin their escape. When the pine cone burns, the angry moon pursues them. A fish eye becomes a lake to block the moon's progress and a rose turns into a tangled thicket to slow the chasing moon. A stone grows into steep mountains and the children make their escape and return to earth to tell their story to succeeding generations. 2–3.

New Vocabulary: Lupan, Lapowinsa, angry, pine cone, chain of arrows, smoke hole

Materials: drawing paper, pencils, crayons, pictures of the folktale

Motivation (linking prior knowledge; "into" the reading activities): Ask children to discuss their interpretation of the book's title.

Purpose for Reading or Listening: "You are about to hear the story of a young girl who angers the moon and her subsequent rescue by a boy who shoots his arrows toward the moon, makes a ladder from the arrows and climbs into the sky. Read (listen) to find out how she was rescued."

Discussion Questions:

1. The questions/activities that follow are examples of the types which teachers and librarians can prepare to encourage children to talk about how they feel about some of the ideas related to the book before it is read or heard:
   a. Why do some people come to the aid or rescue of others?
   b. Why is a person often punished when he/she angers others?
   c. Without using the word "angry," talk about what the title *The Angry Moon* means to you.

Retelling ("through" the reading activities): Working in groups, suggest that students roleplay scenes from the tale and take turns playing Lupan, Lapowinsa, and the angry moon.

Extended Activities ("beyond" the reading activities):

1. Create an "angry" research project. Make a list of words that best describe an angry person. Make a list of things that cause a person to become angry. Tell how you recognize anger. Tell what you could do to overcome anger in another person.

2. After reading or listening to the story, the students may be asked to think back to the rescue event and then write their impressions about a person who came to the aid or rescued another person. Take time to discuss the children's work and point out examples that modify gender stereotypes. Have children write their own impressions to be put into a book for others to read and comment on.

3. With the children, a teacher or librarian may read these sentences about some of the things Lupan experienced in the story. After hearing each sentence, invite the students to "tell how you think Lupan felt and more about what he did" and "As Lupan was feeling this way, tell how you think the young girl felt."

   a. Lupan discovers that a rainbow appears and takes Lapowinsa to the sky when she angers the moon.
   b. To retrieve the girl, Lupan shoots his arrows toward the moon.

Interdisciplinary Ideas

Social Studies: With children, review the episode in the story where Lupan notices a chain of his arrows makes a ladder on which he climbs into the sky and is taken by a small boy to his grandmother's house where he receives four objects to aid in the rescue of Lapowinsa. Have children find books in the library that tell how the elderly have helped others.

Science: After reading about the episode in which Lupan follows the sobs of Lapowinsa to the moon's home and substitutes a burning pine cone in her place in a smoke hole to allow them to escape, the students may inquire into reasons why a pine cone burns and investigate the characteristics of "objects that burn" and "objects that do not burn."

With adult supervision and the directions for "The Flame Test" in *Chemically Active* (Lippincott, 1985) by Vicki Cobb, students can be chemical detectives and observe that when certain metals are heated, the metals give the flame a distinctive color. The color is a way of identifying a metal (i.e., a copper penny will give off a bright green color).

Art: Have girls and boys cut out paper shapes of "the transformations" that Lupan sees: a fish eye becomes a lake to block the moon's progress, a rose turns into a tangled thicket to slow the chasing moon, and a stone grows into a steep mountain.

Math: Chart the children's favorite Native American tales that include escapes similar to the escape of Lupan and Lapowinsa before their return to earth.

Language Arts: Engage the boys and girls in an activity, "Tell Us a Story," and encourage them to roleplay listening to Lupan and Lapowinsa as they tell their story to the "succeeding generation."

Recreational Reading: Have children look for other folktales about pursuits with a setting in a country other than the United States.

229 Paul Goble. *Her Seven Brothers.* Boston: Bradbury, 1988.
   Theme: This is a story of a rescue.
   Overview: A girl and her seven chosen brothers become part of the Big Dipper. 2–3.
   New Vocabulary: porcupine, quills, moccasins, immensity, tipi, Buffalo Calf, Buffalo Nation, horizon, clambered, quivered, boundless, star-prairies, Big Dipper
   Materials: drawing paper, pens, watercolor, pictures of the tale
   Purpose for Reading or Listening: "You are about to hear the story of a young girl who traveled to find her seven brothers. When the chief of the Buffalo Nation wanted the young girl for his own, the brothers defended their sister. Listen (read) to see what the brothers did to protect her."
   Discussion Questions ("through" the reading activities):
   1. The questions/activities that follow are examples of the types which teachers and librarians can prepare to encourage children to talk about how they feel about some of the ideas related to the book:

      a. Why do some people wish to impose themselves on others?
      b. Why is a person often punished when he/she angers others?

   Retelling ("through" the reading activities): Working in groups, suggest that students roleplay scenes from the tale and take turns as the sister, the little brother, and Buffalo Calf.
   Extended Activities ("beyond" the reading activities):
   1. Create a "Big Dipper" research project. Make a list of words that best describe the Big Dipper. Tell how you recognize this constellation.

2. After reading or listening to the story, the children may be asked to think back to the moment when the boy's arrow caused the pine tree to grow higher until they were carried up among the stars. The children can then dictate or write their impressions about the moment when the sister and her seven brothers all jumped down from the tree's branches onto the star-prairies of the world.

3. With the children, a teacher or librarian may read sentences about some of the things the sister experienced in the story. After hearing each sentence, invite the students to "tell how you think the sister felt and more about what she did" and "As the sister was feeling this way, tell how you think the little brother felt."

    a. The girl discovers that she can see seven brothers who live by themselves in her mind when she closes her eyes.

    b. The girl finds the trail and leaves her mother to go on alone to the North Country.

    c. The girl arrives at the tipi of the seven brothers and the little boy greets her.

    d. The girl gives her gifts to the brothers and the little boy admires his new shirt and moccasins.

    e. The girl stayed and the brothers looked after her.

    f. The girl went out for water and gathered firewood and the little boy would take his bow and arrow to protect her.

    g. The girl runs with her brothers to escape the stampede of the Buffalo People.

    h. The girl lifted her little brother onto the lowest branch of a pine tree and climbed up after him. Then the other brothers climbed after them.

    i. The little boy shot an arrow and the tree grew taller and they were carried up among the stars where they could jump onto the star-prairies. The Brothers are now the seven stars in the sky called the Big Dipper.

Interdisciplinary Ideas

Social Studies: With children, point out the social context of Cheyenne storytelling. The stories were told after dark when the listener's "mind" could "see" the story. In the glow of the fire in the middle of the tipi, a Native American storyteller would rub his body with earth to show others that the people came from the earth and that it would be the witness to the truth of his story.

Science: After reading that the brothers are now the Seven Stars in a constellation in the Northern sky, distribute pictures of the constellation to the children and ask them to look carefully at the stars in it. Help the children discover that there are really eight stars in the Big Dipper and that close to one of the stars is a tiny star. Point out that the legend maintains that the tiny star is the little boy walking with his sister who is never lonely now. Another part of the legend maintains that the North Star is the Star Which Always Stands Still and that the sister and her brothers are forever turning around the North Star.

Art: Have girls and boys review the designs of the shirts, dresses and other articles in the book that are based on Cheyenne designs. Point out that the living creatures share the earth with Native Americans and so they are included in the pictures.

Suggest that the children look carefully at the pen-and-ink drawings filled in with watercolor. Invite them to work in the manner of Paul Goble and create drawings related to the story with ball point pens and watercolor.

Suggest that the children embroider designs to simulate the embroidery that the girl did to decorate deer and buffalo skin robes and clothes.

Math: Point out the value of collecting information on a chart and chart the children's favorite Native American tales which include "sky stories" similar to this one.

Language Arts: Suggest that the children visit the library and meet with the librarian to find books that tell them more about the Cheyenne people. One of the titles that might be suggested is *American Indian Myths and Legends* (Pantheon, 1984) by Richard Endores and Alfonso Ortiz.

Recreational Reading: Have children look for other folktales about "sky stories" with a setting in a country other than the United States.

Extended
Activity Unit:
Grades 4–8

AFRICAN AMERICAN HERITAGE

230 Scott O'Dell. *My Name Is Not Angelica*. Boston: Houghton
    Mifflin, 1989.

Theme: Raisha, a girl who is a survivor, is captured in Africa and
sold as a slave. She hates her new name and slavery but is strong and wants
to retaliate. She realizes that rash action is dangerous for her, however, and
so she survives through other strategies.

Overview: In Barato, Africa, Konje, Raisha, and Dondo are captured
at a rival king's feast and sold as slaves. They are unloaded in St. Thomas
(Danish Virgin Islands), participate in the slave revolt on St. John
(1733–34), see the suicide leap by slaves into the sea, and hope for a better
future. 4–8.

New Vocabulary: survivor, Barato, St. Thomas, St. John, Danish
Virgin Islands, revolt, Mary Point, Martinique

Materials: chalk, chalkboard, paper, pencils, books for further reading, African-American folk literature, materials for constructing a mural

Motivation (linking prior knowledge; "into" the reading activities):

1. Ask students to imagine/sketch this scene: "You have been invited
   to enjoy a dinner and spend the night at the home of an acquaintance
   in a nearby town. Suddenly while you are sleeping, you and two of
   your friends are dragged from your bed and put aboard a ship
   bound for another land." In small groups, ask them to tell their
   classmates their feelings about this scene and what they would
   have done in the situation.

2. Discuss the custom of each of the slaves receiving a new name
   when purchased by a planter and the ways each African responded
   to this captivity in the strange surroundings. Encourage them to
   locate incidents that show that Dondo was docile and obedient on
   the outside while angry inside; that Konje showed his kingly bear-
   ing and attitude and escaped to Mary Point, the gathering place for
   runaway slaves on the island; that Raisha hated slavery but realized
   the danger around her.

Purpose for Reading or Listening: "You are going to read (hear) a story
about a girl named Raisha who was renamed Angelica when she was sold
as a slave. Read (listen) to find out how Raisha changed her attitude from
one of despair to one of "life forever." How did Konje's love help her make
this decision?

Discussion Questions ("through" the reading activities):

1. In Africa, what trickery was played on Raisha, her family and
   friends at the rival king's feast?

2. Describe how you think a day in Raisha's life must have been before she became a slave.

3. How do you think Konje felt when he escaped to Mary Point, the stronghold of the runaways on the island? What might *you* have said or done if you had been with him when he escaped?

4. Why did Raisha continue to work as a personal servant for Jenna Van Prok and not escape? How did she finally escape?

5. What were Raisha's feelings about Konje by the end of the story? How do you think Konje felt about Raisha?

6. What are some ways you can help someone who may have no hope for a better life?

Retelling ("through" the reading activities): Pairs of students roleplay the story taking turns being either Raisha or Konje.

Extended Activities ("beyond" the reading activities):

1. Taking the role of Raisha, have students write a letter to smuggle back to her homeland telling about the day when Jost Van Prok, a planter of Hawks Nest on the island of St. John, purchased Konje, Dondo, and Raisha. Explain how Raisha felt and what actions she planned to take.

2. Have students take the role of a participant who was there to see the day when Captain Dumont arrived at Mary Point with the soldiers. Ask students to rewrite the event from their point of view.

3. Have students discuss the story from the point of view of Captain Dumont and the planters. Help them to imagine that the planters and the soldiers were afraid of the slaves in their revolt and needed the laborers to work in the fields.

4. Have students interview a student playing the role of Raisha. Questions can include, "What is a day in your life like?" What are some of the things you do to survive?" Help students to compare their lives of freedom with that of another who is not free.

5. Have students write a letter to Konje from Raisha telling of her plans to escape.

Interdisciplinary Ideas

Social Studies: Suggest students find books in the library that tell how African Americans were treated in slavery.

Science: Investigate the ways that people can send secret messages. Have students write expository paragraphs explaining the use of secret writing, secret codes, secret signals.

Art: Engage students in construction of a diorama of the capture of Raisha and her family and friends at the rival king's feast in Africa.

Math: Count the number of books the students find that tell about slavery. Graph the information in categories (e.g., informational books, historical fiction, and biographies).

Recreational Reading: Ask students to look for folklore about the desire of people to be free. Discuss how freedom is seen in these folktales and legends. Why do they suppose this is so? Select *The People Could Fly,* a collection of African American folktales. The title tale tells of the ability of field laborers to fly away from the harsh life as slaves.

231 Ed Clayton. *Martin Luther King: The Peaceful Warrior.* Ill. by David Hodges. New York: Archway, 1968.

Theme: Dr. King chose nonviolence as the keystone to his civil rights movement.

Overview: Dr. Martin Luther King helped to organize the civil rights movement. As a result of his activities, the United States Congress passed an historic civil rights bill. Because of his remarkable achievements through nonviolent means, Dr. King was awarded the Nobel Peace Prize.

New Vocabulary: belittling, venerable, prejudice, segregated, Emancipation Proclamation, oppressive, jubilant, boycott

Materials: Copy of "I Have a Dream" (tape or transcript, copyright 1963 by Martin Luther King, Jr.), or tape or record of "We Shall Overcome" (Ludlow Music, Inc., 1963). Other books on the civil rights movement: *The Peaceable Revolution* (Houghton Mifflin, 1976) by Betty Schecter and *Martin Luther King* (Messner, 1982) by Doris and Harold Faber

Motivation (linking prior knowledge; "into" the reading activities):

1. Martin Luther King was deeply influenced by the teachings of Jesus Christ ("Love your enemies"), Henry Thoreau (Civil disobedience), and Mahatma Gandhi (Passive resistance—"love the oppressor"). To fully understand what they are about to read (listen to), have groups of students research the philosophies of these three great teachers.

2. Have the students look up the meaning of "prejudice" in a dictionary. Explain that the word comes from two Latin words—prae (before), and judicum (judgment). Ask the students if they have been victims of prejudice.

3. Ask the students to imagine that one day they are told that they can no longer play with their best friend because the best friend's parents don't like the color of their hair, skin, eyes, etc. How would they feel? What would they do to rectify the situation?

4. In an early chapter, Martin is described with a racial slur by an adult lady who accuses him of stepping on her toe. Read this episode (p. 23) to the students. Ask them if they can think of a peaceful way to handle such an incident.

Purpose for Reading or Listening: "You are going to read (listen to) a book about a man who experienced terrible things happening to him, his family, and his people, simply because of the color of his skin. Instead of fighting people, he chose to follow a path of nonviolence to try to change people's hearts. Read (listen) to find out how he accomplished this."

Discussion Questions ("through" the reading activities):

1. What do you think made King decide to become a minister?
2. Explain how he learned about prejudice early in his life. How do you think these incidents shaped King's later career?
3. How did King find that the North was different from the South in attitudes and behavior toward blacks? Why did King return to the South?
4. How did the bus strike cause change in the South?
5. How was Dr. King influenced by his religion? By the teachings of Mahatma Gandhi? By the philosophy of Henry Thoreau?
6. Why do you think the author of this book calls King "the peaceful warrior"? Do you think this is an apt title? Why or why not?
7. What was Dr. King's dream? In what ways do you think his dream has been realized today? What other examples can you give?
8. On page 105 of the text, there is a picture of Dr. Martin Luther King, Mahatma Gandhi, and Abraham Lincoln, all walking together hand in hand. What do you think is the significance of this illustration? In what way did each of these great leaders make the world a more peaceful place?

Retelling ("through" the reading activities): Have students make a timeline of the events in the life of Dr. Martin Luther King, Jr.

Extended Activities ("beyond" the reading activities):

1. Invite students, through the publisher of this book, to write to Dr. King's widow, Coretta King, telling her of their impressions of King's life.
2. Obtain a copy of King's "I Have a Dream" speech either on tape or the transcript. Discuss King's dream and how close the people of the United States are to achieving this dream.
3. Encourage students to write about their own dreams for a more peaceful world. Have them start and end their dream with "I have a dream . . ." as King did.
4. Have students resarch the beginning of the Nobel Peace Prize. Have them draw up a list of other awardees and find out what deeds caused them to be considered for the prestigious award.
5. Have students write an epitaph for the tombstone of Dr. King.
6. Stage a mock meeting between Mahatma Gandhi, Abraham Lincoln and Dr. King. Have volunteers research the lives of each of the three leaders. When the three volunteers are thoroughly re-

hearsed in the lives of the three characters, have them sit in the front of the room in a panel. Invite classmates to ask questions of one of the three that will spark a conversation among the three. Let each "leader" answer questions about modern-day problems with peacekeeping suggestions as they think that leader might have answered it.

Interdisciplinary Ideas

Social Studies: Help students make a time line of the events of Martin Luther King's life.

Art: Using butcher paper, have students make a mural of the events in Dr. King's life.

Music: Share with students the freedom movement song that was always sung at the close of civil rights meetings, "We Shall Overcome." The last verse of the song suggests that peace will someday come. Ask students if they think that if Dr. King were to return today he would feel that that day had arrived. Why or why not?

Language Arts: Have pairs of students act out the following scenes:
1. the scene between young King and the shoe salesman who wouldn't serve "colored" in the front of the store (pp. 19–20).
2. the scene between King and the student from North Carolina at Morehouse College who accused him of upending his room (p. 48).
3. the scene between Dr. King and Gunnar Jahn when King was awarded the Nobel Peace Prize.

Recreational Reading: Introduce students to other leaders in the civil rights movement (e.g., Medgar Evars, Ralph Abernathy, Jr., Rosa Parks, and Malcolm X). If interested, have them find trade books about these leaders in the library. Encourage them to present information about the leaders' lives to their classmates.

ASIAN AMERICAN HERITAGE

232 Laurence Yep. *Dragonwings.* New York: Harper & Row, 1975.

Theme: An eight-year-old boy tells his family's story about his father, Windrider, who tinkers with mechanical inventions.

Overview: In 1903, in San Francisco, Moon Shadow Lee and his father,

Windrider, study aeronautical books and build gliders. They turn all their energies into building a flying machine, Dragonwings. After three years, the machine is finished and Windrider makes a successful flight. 6–8.

New Vocabulary: Moon Shadow Lee, Windrider, Dragonwings, Mrs. Whitlaw, Uncle Bright Star, revolt, San Francisco

Materials: chalk, chalkboard, paper, pencils or pens, related books for further reading, Asian American folk literature, materials for constructing a mural

Motivation (linking prior knowledge; "into" the reading activities):

1. Ask students to sketch this scene: "You have been invited to visit a barn in the foothills of nearby Oakland where Moon Shadow Lee and his father, Windrider, live and build a flying machine, Dragonwings.

Purpose for Reading or Listening: "You are going to read (hear) a story about a young boy named Moon Shadow Lee who helped his father build a flying machine. Read (listen) to find out how the boy and his father did this.

Discussion Questions ("through" the reading activities):

1. In San Francisco in 1903, what work did Moon Shadow Lee and his father do to earn money to build the flying machine?
2. Describe how you think a day in Moon Shadow Lee's life must have been in those days in San Francisco.
3. How do you think Moon Shadow Lee felt when he became a friend of Robin, Miss Whitlaw's niece? What might *you* have said or done if you had been with him when he was learning to read and write English?
4. What damage did the 1906 earthquake do?
5. What were Moon Shadow Lee's feelings when his father was injured in the crash of Dragonwings?

Retelling ("through" the reading activities): Pairs of students may roleplay the story taking turns being either Moon Shadow Lee or his father, Windrider.

Extended Activities ("beyond" the reading activities):

1. Taking the role of Moon Shadow Lee, have students write a letter to send back to his homeland telling about his father's interest in building a flying machine. Explain how Moon Shadow Lee felt and what he did to help his father.
2. Have students take the role of a participant who was there in 1906 on the day the earthquake hit San Francisco. Ask students to rewrite the event from their point of view.
3. Have students discuss the story from the point of view of an inanimate object, the flying machine.
4. Have students interview a student playing the role of Miss Whitlaw

who was teaching Moon Shadow Lee to read and write English. Help students to compare their lives as citizens of America with that of a newcomer who has to learn to read and write a language different from his own.

5. Have students draw a blueprint of an original flying machine.

Interdisciplinary Ideas

Social Studies: Suggest that students find books in the library that tell about other flying machines.

Science: Investigate the ways that people experimented with flying machines.

Art: Engage students in construction of a paper-engineered flying machine.

Math: Discuss what mathematics is needed to construct and fly a flying machine.

Recreational Reading: Ask students to look for folktales about people's desire to fly. Discuss how flight is seen in these folktales and legends. As an example, introduce *The People Could Fly,* a collection of African American folktales. The title tale tells of the ability of field laborers to fly away from the harsh life as slaves.

233 Toshiko Uchida. *Journey Home.* Illustrated by Charles Robinson. New York: Atheneum, 1978.

Theme: Multidimensional Japanese characters are presented; the pain caused by the Japanese American concentration camps is shown through the eyes of Yuki and her family. Overcoming pain and bitterness caused by prejudice and ignorance is a major theme.

Overview: When Yuki and her parents are released from a concentration camp near the end of World War II, they meet with prejudice and violence as they try to begin life again in this realistic and poignant story.

New Vocabulary: famished, contemplated, agitators, contraband, curfew, vigilantes, counterirritant, samurai, evacuated, inconspicuous, brusque

Materials: Pictures of Japanese concentration camps; Lodestar's "Jewish Biography series."

Motivation (linking prior knowledge; "into" the reading activities):

1. Write the word forgiveness on the writing board or on transparency for the overhead projector. Ask the students to think of a time someone did something upsetting to them and then asked for their forgiveness. How did the person ask for forgiveness? How long did

it take them to forgive the person? How did they demonstrate to the person that they were forgiven? Invite students to share their episode of forgiveness with a neighbor.

2. Tell the students that they will soon be reading a story about an entire family who was put in a concentration camp. The family had done nothing at all; they were simply Japanese Americans, and America was at war with the Japanese at that time. Discuss how the students think the members of the family must have felt knowing that they were imprisoned, although they had done nothing wrong.

3. Show students pictures of Japanese Americans in concentration camps or being taken there (many pictures have surfaced since the recent fiftieth anniversary of the World War II tragedy. Have students imagine conversations that might have taken place among the people in the pictures.

Purpose for Reading or Listening: "You will read a story about a young girl and her family who are trying to resume their former life after being released from a concentration camp. Read to find out how each character in the story coped with their bitterness."

Discussion Questions:

1. Why were the Japanese Americans put into concentration camps? Were the suspicions of other Americans founded or unfounded?
2. Why did Yuki feel that Mrs. Henley never quite trusted them?
3. Why had Papa kept the newspaper hidden from Mama?
4. Why was the family overjoyed after receiving the telegram stating that Ken had been wounded?
5. What things had changed when Yuki returned to Berkeley?
6. Who do you think set the grocery store on fire?
7. Why did the Olssens hesitate before telling Yuki's family that their son had been killed in the war?
8. Why did Yuki feel "empty" when Ken returned after she had anticipated his coming home for so many months?
9. What did Grandma Kurihara mean by her statement, "What Ken needs is a 'counterirritant' to get rid of the ache inside his soul"?
10. What finally made Ken feel better?
11. Tell why you agree or disagree with Mr. Oka's statement, "I guess forgiving does take the bundle of hate off your back."
12. What made Yuki decide she was finally home?

Retelling ("through" the reading activities): Invite the students to paraphrase conversations that took place between characters in the story:

1. Papa and Yuki, as they discuss what they would do when they returned (pp. 8, 9);

2. Mrs. Henley and Yuki, discussing why the President made all Japanese Americans leave the West Coast (pp. 15, 16);
3. Mama and Yuki, after Yuki broke Mama's vase (pp. 31, 33);
4. Mr. Oka and Ken, as they discuss why Ken joined the Army (pp. 117, 119);
5. Mr. Olssen and Mama, as Mr. Olssen tells them their son was killed in Iwo Jima.

Extended Activities:

1. Mr. Oka tells Mr. Olssen that "...there are ways to fight back without destroying yourself" as alternatives to hating people who have wronged you. Call students' attention to recent "hate crimes" that have been in the news, or even happened in their city or area. Have students brainstorm some ways that the victims of these crimes could "fight back without destroying themselves" or "fight back in nonviolent ways."
2. Ask students to write a character sketch of what they think Yuki will be like when she grows up. Have them envision her career, family, friends, and particularly the way she looks back on the concentration camp and ensuing prejudice and violence.
3. Help students draft a letter to President Harry Truman, who was president at the time of the Japanese American internment, telling him how unfair the policy was.

Interdisciplinary Ideas

Social Studies: Japanese Americans were not allowed to be U.S. citizens, as reflected in Mr. Oka's exclamation: "Imagine having a law that keeps all Asian people from becoming citizens. What utter nonsense!" Have students research times in history when other groups were similarly disenfranchised.

Language Arts/Social Studies: Have students memorize some of the Japanese words and phrases interspersed throughout the book such as "shikata ga nai" (It can't be helped); "hakujin" (white people); "moxa" (soft, burning herb). Through research in the library or by brining in Japanese American speakers, introduce children to additional Japanese words and phrases.

Recreational Reading: Discuss the parallels of the Japanese concentration camps and the concentration camps for Jewish people in World War II in Germany. Refer the students to books in Lodestar's "Jewish biography" series such as *One Man's Valor: Leo Baeck and the Holocaust* by Anne E. Neimark.

EUROPEAN AMERICAN HERITAGE

234 Leighton, Maxinne Rhea. *An Ellis Island Christmas.* Ill. by Dennis Nolan. Viking, 1992.

Theme: At Ellis Island, Krysia, a young Polish girl, sees a crying woman, turns away, and worries if she will be allowed to stay in America and see her father.

Overview: In Poland, Krysia wants to see her father again and Mother says, "First we must cross the ocean to get to Ellis Island in America." Papa is waiting for them in America and the rest of the family journeys on a long, stormy ocean voyage. On Christmas Eve, the passengers are on deck to see the Statue of Liberty as the ship approaches the dock where long lines of people are waiting to be accepted into America and a "new world." Krysia sees a woman crying, turns away, and worries if she will be allowed to stay in America to see her father. Historical fiction. 4–5.

New Vocabulary: Poland, Krysia, Ellis Island, immigrant, Statue of Liberty

Materials: a favorite book

Motivation (linking prior knowledge; "into" the reading activities): Ask students to sketch a scene about one of the following:

1. Krysia, a young immigrant traveling to a new place, shows her uncertainty.
2. The members of her family stare in wonder at the Statue of Liberty in America.
3. Other feelings and messages.

Purpose for Reading or Listening: "You are going to read (hear) a story about a girl in Poland named Krysia who wants to see her father again, and Mother says, "First we must cross the ocean to get to Ellis Island in America." Listen to find out what happened on their journey across the sea and what happened when they reached America?

Discussion Questions ("through" the reading activities):

1. What did the title mean to you when you first saw the book?
2. After hearing/reading the story, what did the title mean to you?
3. How did the meaning of the title change for you?
4. In all cultures and in different time periods of history, children's fathers have had to leave their families for various reasons. What are some of the reasons from your point of view?
5. Describe what the sea journey might have been like.
6. If you had been there, how could you have helped the girl and her family?

Retelling ("through" the reading activities): Pairs of students roleplay the story taking turns being either Krysia or another child who meets Krysia on the journey.

Extended Activities ("beyond" the reading activities):

1. Taking the role of Krysia, have students write a letter to send back to friends in her homeland telling about the journey to America. Explain how Krysia might have felt while leaving her friends in Poland.

2. Have students take the role of a new friend who was there on the ship traveling to America as Krysia was. Ask students to tell and write about the journey from their point of view.

3. Have students discuss the story from the point of view of the mother who kept her family together. Help them to imagine the financial hardships of a single parent family.

Interdisciplinary Ideas

Social Studies: Suggest students find books in the library that tell how newcomers from different cultures might have been treated when they arrived in America.

Science: Investigate the scientific technology and its related products that Krysia would see when she arrived in America. Have students write expository paragraphs explaining the use of some of these products.

Art: Engage students in construction of a diorama of the journey of Krysia and her family.

Math: Count the number of books the students find that tell about "a young newcomer's experience" and graph them according to the heritage of the main character. With the girls and boys, a teacher may discuss a book's illustrations and engage them in searching for evidence that points out some of the messages felt by newcomers. Record the students' interpretations on a writing board or overhead transparency:

Book Title	Uncertainty of Newcomer	Wonder at "New World"	Other Feelings
a.			
b.			

Recreational Reading: Ask students to look for other stories about newcomers. Discuss how newcomers are seen in contemporary realistic stories. Why do they suppose this is so? To surround the students with books about other young immigrants and newcomers, a teacher may initiate an author or author/artist study in the classroom with some of the following:

Book Titles	*Message*
For K–3	
Felita (Mohr)	Felita is an unhappy newcomer when her family moves into a new neighborhood.
Going Home (Mohr)	Felita is made to feel like a new-comer again when she visits relatives in Puerto Rico and is called a "gringa."
The Hundred Dresses (Estes)	Wanda, a Polish girl, is laughed at because she wears the same faded blue dress daily.
Mail-Order Kid (MacDonald)	Flip's parents adopt his little brother from Korea.
New Neighbors for Nora (Hurwitz)	New people move into a New York City apartment building and seven-year-old Nora feels the need to expand her circle of friends.
Through Moon and Stars and Night Skies (Turner)	Clutching a picture of his new momma and poppa, a white house, a dog, and a teddy bear quilt, a small boy remembers how he left the orphanage in the Far East and went to his new life.
For grades 4–8	
Angel Child, Dragon Child (Surat)	A Vietnamese girl adjusts to her American home.
A Brown Bird Singing (Wosmek)	A nine-year-old Chippewa Indian girl adapts as a newcomer when she is left in the care of an Irish-Austrian family who lovingly care for her.
The Crossing (Paulsen)	A fourteen-year-old street child from Juarez, Mexico, wants to cross the Rio Grande into the United States.
Dogsong (Paulsen)	Russel, a contemporary Eskimo boy, leaves the people who hunt

animals with snowmobiles and returns to the old Eskimo ways. An elderly Eskimo mentors Russel, a "newcomer" to the old ways, as the boy faces his ordeals with nature, visions, treks and learns the old ways.

The Happiest Ending (Uchida) — Rinko, a twelve-year-old Japanese American girl, rescues Teru, a family friend from Japan, from the arrangement of marrying an older stranger.

In the Year of the Boar and Jackie Robinson (Lord) — A love of baseball helps a Chinese girl make friends in America.

It's Only Goodbye (Gross) — Umberto and his father travel by boat from France to New York City in 1892.

My Name Is San Ho (Pettit) — During the war in Vietnam, San Ho's mother sends him to Saigon for his safety and he leaves behind all he knows and loves.

Sea Glass (Yep) — Craig faces the problems of leaving the Chinese community and learning to live in another place.

To Stand Against the Wind (Clark) — An eleven-year-old boy's memories turn to his beautiful Vietnam land before it was destroyed by war.

Trouble Half-Way (Mark) — Amy realizes that regional dialects make her a foreigner in her own country.

235 Robert Innocenti. *Rose Blanche*. New York: Stewart, Tabori & Chang, 1985/Creative Ed., 1986.

Theme: A girl, who is in every way a heroine, shows great bravery, as well as selflessness and compassion in this moving story.

Overview: During World War II, a young German girl's curiosity leads her to discover something far more terrible than the day-to-day hardships and privations that she had been experiencing — she discovers a concentration camp full of cold, hungry children. 4–6.

New Vocabulary: holocaust, crocuses

Materials: 3″ × 5″ cards, pictures from concentration camps, pastel chalks, construction paper, Vivaldi's *Four Seasons,* tape recorder

Motivation (linking prior knowledge; "into" the reading activities):

1. Write on the writing board the phrase "All tyrannies begin and end with thoughts uncritically accepted." From what students already know about Adolf Hitler and World War II, ask them how they think this quote relates to the actions of the Nazis in Germany in World War II.

2. Play a game called Heroines with students. On 3″ × 5″ cards, write the names of famous women who have done brave things and could be considered heroines, one per card. Tape a card to each child's back. By asking questions that could only be answered with "yes" or "no," have students try to identify the heroine on the card taped to their backs. Some possible heroines include:

Sally Ride	Indira Gandhi	Golda Meir
Elizabeth Kenny	Corazon Aquino	Margaret Thatcher
Mother Teresa	Eleanor Roosevelt	Barbara Jordan
Harriet Tubman	Clara Barton	Pat Schroeder
Florence Nightingale	Maya Angelou	Shirley Chisholm

3. Encourage students to do research on the heroines with whom they were unfamiliar.

4. Ask students to think back to a time when *they* did something brave or heroic in their lives. Have each student turn to a neighbor and relate that experience, beginning with, "I was a hero/heroine when _____."

Purpose for Reading or Listening: "You are going to read (hear) a story about a brave girl whose curiosity leads her to make a startling, horrific discovery. Read (listen) to find out what Rose Blanche does for which you would give her the title of 'heroine.'"

Discussion Questions ("through" the reading activities):

1. How did Rose Blanche's life change when the soldiers came to town?

2. Why did Rose Blanche follow the little boy?

3. Would *you* have followed him? Why or why not?

4. Rose Blanche was stealing food from her house and sneaking out of school early to go to the camp. Were these actions right or wrong? Why do you think so?

5. Have *you* ever deliberately gone hungry so that someone else could eat? Can you imagine a situation where you would?

6. How do you think Rose Blanche felt when she saw the children getting thinner and thinner?

7. Why do you think Rose Blanche didn't tell her mother what she was doing?
8. Why did all of the people suddenly disappear? What had happened?
9. Why did the soldiers shoot Rose Blanche?
10. Why does this author begin the story in wintertime and end with vivid descriptions of springtime? Was this an effective technique?

Retelling ("through" the reading activities): This story begins through the voice of Rose Blanche and then, halfway through, is told in the third person. At no time are Rose Blanche's feelings described. Have pairs of students reread the story one page at a time. As one page is completed by the reader, have the listener take the part of Rose Blanche and say, "I am feeling _____." Have the pairs of students alternate reading and responding in the voice of Rose Blanche.

Extended Activities ("beyond" the reading activities):

1. Have students rewrite the story from the point of view of one of the hungry children in the concentration camp; from the point of view of Rose Blanche's brother; from the point of view of a Nazi soldier.
2. Instruct students to write an epitaph for Rose Blanche's grave that would appropriately summarize the brave circumstances of her death.
3. There is no dialogue in this book. Have students choose a scene from the book and create a conversation between the following people: Rose Blanche and her mother; Rose Blanche and one of the children in the camp; Rose Blanche and a soldier. Have groups of students present their dialogues to the rest of the class.

Interdisciplinary Ideas

Social Studies: Bring in pictures of the holocaust and concentration camps. Encourage students to find out about the Jewish religion through research or by interviewing a Jewish person. Ask students why they think the Jews were killed.

Art: Ask students to close their eyes and listen to the final words from the book:

The crocuses finally sprang up from the ground. The river swelled and overflowed its banks. Trees were green and full of birds. Spring sang.

From this imagery, encourage students to draw a picture of springtime as the author describes it, using pastels and construction paper.

Music: Obtain a copy of Antonio Vivaldi's *Four Seasons*. Play the sections entitled "Winter" and "Spring." After each, allow students to brainstorm some words and open-ended phrases that the music brings to their minds. Discuss how the composer makes the listener think of the appropriate season through his use of instruments, volume, tempo, etc.

Recreational Reading: Have students find books in the library about Hitler, Nazi Germany, and World War II. Ask them to write a paragraph about why they would/would not have liked to have lived in Germany at that time.

LATINO AMERICAN HERITAGE

236 Gary Soto. *Baseball in April and Other Stories.* New York: Harcourt Brace Jovanovich, 1990.

Theme: The smart, tough and vulnerable kids in these stories are Hispanic; their dreams and desires are universal.

Overview: This collection of short stories focuses on poor young people growing up Mexican American in California's central valley. The stories describe events in everyday life, but address larger themes — youth and age, love and friendship, success and failure — with which every young person can identify. 5–8.

New Vocabulary: conviction, catechism, guitarron, solitaire, reassurance, nonchalantly

Materials: glossary in appendix of *Baseball in April and Other Stories*

Motivation (linking prior knowledge; "into" the reading activities):

1. Ask the students to brainstorm some of the major concerns of people their own age. List those items on the writing board or overhead (e.g., having friends, clothes, making a sports team, etc.). Ask the girls and boys if they think young people in all cultures have these same concerns. Encourage them to explain their answers.

2. From the list created from #1, ask the students to select what they consider to be their most significant personal concern at this particular moment. Ask them to write a short paragraph about how that concern is making them feel. Invite any student who is willing, to share their paragraph with the class, a small group, or a neighbor.

3. Read the table of contents in which the titles to all the stories in *Baseball in April* are listed. Ask the students if they can guess what group of people the stories are about, explaining the reasons for their hunches. Tell the students that the stories all concern Hispanic Americans. Discuss any surprised reactions.

4. Ask students to discuss any preconceived notions they have about what Hispanic Americans are like. Allow any Hispanic American students in the class to react to their classmates' preconceived notions. *Note:* This discussion must be handled sensitively and can only take place in a "safe" environment where students are never allowed to "put down" other students or cultures.

Purpose for Reading or Listening: "You will read (hear) about many young Hispanic students and their daily lives and concerns. Read (listen) to find out how the concerns of their daily lives compare with yours."

Discussion Questions ("through" the reading activities):

1. "Broken Chain": How is the relationship between Ernie and Alfonso like or different from the relationship you have with a sibling or a close friend?
2. "Two Dreamers": Why did Hector always go along with his grandfather's schemes even though he thought they were ridiculous?
3. "Barbie": What about Barbie captivated Veronica?
4. "The No-Guitar Blues": Why did Fausto give the twenty-dollar bill away? Why did he wish he hadn't?
5. "Seventh Grade": Why did Victor sign up for French class? Did he regret it? Why or why not?
6. "Mother and Daughter": Why did Yollie think Ernie would be mad at her when the dye ran from her dress?
7. "The Karate Kid": Why did Gilbert identify with "The Karate Kid"? Did karate lessons turn out to be what he expected? Why or why not?
8. "La Bamba": Why did Manuel volunteer for the talent show? Why did he wish he hadn't?
9. "The Marble Champ": Why was winning at marbles so important to Lupe?
10. "Growing Up": Why did Maria feel "snappily" dressed in Fresno, but poor in Disneyland?
11. "Baseball in April": Why do you think Jesse persisted at baseball even though he wasn't very good at it?

Retelling: Have small groups of students select one of the brief stories to act out in a skit.

Extended Activities ("beyond" the reading activities):

1. Invite the students to rewrite their favorite short story with themselves as the main character. Encourage them to see how the ending to the story differs as their character creates its own personal dialogue and reaction to problems.
2. Write down all the main characters on the board or overhead. Brainstorm some events typical in the lives of young people that were not addressed in these stories. Ask the girls and boys to

select one character from two different stories. Have them create a short story with one of the brainstormed events using the two characters.

3. Engage the students in writing a letter to Gary Soto, the author of this book, telling him what they learned about Hispanic American young people living in the central valley in California, from his stories.

Interdisciplinary Ideas

Language: A glossary containing words, phrases, and expressions in the book can be found on page 109. Have the students pronounce the words, talk about the meanings, and discuss how they differ from English words. If there are any Hispanic Americans in the class, invite them to teach their classmates some other words and phrases to add to the glossary.

Music: Obtain a record or tape of Richie Valens' "La Bamba" (*Picture Our Music,* 1958) and play it for the students. Invite them to "lip synch" the words (or sing them if they can) the way Manuel did. Invite the students to bring in other music that is sung in Spanish or written by a Hispanic composer.

Social Studies: In "Seventh Grade," Victor thinks that ". . . some day he might travel to France, where it was cool; not like Fresno, where summer days reached 110 in the shade." Using an atlas or an encyclopedia, have the students research the relative weather each month in France and in Fresno.

Math: After having the girls and boys read or listen to all the stories in *Baseball in April,* graph which ones are preferred. Compare the favorites of the girls and boys.

Language Arts: Have students consider which of the characters in the stories they felt most like. Ask them to write a short paragraph defending their choice, beginning with the sentence stem, "I feel that in many ways I am very much like _____, because _____." If they wish, allow students to share their paragraphs with the rest of the class.

237 David Nelson Blair. *Fear the Condor.* New York: Lodestar, 1992.

Theme: In Bolivia in the 1930s, Bartolina and the Aymara Indian people are caught up in the struggle during these times of great upheaval.

Overview: On the Patron's land, Barotlina Ch'oke, a young Indian girl, faces the hardships of her life as she is confronted by the adversaries of the Aymara Indian people. She bears the work load of duties in the hacienda house, sees her father sent away to fight in a war, sees the death of her grandmother, and begins a friendship with the distrusted Canadian Baptist missionary.

New Vocabulary: condor, Bolivia, Bartolina Ch'oke, Aymara Indians, hacienda, inkweaving, Canadian Baptist, mayordomo, Patron, Yareta (sack), oficina

Materials: copies of *Fear the Condor*

Motivation (linking prior knowledge; "into" the reading activities): A teacher might ask, "What thoughts does the word condor bring to your mind?" The girls and boys are asked to sketch a scene about their interpretation of a condor.

Purpose for Reading or Listening: "You are going to read (hear) about the dangers and hardships faced by Bartolina, a young Indian girl in Bolivia in the 1930s. It is a time of war, of brutal landowners, and of strangers coming to the land. Listen (read) to find out how she faces her adversaries."

Discussion Questions ("through" the reading activities):

1. What power did Don Luciano have over Bartolina's uncle and the other Indians on the hacienda?
2. Why did Uncle Jacino and his family leave their home during the night?
3. Recall what Grandmother said, "A twin never came to any good." What is your interpretation of Grandmother's saying? What were some of Bartolina's negative reactions toward the twin, Simona Paez?
4. Recall the ways the mayordomo spread fear among the people with his story of "a condor who tells unusual things and appears as a man but eats children." How do you think this relates to the title, *Fear the Condor?*
5. Describe the parallel that was drawn between the Canadian Baptist missionary and the condor.
    The priest's description — wore a black coat, white collar, was long necked, and had red hair
    The condor's description — had a red comb, white collar, long naked neck, and huge black wings, savage talons and beak
6. How could you have helped the girl and her family?

Retelling ("through" the reading activities): Pairs of students roleplay teaching one another to write, a simulation of Bartolina's learning inkweaving (writing on paper) from the Baptist missionary.

Extended Activities ("beyond" the reading activities):

1. Taking the role of Bartolina, have students do inkweaving (e.g., write a letter to send to her friends in the city). Explain how she might have felt not knowing what happened to her father in the war.
2. Have students take the role of the twin, Simona, who was waiting for her in the big city. Ask students to tell and write about the journey to the city from Bartolina's point of view.

3. Have students discuss the story from the point of view of Bartolina who tried to help keep her family together. Help them to imagine the hardships of the family living on patron-owned land.

Interdisciplinary Ideas

Social Studies: Suggest students find books in the library that tell about the Feast of Corpus Christi that the people celebrated. Wearing kilts of jaguar fur, the people celebrated with a spear dance, songs, and music from short reed pipes, drums, and whistles. Students may research another celebration, the Feast of the Nativity, where Bartolina and her people enjoyed hard sweets, coca and chicha.

Suggest that the students research the role of the curer among the people. In the story, Bartolina visited Arturo, the curer, so he could call back Bartolina's weaving soul, the one Bartolina believed her grandmother had taken with her when she died.

Suggest that the students discuss the return of Bartolina's father from the war and his interest in the people's gathering to discuss land rights. What importance can be given to the words of another Aymara man who spoke or a rural union among hacienda farmers?

Suggest that the students turn to the detailed map of South America and find the location of the Aymara people. The people have kept their language and survived in spite of their rulers and the religious leaders of Catholicism.

Suggest that the students find books to tell them more about the later 1950s when Bolivars of all ethnic backgrounds won their civil rights and gained meaningful citizenship in their country.

Science: Suggest students find books in the library that tell about chuno-making (crushing potatoes and preparing a mash). Have students write expository paragraphs explaining the use of the mash.

Art: Engage students in simulating weaving by asking them to weave paper strips together to make a mat.

Language Arts: In groups of two, discuss the meaning of the word ink-weaving and write original definitions.

Music: Engage students in construction of a pipe. Use reeds (plastic pipes) tied together. The pipe should be similar to the one played by Grandfather when Bartolina chanted along softly. Invite the students to experiment with the notes and to create a chant to go along with the music.

Research the drums and pipes and other musical instruments used at the feasts and the celebrations of the native people.

Math: To plant the fields, Bartolina and the others used a measuring stick to plant the beans. Bartolina drove a hole with a stick, dropped in a seed and pressed a mound of dirt over the seed. Invite the students to discuss why the stick was called a measuring stick and tell what they thought was measured, the importance of having a measuring stick, and to predict what depth the stick was to measure for planting.

Recreational Reading: Ask students to look for other stories about the people of Bolivia. Discuss how the people are seen in contemporary realistic stories. Why do they suppose this is so?

NATIVE AMERICAN HERITAGE

238 Martha F. Bryant. *Sacajawea.* Billings, Montana: Council for Indian Education, 1989.

Theme: Sacajawea counteracts the stereotypical notion of the hostile Native American from the pioneer days; she also provides a positive example of a strong and courageous female Native American.

Overview: A Shoshone Indian girl named Sacajawea guides the Lewis and Clark expedition. Her life is documented from childhood to her later years.

New Vocabulary: exodus, belligerent, sanctuary, maneuvered, confluence, bolstered, dowry, authority, foreboding, apprehension, taciturn

Motivation (linking prior knowledge; "into" the reading material):

1. Invite the students to share their impressions of life in the pioneer days when people were heading Westward. What have they heard about the relationships among the pioneers and the Indian people? Have they been led to believe that the Native Americans were always the hostile aggressors? Why do they believe this is/is not so?

2. Lead the students in a visualization exercise of life as a "camp drudge" as Sacajawea was for many of the early years of her life: "You have been taken captive by the Mandan Indians because your parents died. By day, you gather tuba plants and carry water for cooking. You speak Shoshone, so you don't understand everything that goes on. At night, you are tied up so you cannot run away. You are told that in a few years, when you grow up, you will be sold to a French or English hunter as a squaw."

3. Ask the students to respond to the above visualization. Would they try to escape? How would they feel?

4. Tell the students that Sacajawea survived her captivity by reciting the following mantra: "My father is chief of the Shoshones. I am his daughter. I am Sacajawea and I will survive." How do students think that repeating this phrase over and over again helped Sacajawea to keep up her courage?

Purpose for Reading or Listening: "The book you are about to read (listen to) tells about the life of a Shoshone Indian girl who is forced to live among another tribe of people. Read (listen) to find out how she overcomes her fear to become one of the most well-respected Native American women of all time."

Discussion Questions:

1. What was the meaning of Sacajawea's name in the Shoshone language? Why was it a fitting name for the child?
2. What had happened to Sacajawea's parents?
3. How did Sacajawea come to be married to Charbonneay? How would you describe their relationship?
4. How did Lewis and Clark come to respect Sacajawea's skills?
5. Why did Sacajawea convince her husband that their sons must learn to speak English?
6. How did white men use liquor with the Indian people?
7. What motivated the French and English pioneers to move to a new land?
8. How was the motivation of the Native American people different from that of the white people?
9. How did Sacajawea respond to her eventual reunion with the Shoshone people?
10. What reasons did the settler women give Sacajawea as to why she could not vote? Were they *real* reasons? How was this situation similar to the Southern blacks who were discouraged from voting after the Civil War?

Retelling ("through" the reading activities): Invite students to dress up as Sacajawea as an eighty-year-old woman and reflect upon the events of her life. Allow other students in the class to ask the questions.

Extended Activities ("beyond" the reading activities):

1. Have students write a letter to Sacajawea describing what life is like today for white women and Native American women.
2. Divide students into small groups. Have them act out conversations between/among the following people:
   a. Sacajawea and Grass Woman (pp. 21–22).
   b. McKenzie and Captain Clark (pp. 49–50).
   c. Lewis andf Clark (pp. 53–54).
   d. Jean Baptiste and the Reverend Mother (p. 174).
   e. Sacajawea, Jerk Meat and Jerk Meat's mother (pp. 193–194).
   f. Others identified by the students.
3. Have students write an epitaph for Sacajawea's grave that would epitomize her brave life. Show the students the photograph of her real grave (p. 250).

4. Ask students to write a paragraph expressing their thoughts about the forced marriages that took place between very young Indian women and the traders who could provide their captors with the most beaver skins or horses. Have students include their answers to the following questions:
   a. Was this a good way to arrange a marriage? Why do you think so or not think so?
   b. Could the Indian women ever be happy this way?
   c. How does this custom differ from tribe to tribe? How was it different when the girl was raised in the tribe? how does it differ from marriage customs in our society?

Interdisciplinary Ideas

Science: Ask for reactions to Prairie Woman's concern: "Some of these strangers will be bad for us Mandans; for they will bring the bitter water that makes our warriors weak. Then the white man will cheat us." What is the "bitter water" that Prairie Woman is referring to in this quote? In what way would it make warriors weak? Discuss the detrimental effects of alcohol abuse on the human body.

Art: Give each student a charcoal pencil and a piece of manila paper. Ask them to sketch their impression of Sacajawea from the imagery on p. 31: "She was small and her hair hung in two thick braids over her buckskin tunic down to her waist. Across the front of her tunic, she'd stitched porcupine quills and streaks of red and black dye."

Social Studies: From trade books found in the library or a reference text such as *Fodor's Indian America,* have students find out about the Native American tribes mentioned in this book: Shoshone, Blackfeet and Mandan. Using a matrix, have the students chart the differences and similarities in language, ways of getting food, customs, etc.

Math: Using encyclopedias, have students make a bar graph showing the population of the three Indian tribes mentioned in this book.

Recreational Reading: Refer interested students to other books on this topic, such as *American Indian Women* (Hawthorne, 1974) by Marion Gridley, and *Bird Woman: Sacajawea, the Guide of Lewis and Clark* (Riverside, 1918) by James Willard Schultz.

239 Elizabeth George Speare. *The Sign of the Beaver.* Boston: Houghton Mifflin, 1983.

Theme: A white boy begins to appreciate and respect a resourceful Indian boy who helps him to survive in the forest. Prejudice and stereotypes of Native Americans are modified. Mutual respect is highlighted.

Overview: Thirteen-year-old Matt is left alone in the wilderness and begins to rely upon the kindness of members of the Beaver Clan while he learns how to survive.

New Vocabulary: solemnness, tribute, contemptuous, hemlock, dumbfounded, lamely, grudgingly, breechcloth, rummaging, sledge, caribou

Materials: charcoal, construction paper, video of Western (e.g., *The Witch of Blackbird Pond, The Cay, Calico Captive, The Bronze Bow*)

Motivation (linking prior knowledge; "into" the reading material):

1. Ask the students to close their eyes and visualize their parents having to go away on a journey and leaving them to fend for themselves in a cottage in the woods. How would they feel? How would they get food? What would they do? Ask the students to open their eyes and discuss answers to the questions in small groups of three or four.

2. Show a videotape of an old Western that depicts stereotypical conflicts between cowboys and Indians. Ask the students to brainstorm why they think American Indians were always presented so negatively. Were cowboys always good? Were Indians always bad?

3. Show the students the painting on the book jacket of *The Sign of the Beaver* (the jacket shows thirteen-year-old Matt looking apprehensively at a shadowy form—a young Indian boy—in the woods). Have pairs of children select to be either Matt or the Indian boy, Attean, and create the conversation that each must have been having with themselves while peering at one another.

Purpose for Reading or Listening: "You are going to read (hear) a story about a thirteen-year-old boy whose father and mother left him in the wilderness to guard their house. He has been taught to be afraid of the Indians. Read to find out how he overcomes his fear of the Indians and begins to respect and appreciate the Beaver Clan."

Discussion Questions:

1. Why had Matt's family left him? Do you think this was a responsible plan? Why or why not?
2. How did Matt keep track of the time while his family was gone?
3. The renegade white stranger stole Matt's guns. Why had Matt so easily trusted the stranger?
4. What were Matt's fears when he found his guns were stolen?
5. What did Matt learn about being careful with his food?
6. How did the Indians save Matt's life?
7. What things did Matt learn from the Beaver Clan? Why did he feel ashamed?
8. How did Matt decide to teach Attean to read?

9. What was the basis of the friendship between Matt and Attean?
10. Why was Attean offended by excerpts from Robinson Crusoe?
11. How did Matt understand the Feast of the Bear, even though he couldn't understand the Indian's words?
12. Why did Matt have a difficult time explaining his relationship with the Beaver Clan to his parents?
13. What's were Matt's fears for the Indians?
14. How had Matt overcome his fear of the Indians? Do you think such a method would work between any two cultures that are experiencing conflict?

Retelling ("through" the reading activities): Have individuals recount the story in their own words to small groups of children in a younger grade, to their parents, or to a staff member.

Extended Activities ("beyond" the reading activities):

1. Have the students break up into pairs and reenact conversations, in their own words or using the actual text, between the following duos:
   a. Matt and Ben
   b. Matt and his father
   c. Matt and Attean
   d. Matt and Saknis
2. Have the students write an entry in a journal that Matt might have kept during his months in the wilderness. Collate the entries into a class book. Invite the students to illustrate the book.

Interdisciplinary Ideas

Social Studies: "Indian" and "Native American" are global, generic terms and tell nothing of the values, beliefs and customs of any particular tribe. Ask groups of four or five students to select a Native American nation and research that nation, finding out specifics about its rites, folklore, language, customs, etc. Have each group share its findings with the rest of the class.

Language Arts: Have the students make a Beaver Clan dictionary containing all of the words of that clan that are interspersed throughout the text.

Science/Health: Discuss the four food groups and whether Matt managed to have a healthy diet in the wilderness by himself. What foods was he missing? How could he have gotten these foods?

Art: This young adult novel contains no illustrations except the impressionistic jacket cover. With charcoal and construction paper, have the students select one of the following scenes to sketch from the description given in the text:

1. "Women in bright cloth skirts and odd pointed caps moved about without a sound . . . light glinted on their silver armbands and necklaces. . ." (p. 78).
2. "It was Saknis, his paint-streaked face barely recognizable. He wore a long red coat decorated by a handsome beaded collar and metal armbands. A crown of features rose from the beaded band around his forehead. . ." (p. 79).
3. "All around him in a circle rose the dim shapes of cabins and cone-shaped wigwams. In the center of the circle a long, narrow fire was burning between walls of logs. Suspended on timbers hung three iron pots, sending up rosy curls of steam in the smoky air. . ." (p. 78).

Recreational Reading: For students who are interested in more books by Elizabeth George Speare, introduce them to *Calico Captive, The Witch of Blackbird Pond,* and *The Bronze Bow.* For those students interested in reading a book with a similar theme of overcoming prejudice through personal experience, lead them to *The Cay* by Theodore Taylor.

INDEX

References are to entry numbers, not pages.